Tony,

Way to take action &
work with me for your
growth. I'm so excited to
see your results come in.
Keep growing & learning I believe
in you & I'm proud of you.

Your Friend

Connor "Juke Jivis" McClellan

WAKING
The CORE
Of MAN

A Hardwired Series

Waking The Core Of Man

The Gateway To Separating Yourself From The
Average Man With Dating, Attraction, & Love

Connor (Selna Kim) McCanless

Waking The Core Of Man
COPYRIGHT © 2020 by Connor McCanless

McCanless Companies LLC
Selna Kim Studies

....

Cover art direction and design by *Marian Wolff*
Cover portrait identities (left to right) and special thanks to

Sophia Manor | *Bérénice Cleyet-Merle* | *Brittney Williams*

(Not Affiliated With the Story)

....

ISBN: 9798408163175

Acknowledgments

To my *mother*, thank you for passing your optimism onto me, your giving nature, and your care for all people. You are strong.

To my *father*, thank you for teaching me that there's always a way and to find it. You've guided me, believed in me. Your wisdom is incredible.

To my *stepfather*, you taught me the ability to stand up for what I want, knowing my value, and cutting right through the bullshit.

To my *stepmother,* thank you for showing me never to fear being vulnerable, loving who I am, flaws and all.

To my brother, *Cameron*, I believe no one but you can understand yourself fully, but those who can relate the most usually become best friends. You are the only one who can understand me closest to my understanding of myself.

I love all five of you very much.

I'd like to thank my former coaches, *Kristina* and *Nathan*. You were among the first to ever see potential in me when I had nothing. You changed my life. Also, *Mark* and *Linda*. Your relationship inspires me to love and give just like you do for each other.

I've had other people behind the scenes helping me and supporting me too. I'm grateful to them all, but specifically,

thank you, *Ace, Josh, Kyle, Brittney, Adrian, Greg, Alec, Evan, and Lewis.*

I'd like to take a moment to thank my *grandparents, aunt, uncle, and cousins.* I love you all so much.

Thank you, *Tony Robbins, Jason Capital, Gary Vee,* and especially *Corey Wayne*, a life coach, for being a role model and a huge inspiration in my life. Also, a special thanks to the Letters. H, X, N, Z, Jay, and especially Letter-V for showing me who I was but also who I needed to become.

Thank you, *Masashi Kishimoto,* for your work. When I was a small boy, it helped keep a fire burning in me to push through the most difficult times of my life. You and *Neil Strauss* have inspired my writing.

For the *women*, thank you for being a part of this, because without you I wouldn't be the man I am today. I wouldn't be able to share this book. You know who you are.

Lastly, *you the reader*, thank you for being the difference that makes the difference.

Constant growth and change aren't for everyone. There are those who do and those who do not. Chances are you feel something calling you from afar. That same voice is challenging you to reach new levels no matter the difficulty. You may hesitate at first, but it guides you through. It's brought you to this book, where this may be your next obstacle to master and overcome.

To the people I hurt

To those I left heartbroken

To my friends who never understood

To my family who only saw one side to me

And for those I deceived until the very end...

This is my rawest self...

I beg for your forgiveness in advance.

Don't try to fix someone

Fix the society that created them…

TABLE of

CONTENTS

Introduction

The trigger clicked. The gun fired.

The flash painted the walls for a split second. The bang echoed off the cement in the parking garage, slowly dissipating into silence.

This moment would feel like hell's eternity when trapped inside of this reality, but only lasted seconds.

He held his chest.

Drip.

Drop.

The unforgiving grey of the cement merged into maroon after each trickle.

This eternity would be his final moments as his wife watched him get shot in the chest, the image tattooed to her brain forever.

Moments before, the wife woke the husband up from his slumber.

It was around midnight; they were sleeping in their apartment in downtown Chicago.

"Oh my gosh, is it happening?" he gasped, throwing the covers off him. He put on some clothes and grabbed his car keys. "We need to go now."

Helping her down and into the parking garage, they finally stumbled to his car. He helped her in. He ran to the other side of his car and hopped in. The engine purred as he pressed the 'Push to Start' button. Just before he clicked his seatbelt, his wife pointed out the window and asked, "Who is that?" The husband turned his head and looked. A man appeared in front of their car, his shadow elongated behind him from the strength of the headlights.

Another man came alongside the driver's side, tapping on the window. It startled the couple, and when they saw the gun in his hand, they knew what was happening. They were being robbed. The robber motioned him to step outside. The husband put his hands up and began to open the door. He looked back to his wife before he stepped out.

"Don't worry, honey, everything will be alright. Just stay in here."

He smiled at her, and before she could utter a word, he stepped out of the car.

"Please, we don't have time," he tried to sympathize with the robber. "She needs to go to the hospital. I'll give you anything you want!"

He pulled out his wallet and gave him all the money he had in it.

"Two tens, a five, and two ones?" the robber said, looking puzzled at the husband. "I'm going to need more than this."

"That's all I have," the husband said, practically begging at this point.

The robber pointed the gun at him. "I want something else." His eyes slowly looked in the direction of his wife.

"W-What?" the husband said, darting his eyes to the car, back to the robber, and then at the car again.

"Is that your wife?" he smiled lasciviously. "She's coming with me."

"No, anything but that." He was panicking because he wondered what he would do to her. *Was he going to take her...rape her...kill her...something else?* "Shoot me instead, take me, but please don't do anything to her!" he pleaded.

"No," the robber said, moving in closer. "I want her right now. Give her to me, or I'll kill you both."

The wife watched as her husband began to come back towards the car with the robber following right behind.

In the reflection of the window, the husband saw that he was pointing his gun directly at his back. The wife was on the verge of passing out when she saw, in a flash, the husband spinning around grabbing the gun.

They wrestled for it, and suddenly it went off.

It seemed as if time froze for a second. The two men, motionless. Then the husband fell to his knees, and then onto his chest, gasping for air. The two robbers took off running. She leaped out of the car and fell by his side. She couldn't see what had happened from behind, but she rolled him over and her eyes grew large with tears. His grey T-shirt was soaked with blood.

She began to cry uncontrollably. She wanted to believe it was all a bad dream and pinched herself to wake up.

He looked up at her. In the distance, red and blue lights illuminated the streets outside.

She faintly heard the sounds of sirens.

He was still alive, but he was growing weaker. She tried to think of anything to escape this reality, but it was his time. Every moment that passed, he continued to die slowly in her arms.

"I don't think I'm going to make it," he let out. "The bleeding isn't stopping." Her tears soaked into the few dry spots left on his shirt.

"You're going to make it, please don't leave me now!" she cried.

The ambulance and police cars had almost reached the scene.

She buried her face in his arm and continued to cry. "Our baby is on his way right now."

She was pregnant, and her water had broken just moments before. It was almost time for their baby to arrive.

He cupped his hand over her face.

His voice gave out, and he passed away in her arms.

When I was 21, I attended a seminar at the United Center, where the Blackhawks play. Gary Vaynerchuk, Tony Robbins, and other well-known speakers were at this event to speak life into people. The line was huge to get in, and it was freezing outside.

The line wasn't moving, so I began to look around at all of the people surrounding me. It was packed, and you could see everyone's breaths exhale into the air and then disappear at random intervals.

The sun was just rising over the city.

I squinted as I looked at it.

The morning sun brought some heat to me. My hands were tucked away inside of my dark-brown bomber jacket.

How long is this line? I thought, slowly following the trail of freezing people snaking around the corner. When I couldn't see more, I followed the trail back. I locked eyes with a beautiful woman. Her gaze was so powerful, I almost couldn't handle it.

Two seconds passed... The morning sun illuminated her blue iris.

Three seconds passed... "Hey buddy, the lines moving," a guy said to me.

"Oh, right," I said, turning around. Finally, I was warm inside the building. It was even crazier inside with all of the people. I couldn't help but think, *Who was that woman?*

The presentations started, and I quickly found my seat, putting her in the back of my mind. I probably wouldn't ever see her again anyway. Or so I thought.

During the break, I went outside to purchase a rib sandwich from one of the stands. After I finished eating, I threw the trash away and began to walk back to my seat, but there she was.

The woman I locked eyes with from earlier, sitting alone.

Her left hand was in the pocket of her white North Face jacket as she held a cup of coffee in her right hand. She looked to be about 25, and I thought she was stunning.

I had a way with women, so I decided to go up and see what could be done. She sat alone at a high table with two chairs, her face was almost level with mine when she looked up and saw me coming.

"I couldn't help but notice you earlier today outside." I smiled at her and that same gaze of hers stared into my eyes, "I don't have a lot of time to talk, but were you checking me out?"

She laughed. "Honey, I'm probably double your age."

"So?" I shrugged my shoulders.

She was smiling, "If they had a picture of bold in the dictionary, it would have your face next to it," she said. "You're quite the guy."

She took her left hand out of her pocket and started to fidget with her coffee cup. A huge diamond ring glistened in the light. She was

4

married. Looking down at her coffee, I could see a shift in her body language.

"Oh," I said. "I'm sorry, I didn't realize…"

"No," she cut me off. "It's okay. I was going to say that you are the spitting image of my late husband."

So, she was a widow.

"I remind you of him?" I asked.

"He was the flirty type, kind of like you." She smirked. "When he tried, I declined him over and over, but eventually something about him made me fall madly in love with him."

"What made you fall for him?"

"I thought he was an asshole at first. He was cocky and acted like he had a lot of girls," she continued. "He would ask me out all the time, and I turned him down two or three times. I said the meanest things to him like, 'I'll *never* go out with you.' I'm not sure why I decided to go out with him, but in the winter, I saw him do something that touched my heart." She put her hands on her heart as she talked.

"What did he do?" I asked.

"We were in college together, and I was walking back from class. I saw him going in the same direction I was. Far in the distance, a boy was struggling in a wheelchair. His hands must've been numb from the cold by pushing it. My husband began to pick up his pace and eventually stopped the kid in the wheelchair. He took the gloves off his hands and gave them to the kid. Then he pushed the kid back to his dorm room."

She told this story as if she had just experienced it yesterday.

"Then what?" I asked her, sitting in the chair across from her.

"I was at a party one night, and one of his friends was there as well. I told his friend that he should invite the man who would become my future husband. He showed up, of course." Her smirk conveyed to me that he couldn't resist coming knowing she was there.

"Who's bold now?" I said, rolling my eyes.

She laughed and continued. "I was interested, but I tried to act like I wasn't. He was the type of man who could make you fall for him; he was dangerous. The more I tried to push him away, the more I kept thinking about him. I took him from the party into a different room so we could be alone and talk."

"Oh," I said, beginning to smile. "Took him to the bedroom to 'talk,' huh?"

"No," she glared at me even as she smiled. "I just wanted to talk."

"Yeah. Talk, I'm sure," I said skeptically as I rolled my eyes again. "Go on."

"I wasn't sure about him, but after that night, we went out on one date, and from there he couldn't get rid of me. We got married a couple years after college."

"Wait," I said. "What happened to him?"

"Eight years ago, he was shot one night a couple miles from here."

I started to think. She looked as if she had just graduated from college. Just how old could she be? I began to do some calculations out loud. "So, if you married him when you were around 26 and he passed away almost eight years ago then you must be around…"

She cut me off. "Do you need a calculator? I'm almost 41."

She looked to be 23 at most. I couldn't believe she was in her forties. At this point, she had hooked me.

I had a way with women. They would open up to me and tell me things, but this far exceeded my expectations. I couldn't believe it when she told me about her husband.

"He was shot one night," she said. "I was pregnant when it happened," she told me as my heart sunk and my eyes began to grow misty.

"After my husband passed away in my arms, all I could remember was seeing the red and blue lights coming into the building. I passed out holding my tummy. My baby was ready to come out, and I prayed that he would live. If I had to make a choice, I prayed that my child would live and to take me instead. I woke up in the hospital, but my tummy was deflated. They must have removed the baby via C-section, I thought."

"Where is he now?" I asked.

She pointed up to the ceiling. "He's with his father," she said.

I had no words. The child hadn't survived. I just stared as she talked some more.

"The doctors came into my room, and I demanded to know where my baby was," she continued. "They told me that due to the traumatic experience and the stress of the whole situation, the baby passed away before they could deliver him."

They let her hold her child for one last goodbye.

She cried harder than she ever had as she held him.

A lifeless infant laid in her arms. She had spent nine months carrying him, talking about names, and assuming they would soon be a family of three. They were going to teach him to play baseball just like his father. But in one night, what they spent half of their lives building came crashing down.

Now it was only her.

As she held her son in her arms, the doctors told her that during the procedure, they still detected a faint heartbeat in him. They did everything they could, but his heart kept growing weaker and weaker.

After what she had just gone through, the doctors couldn't believe the child was still alive when she arrived at the hospital. They knew he wasn't going to live, but they got a small glimpse of what he inherited from his mother.

As she held him, one of the doctors spoke up: "The child was a fighter."

That child wanted to live for something, but this woman...she was a fighter too. Her world was destroyed in one night, and she rose from the ashes of that hell. This was one hell of a woman sitting right in front of me. Her baby was a fighter just like Mom. He wanted desperately to open his eyes and see the world and live his life. Just to have one opportunity. All people are alive, but are they truly living?

What was this baby fighting so hard for? He was fighting as hard as he could to live, but for what? And it made me wonder...

Before we parted ways, she told me one last thing about her husband. "He learned to love life as it is. He spent his days always trying to become the best version of himself. He took the time to understand me, and our marriage was difficult at first, but he figured out a way. He always knew that there was an answer and didn't stop until he found it."

She took the cardboard sleeve off her empty coffee cup.

Unraveling the holder, she held it flat on the table. Clicked her pen and began to write on it.

She stopped and looked back up at me. "I feel as though my husband and child are still with me. When they were taken from me, it took me years to recover, but I inherited something from them. Everyone is searching for something."

She took the cardboard, crumbled it up, and placed it in the palm of my hand. "You're seeking an answer, and I think it's because somebody hurt you a long time ago." My heart thumped a little harder when I heard this. Could it be true? She began to walk away, placing her hand on my shoulder. "You're going to find it. If you need me then I'm only a phone call away."

I stared at the cardboard. Her number and her name stared back at me. Dana. What a mesmerizing name.

Litost

"You can't connect the dots looking forward; you can only connect them looking backwards. So, you have to trust that the dots will somehow connect in your future." – Steve Jobs

[Litost: A Czech word meaning, "A state of regret created by the sight of one's own misery."]

I flipped the engagement ring like a coin, caught it, and threw it into the lake.

She left before I could ever ask her.

Of everyone I had dated – models, cheerleaders, Pacemates (the Indiana Pacers' dance team) – I ended up falling in love with someone people would say was just an ordinary girl.

She had straight and silky dark-brown hair that matched her brown eyes but was offset by the vibrance of her sassy personality. She was five-foot-six and always worried she was too tall for a girl, but her height also brought out her body's curvature, especially when she would wear jeans or a leather dress so tight it was as if they were glued to her skin. To me, she was everything I had been searching for. Her name was a city in England – Londyn – replacing the 'o' in the latter half of her name with the letter 'y.'

I sat here and asked myself *why?* It felt like love came and then, just as quickly, it left. I had been searching a long time for it ever since.

It always hurt when it left. But I never showed how much it did until that breakup.

For the first time since I was young, my mom saw me cry.

To comfort me, she told me a story about when I was a baby. She had gone to Colorado for a week, leaving me with my grandparents.

When she returned home, I was asleep in my crib, and she woke me up gently. She said that when I opened my eyes, I had the brightest smile beaming across my face, and – even though I couldn't talk – she knew that I loved her. I didn't have to say it because she could see it and feel it.

At the very end of her story, she asked me a question that changed me.

"When did you…" she paused, "forget how to smile like that?"

She brushed her curly blonde hair out of her eyes after a gust of wind. She looked into my blue eyes. We both had the same color of eyes, her gift to me. The same eyes that the women I charmed said were dreamy, romantic, and soul-gazing.

But somewhere along the line, that radiant smile faded away, and I didn't know who I was anymore. I gained everything I wanted, but out of greed, I lost myself.

I felt that this was my own doing.

They say there are three parts to a person. The first is *how you see yourself.*

I lacked confidence in my physical appearance. I felt I was too skinny – so skinny that I looked malnourished. I had a runner's body – tall and lengthy with muscles like a stick bug's – because no matter how much I ate, I couldn't pack on a lot of muscle. I have an almost unnoticeable mark on my left cheek from being heavily bullied as a kid that drained my confidence down to zero. I am not balding; in fact, I tended to grow my blond hair longer like a skateboarder, lightly covering one of my eyes. I also have a weird obsession with pinstripe clothing.

The second part is *how people see you.*

To say I sucked with girls was an understatement, but over time it completely reversed.

I created an alter ego. Thanks to a man known as 'Letter-Jay,' I became a different person. People saw me as a player, a womanizer, and a robot. Inside, deep down, I was fragile, but I covered it up by changing my personality and adding charm. I became charismatic. I learned everything there was about seduction and attraction and invented my own style, which worked like magic. After 'performing,' I'd win a woman's heart every single time. It was simple. People saw me as a man who had everything. I knew how to win the heart of the finest women, and I was recruited to do it for some of the Midwest's top club promoters.

After Jay taught me, he introduced me into the community, and they named me, 'Letter-C.' My partners included Letter-Z, a man with greased-back black hair, and Letter-H, a man who resembled Jack Frost. Despite our looks, we all had talent, and it showed.

The strategy I perfected was a simple three steps: 1) Get the most attractive and eye-appealing women into the club. 2) When the guys saw the girls go into a club, what would they do? Pay to get into that club. 3) Leave that night with a percentage of the cover charge because, when Jay and I used this strategy, the club tended to quadruple net revenues each night.

I would then bring the girl of my choosing back to the suite where we usually stayed, and that's where I discovered, over time, the two things that brought confidence in my looks back. Usually, late into the wee hours of the night that tended to bring out the best in romance, she would tell me one of two things: "I love your eyes" or "I love your smile."

The third and final part of someone is *who they truly are.*

I put a Grand Canyon between my two lifestyles. The dark part of me and the light.

I thought that I had a simple destiny. That I would marry right after university, get a great paying job, find 'the one,' make babies (my mother's terminology), get a decently nice house, and complain to my wife every now and then about why work sucked that week. Then, finally retiring at 65, and eventually dying.

That was until I met people who had something I never had – Letter-Jay and Ace. They tended to always get the ripest apples on the tree, and I was barely able to get the ones lying on the ground and rotted. I felt like there was a divide. In high school, I had two big dreams. The first was to date the most beautiful girl, and the second was to be a varsity starter on the football team.

When I asked my coaches for more playing time, or playing time at all, they said to me, "I'm sorry. The starters just have something that you don't have and never will have. Accept that."

With Jay and Ace, I once again felt those same emotions. They had everything it took to accomplish my first dream. They were the guys who 'had it – who always left the club, or the house, or wherever with the girl everyone had their eyes on. Then there were the guys like me who didn't.

Two simple dreams, and I couldn't accomplish either of them. I never had what it took to get the girl who turned heads when she walked into the bar, probably because I could never be comfortable around them.

Attraction and dating and relationships – but more specifically, women in general – were one of the many areas of my life in which I was an absolute abomination. It brought me some of my greatest joys but also the worst pains in life. I believe that when people experience a pain so great, it calls us to at least subconsciously search for a solution.

There were two parts to me.

On the outside, I was the definition of warmth and light. Bright blue eyes, golden blond hair, and an inviting smile. When I loved, I loved deeply, but when I was heartless and careless, I hurt others deeply. I looked like a typical university boy, and that was one half of my reality. But my looks would fool the average person. My soul was dark. The other half was my secret identity. The one who pulled the strings in the clubs. The person who became addicted to the feeling of being desired by women.

This identity, this obsession, was my darkest secret. The one I kept from everybody.

There are two metaphors for fire, or more specifically, power. Fire is capable of burning a new path in order to create a new life for yourself or it can destroy everything.

I truly wanted good, I truly wanted love, but I tended to go about getting it through dark ways. I wanted to feel what it was like. I desired the feeling to feel desired by somebody. I knew every way how to make her mine. Every line. Every direction to move your eyes that made her chase you or feel like you desire her. Not just somebody. But the most beautiful, the hottest, the girl who put guys' heads on a swivel when she walked in.

But sometimes to get what you want, you must sacrifice what you love.

"Never lose that smile," my mother told me. After I lost everything, I craved power, the power to have any girl I wanted. But the sacrifice needed to obtain it was my character, my honor, and everything I cherished. It became a ticking time bomb. Eventually, this way of life destroyed everything.

So, be different from me.

With the gift of power comes the double-edged sword of greed. I will show you everything that I have, but use it responsibly, for if you let it use you, it will take advantage of your carelessness and lack of responsibility. You will become a pawn of the devil. It will have its way with you…grinding who you once were away, leaving somebody who looks like you, but you have no idea who they are. You will turn numb and unable to recognize yourself.

Use this awaiting power to create a life full of love, full of generosity and giving, and full of nothing but light.

I wasn't always heartless or cold, but three specific stories just kind of changed me. They wounded me deeply.

Remember that with any light, there is also a shadow of darkness.

Allow me to share mine, but let's start from scratch.

This is my story…

Chapter I

Toska

Scars from the Past & Lessons In Pain

"Sometimes you must hurt in order to know. Fall in order to grow. Lose in order to gain because life's greatest lessons are learned through pain." – Masashi Kishimoto's Nagato

[Toska: A Russian term defined as "A pain so deep that it can't be put into words. A spiritual anguish and suffering."]

"I don't think you would necessarily want to be me... It's very hard to turn my brain off."

Those were the words of Elon Musk – creator of Tesla, SpaceX, and PayPal – on the Joe Rogan podcast. But I felt those words because I always found it difficult to turn my brain off ever since I was young – because it was when I was young that I lost everything.

After the age of eight, I always tended to admire the villains in the cartoons or the anime I'd watch. I didn't just enjoy them; I felt like I understood each of them deeper than most of the characters. I felt connected to them. It was because the best villains had the deepest backstories.

Usually, we hate them at first because they seem purely evil, but once we see what they went through and why they are doing what they are doing, our perspective begins to change.

For example, The Joker had to commit a crime in order to support his pregnant wife, but later she died an accidental death causing him to go insane. Darth Vader we perceived to be cold and heartless, but we later realized he became dark because he lost the person he loved. Then there's Sasuke, who witnessed the killing of his entire family before becoming heartless in order to gain the power to kill those who put him through that.

Each seemed like a normal person until something changed them – some event that turned them cold.

Everyone has a story that changed them, and it becomes their primary driver. I admired the villains only because I *was* one.

In my eyes, I'm no different than most people. I seek love. I desire happiness and freedom. I get jealous or upset occasionally, and I tend to see my flaws first before my strengths. My ways of achieving love were possibly different from some but could hit home for most.

I was just an ordinary kid from the start. I was born into a rich family. My dad was the crew chief mechanic for the winning car in the 1990 Indianapolis 500. My mother was one of the top real estate agents in the Midwest. I went to school, I had plenty of friends who I played with after school, and my brother and I were spoiled rotten. We were cherished by them, but even as a young kid, I saw that they were falling out of love with each other.

Each day I grew older, their marriage was slowly dying.

At first, it was subtle. I remember noticing my father consistently sleeping in the guest room, and when I asked my mom about it, her excuse was, "He snores too loud." They began to argue more often. The arguments began to grow in consistency as well as intensity. Their arguing was so bad, I tended to put my mind on sleep mode when it happened. I'd stare out the window and fantasize about the days they used to say "I love you" and actually showed it.

When it started to get really bad was when we were all in the car. My brother and I sat in the back seat and my mother in the passenger seat while my dad drove. Once, when they started to argue again, I just looked out the window. I was wakened from my daydreams when my dad started yelling at the top of his lungs, "Do you just fucking want me to jump out right now?!" We were going 55 miles per hour, and he opened his door. My brother and I started crying and begging him not to jump out. He didn't.

Over time, it kept getting worse. Their arguments turned into domestic disturbances, and the police began to come to our house once a week.

The third time that the police came, they threatened to take my brother and me away from them because we were being physically, mentally, and emotionally abused. That was the first time I'd ever heard the word 'abuse.' My mom decided that we needed to leave, and we were brought to a shelter known as Sheltering Wings.

The next morning, my mom looked at me and said, "Your dad and I are just having some problems. We will figure it out." She kissed my forehead and smiled at me. I knew her, though, and I knew that her smile was broken. She was worn down, and it felt like she was trying to convince herself that it would all be okay.

When she left, I went to the shelter's toy room. I sat alone, playing with a bumblebee stuffed animal while watching the people walk up and down the hallway.

What is this place? I asked myself. *Why am I here?*

The kids roaming the halls looked like zombies. They were bruised, cut, their bodies worn down from life, and their eyes had bags under them as if they hadn't slept for days. I was only a few years old, and these images stained my brain. No matter how hard I scrubbed, they'd never come out. I'd remember forever.

I was humbled.

I wanted to help these people, but I was only a few years old at the time. I didn't believe I could help them at all, and while I felt grateful, I also felt useless at the same time because these people desperately needed someone to save them.

I'm not one for boring history lectures, so I'll make this brief. My parents divorced in the early 2000s, and when you take a look at divorce statistics over the past 100 years, you can see that in the 1980s, the rate peaked at around fifty percent. After that, it started to slowly dwindle to the thirty-percent range by the early 2000s.

In my town, divorce was frowned upon. Divorced families became the 'black sheep.'

My neighbors knew about my family's situation. News spread quickly because it was hard to ignore the frequent visits from police officers to our house. My neighbors told their children not to involve themselves with me. I grew up with these kids. I played with them every day after school, but I started to realize the problem when they would stop letting me play games with them and sit at their lunch tables. They would say, "We're not supposed to talk to you."

I sat at a lunch table of eight with seven of my close friends all around me. As news spread of my home life, my friends slowly began to leave my table. Two of them moved to a different table nearby. Within a week, another three decided to leave. I only had two left who I thought were my closest friends, but I knew it was coming. Everyone else was looking at me as if I was weird, and most people want to fit in, so within a day they left me as well.

The next day, I went to my table. I thought they would get their lunch and come sit by me. Instead, they went in a completely different direction and sat at another table.

I really didn't want to be seen sitting alone. I noticed that at their new table, there was a seat open. I took my tray and walked over.

"Hey, uh, can I sit here?" I smiled.

The two friends of mine looked at me but didn't say a word.

Another kid butted in. "Nope," he chided. "Someone else is sitting here."

I looked at the two with skepticism. "Alright," I said, walking defeatedly back to my seat.

I didn't look around the cafeteria; I didn't want to see who was looking at me. I played with my sliced pears and wondered what everyone else was thinking of me. When lunch was just about over, I decided to go put my tray up first so I could leave that hell.

Prior to walking out, I looked back. That seat was never taken by anybody. I fought back tears as I walked out. "Don't cry," I repeated to myself. "Don't you dare cry."

I realized that I wasn't the only one who was hurting. My family was too, especially my brother when he had a birthday. My mother gave him invitations to pass out to his classmates. He invited all of the twenty-four kids in his third-grade class, but when we got to the room that we booked ahead of time, the only people who had shown up were my mother and me.

I felt for him.

Every Scar Has A Story

Running…

I always felt like I was running away from something.

At school, I was treated like a germ, and at home, there was constant fighting or crying. No matter where I went, suffering followed.

"You, me, or nobody is gonna hit as hard as life. But it ain't about how hard you hit, it's about how hard you can get hit and keep moving forward."

These were the words of Rocky Balboa when he gave that speech to his son. I always loved the sport of boxing, and I tended to think it was the sport one could compare to life. I believed that the strongest can survive to the final round. The only difference was that in life, there are no TKOs or bells to stop the round.

When life has you on the ground, it will keep going. When you think the bell is going to ring for the round to end, it never does. Life always kicks you when you're on the ground, and when you think that you've taken all the hits you can take, that's when life smacks you in the face harder than it ever has.

I thought I had taken all the hits I could possibly take, but life was about to smack me in the face harder than it ever had. Two years later, my family had to file for bankruptcy because of the 2008 recession. My mother was a real estate agent and, when the market crashed, we lost everything. We were incredibly poor.

The principal of my school actually told my mom that based on income, we were in the bottom one-percent of the poorest families to attend that school of 600 to 800 students. This meant that only six or eight other students knew exactly how it felt. We lived through the

Indianapolis winters with little to no heat and little to no A/C in the summers.

Sitting alone at lunch with no friends sucked, but sitting at lunch with no lunch and no friends sucked so much more. I remember just looking around and seeing everyone's eyes judging me. I'd look at their lunch trays and see they had packages of Miss Vickie's jalapeño chips.

My stomach growling, I wished I could just have one chip.

My mom was working so hard to just get some sort of food on the table. She went to work three jobs, and sometimes my brother and I would accompany her to help her paint and clean rich people's houses.

In school, especially in my first-grade class, my grades began to suffer as well. My teacher said that it was best to hold me back a grade.

In the neighborhood over from mine, in the rich section of town, there was a basketball court that nobody ever used. We had no money to buy a basketball, but I found one that nobody claimed. I was so happy, I shot it into the basket for hours. That's when a little girl came to the court.

"What's your name?" she asked.

"Connor," I replied, bouncing the ball. "Want to play?"

As we shot the ball around for a while, I found out her name was Madeline. I felt like I finally had a friend again. Another boy came and stood with his fingers wrapped in the chain-link fence.

"Big brother!" she yelled. "Come play!" He glared at me.

"No," he hissed. "Madeline, we need to go home."

She hugged me and ran over to her brother.

As they walked away, he locked eyes with me. I knew who he was. He was one of the kids whose parents told him to never talk to me. He looked at me as if I was a disease.

I continued to shoot hoops until I heard the gate lock behind me. I turned around, and he'd come back but with three other kids. They walked towards me. I backed up. They were way bigger than me. My heart began to race.

"You're that kid!" he steamed.

"That kid?" I asked.

"That kid who I'm supposed to stay away from," he said, walking closer. "Your family is crazy!"

My back hit the fence. All four of them surrounded me.

"You're never going to talk to my sister again."

One of them hit the ball out of my hand and grabbed my arm. Another one grabbed my left arm. They held me against the fence. I tried to kick them away, but they were too strong. That's when he came up to me. I kicked him in the face. He came back and swung at me. I couldn't move. I couldn't protect myself. He swung again and again and again. I tasted blood.

Struggle.

I was beginning to lose consciousness. My movements were weakening. Then he stopped hitting me for a moment.

"As a matter of fact…" he paused, "I do know you on a personal level. You're the kid who got held back from like kindergarten or something." He began to laugh. "How do you get held back in kindergarten? You're hopeless!"

I finally snapped and lost my mind. I laughed with him.

"What's funny?" he growled.

"That no matter how many times you hit me, it won't change the fact that I kissed your little sister." We were young, so this was at an age when a kiss was the biggest deal ever.

Even though I lied because we hadn't kissed, and it wasn't smart to poke the bear, I wanted to have one up on him until the very end.

He cocked his fist back. "You disgust me!" he screamed, lunging at me.

Smack.

There's a birthmark on the left side of my face…at least, that's what I always called it when people asked me what it was. The mark wasn't there before that day.

A mourning dove cooed above and woke me. My eyes opened slowly.

Pain.

I groaned. I was wrapped in golden light from the sunset. My back was against the chain-link fence that I was pinned against earlier. I sat there motionless. I didn't know for how long I had been knocked out.

My lip was swollen and busted open. My eye was black, and the other one swollen shut.

That's when I noticed my basketball. It was popped open and deflated, flat on the ground like a pancake. I just stared at it. I struggled to my feet, and then I fell back to my knees. My head was pounding. I crawled to it and held the ball in my hands like it was a baby.

I couldn't come home because if my mom saw me like this, I knew that it would've broken her heart. She worked three jobs to support us already, and I knew how everyone looked at her as well. In church, they viewed her as tainted. The extended family treated her as an outcast. The divorce and bankruptcy impacted her heavily. If she saw her own creation in this condition, she might have truly given up on life. My brother and I were the strings that helped her preserve hope and kept her from unraveling.

I knew she was always gone. Either she was painting houses, cleaning houses, or figuring out some way to make money to try to put some sort of food on the table. She'd be gone after the sun set, so that's when I came home to keep her from seeing me like this.

I walked in and immediately went to the bathroom. I locked the door behind me. I filled the sink with water and began to wash away all of the dry blood. My eye hurt. My face hurt. My lip hurt. But my heart hurt the most. The clear water in the sink began to cloud brown as I washed my face. I told myself never to cry because crying meant weakness to me…but I couldn't help it. I was crying all over myself.

I was crying harder than I ever had in my life. Partially from the physical pain, majorly from the feeling that I was so unwanted.

Hearing the things that people would say about me or my family felt like my heart being put through a blender. "You're a freak…my parents won't let me talk to you…you're annoying…you're a loser…your parents are crazy." No one knew me or knew the mountains I had to climb at such a young age. They saw me on the outside. But nobody could see my heart. No one could see how badly I was hurting. I worked so hard just for love, but wherever I went, the only thing I got was the feeling that I didn't belong.

I was just a hopeless case, looked at as a result of the worst in the world.

Over time, the isolation and sense of unworthiness caused me to grow envious because I saw the other kids with their families, going on vacation, and doing things together. I couldn't accept that it wouldn't ever be that way for me again.

I suffered because I once had those ties.

When the kids would talk about going to the pumpkin patch or getting Christmas presents, I would just wish with all my heart that I could have that just one more time.

But I knew my family would never be the same.

It affected me heavily because I wanted that human connection so bad. I just wanted friends and a girl to love. Inside, I wanted desperately what everyone else seemed to have. That love and connection. Of course, when I made friends, or at least when I had girls interested in me, I grew attached quickly. I would only seem to push everyone away.

Four letters seem so simple, but the pain I felt was far too complicated. *I was learning that love couldn't be simplified down to a few letters, and it's not just a word, because if love isn't real then why did it hurt so bad when it was taken from me? What was I feeling when I realized that it wasn't there?* I began to believe in it not because I had it but because I didn't have it in the places that I needed it.

Deep down, I loved my parents on a level that I could never put into words. They raised me, they took care of me, but from then on, I found it hard to express my love.

Throughout this process, I felt extremely isolated and alone.

Nobody wanted anything to do with me, and it made me deeply crave the feelings I felt I never had. The feelings that I was important to somebody. That I mattered. That if I left, it would hurt somebody. I felt that if somehow I could make my existence suddenly vanish then it would only do the world a huge favor.

I always felt like I was running away from something, but perhaps I was chasing love, and *it* was always running away from me. Ever since those times as a small kid, I wasn't normal. From then on, I began to chase love heavily. More than the average person ever would.

Part

Rock Bottom

Failure – Rejection – Heartbreak.

Success comes only after we've walked through these gateways.

At least, I had faith that this was true, though I hadn't experienced heartbreak yet.

It was time… The final phase of my transformation.

After my parents' divorce, I was always the odd one out. In team games, I was chosen last, and if there was an odd number of players, I sat on the bench. I always felt like I was just kind of there because I had to be, not because I was wanted to be.

I had never kissed or held hands with a girl. Everyone thinks that the jocks and athletes attract the hottest girls, but I was an embarrassment to that stereotype.

In the football locker room, I wanted to be 'cool' and fit in, but I couldn't talk about experiences with girls because I had none. I couldn't relate to the stories I heard.

One day, a teammate asked me to describe everything I had done with a girl.

I panicked, barely stuttering, "I, uh – I've never had a girlfriend."

"But you've fucked a few, haven't you?"

"No."

"Kissed?"

"N-no."

"Are you gay?"

"No! I'm not gay!"

He thought I was gay.

Desperately trying to get a girlfriend, I knew of only one way, the common movie-script way:

Woman wants the man, but the man doesn't want her. Woman then – for some unknown reason – has to move far away. When she's leaving, the man then chases her down right before she gets into the plane or taxi.

He says something along the lines of: "I see it now! How could I be so blind? You're my everything. You complete me."

She then starts to cry. "Really? I complete you?" Then they make out and live happily ever after.

I had the hugest crush on a varsity soccer player. I bought her a soccer ball, took a golden Sharpie, and wrote something I liked about her in each of the hexagons that made up the ball. In the biggest hexagon, I wrote: "Will you be my girlfriend?" Soon after I gave it to her at school, I was absolutely annihilated.

I got my first girlfriend in high school, but she left me after a few weeks with the words, "I wish I never gave this a chance."

I persistently chased connections, hoping for love, but one particular event really put me in a dark place. I called it 222 Shelton: the house of pain.

It was a small shack in Indianapolis next to a trainyard. It became my home.

My dad had gotten remarried, and I thought everything was starting to pick up in my life. It felt like a fresh start, but a year later, they divorced. A few days before Christmas, we loaded what few belongings we had into a moving truck while it was snowing and left like that house and stepmother were never a part of my life. I felt so dumb at that moment when I watched the house shrink in the mirror.

"Why would I ever choose love when it always ends like this?" I asked myself.

As we drove away, I promised myself that I'd never marry. I'd stop seeking love and focus on power. I wanted nothing to do with love ever again.

Every night for a few years, I fell asleep to the screeching and rumbling of the trainyard.

I only remember a few things about this house, and they pertained specifically to the address. I've always been a spiritual person, and it's said that when one notices a set of identical numbers, it means something.

I tended to notice two specific sets: 222 was the address, and I looked at the clock when it constantly struck 3:33. When I looked into the meanings, I found that 222 is a number associated with relationships and partnership, while 333 meant to have faith and never give up hope.

But I felt like there was no hope.

There's only so much divorce and isolation that a kid's mind can take. It started at first with my mom, but now I had to go through it all over again with my dad.

My brother and I moved at least twelve times before I reached 18; the average number of times an American moves in a lifetime is 11.7. It was one of my biggest pet peeves. I hated moving because I did it so much.

During those times, I dove into drug use to escape my failures and to numb myself. I tried to forget my past and my world, but they always came back. For every high, there is a low that comes.

My family always thought that I was an angel. Because I was held back, I always earned good grades and was the star child in their eyes, but in reality, I was consumed by demons. I never told family members about my drug use because I felt it would have hurt them and distanced myself even further away from them than I already was.

It was like being in prison without the bars. I wondered what I'd done to be put in this position. There's only so much loneliness, pain, and failure a human mind can handle before it goes mad. I never figured out why people hated me – why I was treated as an outcast, a germ – but the only thing I could come up with was that something was very wrong with me.

These series of events were what broke me.

I wanted to feel what it felt like to be loved. I wanted to feel what it felt like to have a girl obsessed with me. I promised myself that I was going to find a way no matter what I had to sacrifice. This journey was going to take more than I would ever know.

In college, it all started with a man who I bonded with during these times. He was heavily connected in club promotion, and the community called him 'Letter-Jay.' He had all the models, all the money, and I needed both.

I believed there were two common endings to love: You either break hearts or you get yours broken. I was going to be the one from now on who did the heartbreaking.

That man was the charmer, the Casanova, the heartbreaker, the alpha, *the villain...*

Chapter II

Odraz

The Reflection of Who You Are

[Odraz: A Czech word that translates to "reflection."]

Throughout a man's twenties and thirties, he is seeking to build his life in a way that revolves around two principles. One is to be recognized and to obtain some sort of certainty or power in his life. The other is to strive towards love, relationship, and potentially marriage.

I strived for power in love, but on this path, I lost a part of me.

When I was young, I would smile and laugh all the time. I had these sparkling blue eyes and this heartwarming smile. I used to be that mischievous kid. The one who disobeyed to get some sort of attention. For example, when I was growing up, my babysitter walked into another room to apparently change her shirt, and she told me not to come in and look. I came in and looked anyway. It was definitely worth it.

I look at myself now in the dirty mirror of a Rock Lobster's club bathroom. There were wet paper towels thrown across the tile flooring and two lights in the ceiling, one flickering with a fly buzzing into it.

I feel like I've changed a lot since I was younger. My mother told me never to lose my smile, but whenever I looked in the mirror, I never was. When I was in grade school, people used to ask me if I had a black eye because I had these dark purple bags that would form due to lack of sleep and stress. I noticed that they were only growing in size and darkening in color as the days went on.

My bleach-blond hair grew out into a mop, darkening into a dirty blond. It was a dirty mop. My sparkling blue eyes had faded into a deep grey, and I doubled my height to about six-foot-two.

I had tracked down Letter-Jay, but I was so intimidated to even go into the club that I stepped into the bathroom to calm myself. I always wondered why I was so uncomfortable around people, but especially women.

It was because being able to attract the opposite sex was the area of my life in which I believed I was a downright failure. This was because when I tried to talk to a girl, I always felt extremely uncomfortable and always got rejected.

Every time I was in a bar, club, or even on the street, I would lock eyes with my desires who wore mascara, tight jeans, high heels, and red lipstick. Everything in me wanted to talk to her, but the other part of me – the part I needed to kill – told me that there was no chance. I knew what I wanted, but I would be frozen with fear when our eyes would lock. All I had to connect were two points – me and her – but I didn't know any way to do that.

Even now, in the bathroom, I was shying away from facing my deepest fears, but that wasn't good enough for Jay.

Letter-Jay was a 24-year-old club promoter who reminded me of Michael B. Jordan – the actor in *Creed* – but he had the personality of a passionate coach who yelled at his team during halftime. He was a person who had the kind of power I desired so deeply. He had the girls, the power, and the resources.

He burst into the bathroom targeting me. "There you are." He grabbed me by the wrist and pulled me out to the club floor.

"There you go," he told me, pointing to a tiny brunette dancing by herself. "She is perfect for you."

Every time he challenged me to talk to a girl, I did one of three things: laugh it off, make an excuse, or deny the spark. This time, I chose to do the third.

Instead, he flipped the roles.

"Fine," he said. "Pick out the hottest girl in here, and I will take her home."

I couldn't believe that he was serious. To me, being able to take a girl from the club to the bed the same night only happened in the movies. I thought it was myth. Only a famous man, or a guy with a lot of money, could have power like that.

Still, I accepted the challenge, scanning the club. I saw two girls sitting at the bar who looked almost identical. They matched silk, skintight hot-pink dresses with jet-black hair and tanned skin. They were giggling at the bar and reminded me of Barbie dolls. Men constantly tried to hit on them as they sat at the bar, but they seemed to brush every guy off like he was dust.

"Her," I said, pointing to one of the girls. I figured that he would pussy out like I would've done. There was no fucking way this could be done, especially with girls like that.

Expecting an excuse, I smirked. But my smirk was wiped off my face when Letter-Jay – without a word – turned around and began to beeline straight towards them. My jaw hit the floor when he not only talked to them but managed to take one of their seats. With every second that passed, the physical escalation rose. One of the girls slapped his arm, laughed at every other sentence, and ordered a drink for all of them.

Jay was the only person I had ever met who, when faced with failure or rejection, didn't even flinch. Everyone else I knew, including girls, family, and most of my other friends said "maybe some other time" or made some sort of excuse. Jay said the opposite. In fact, he rarely talked, but when he did, he spoke passionately. As if he was Gary Vaynerchuk but said the word "fuck" a lot more.

He didn't talk, he just did, letting his actions speak for him. His style and poise read to me like a poem: "I will not fail, I'll make it happen, the time is now." It was addicting to me because "maybe" with everyone else always translated to "never." He was like the human form of cocaine where, if you got a whiff, you become filled with passion, confidence, and hope.

When he pointed to me and the girls turned around, that's when I really needed a whiff. My body turned hot, my face red, and my forehead began to sweat. I awkwardly waved. I wondered what they were saying about me. They turned to him and nodded with a smile.

He walked up to me. "We're leaving," he said. "Back to my place."

In the car on the way back with them, I sat silent. I tried to play coy like I wasn't nervous because one of the first things I heard about being successful with women was to mirror or copy those who already were. So, Jay sat silently and let the girls fill the air with talking, and I copied him – silent as a mouse with one- or two-word replies.

They were softball players from the West Coast for some Division-1 university. One bragged about being verified on Instagram and the other talked about having the blue checkmark on Twitter. When they showed me, I acted unimpressed when I saw thousands of followers with the letter 'k' behind the number. Verified, D1 fucking softball players visiting here in Indianapolis, and Jay acted like it was no big deal that we were taking them home. Perhaps he was playing coy too, and really didn't expect this to happen. Still, after this time, I was doubting him.

I didn't know what to do or what to say, but I didn't have to – yet.

Jay led us all to his basement, and on the way down there, I was practically shaking from nerves. I wanted there to be some sort of excuse he might make. I wanted him to tap out because I was panicking internally. I was waiting for "actually ladies I'm not into this," then I would give a breath of relief, but it never came. Jay was dead serious. For him, this was business as usual.

I had no idea what to do with a girl like this. I was going to be absolutely embarrassed.

They were well-known, sought-after women, and I was, well, I was just me. A skinny 21-year-old who had practically zero experience with women except for when they would say, "Let's be friends" or "It's not you, it's me."

In his basement were two couches on opposite sides of the room.

It was designed for parties with alcohol stains on the floor and two black lights in the ceiling sockets where regular bulbs should go, causing the softball players' white painted nails to glow an ominous purple. Jay took one of the girls to the opposite side of the room, disappearing into the dark.

All I could see were ten glowing white dots – her nails floating in the air, it seemed.

The other softball player pushed me into the other couch, straddling me. She kissed slowly down my neck, and after a few minutes, I looked over to the other side of the room. I saw five glowing and floating dots slowly move south on what I believed to be Jay's chest, and they stopped coming together into a fist. That's when I realized they were already naked, and she was putting a condom on him.

I couldn't take this intensity. I'd never even been fully naked with a woman before, let alone, have sex with two others in the room. I un-straddled her and brought her upstairs, where she re-straddled me on the sofa in the living room.

"Touch me here," she whispered between locking lips, taking my hand, and putting it over her panties.

"Do you have a condom?" she asked.

I did, but I realized I was so nervous that I couldn't even get my dick hard.

I awkwardly rubbed over her panties, too scared to make any move on her, so we made out for twenty minutes. Then she rolled off of me. She saw the real me.

"Actually, I'm not in the mood," she said. "Let's just kinda lay here instead."

Fuck. I blew it.

Jay did something, said something, or talked to her to turn her on so much to me, but then she realized it was all a façade. I tried to reignite the fire, pulling her in for a kiss, but it was done.

"It's okay," she told me, pulling away. "I understand."

Those words crushed me. She saw who I truly was behind the coy act. The timid man who wrote on soccer balls for girls. The sexual rejection only added to my failure.

I couldn't even look them in the eyes when the girls left.

I could only imagine the girls' conversation on the ride home.

"What did you guys do?"

"Nothing, I was so ready to leave. He was so fucking weird."

Jay had the power I had been searching for my whole life. The guy who was the one making out with girls in the club. The guy every other guy watched enviously as he danced with the hottest girl. The guy who had the keys to sexual freedom and the power to walk into a club knowing he had the ability to win her heart for one night or possibly for life.

Chains

I hated rejection.

I figured that most people felt sadness when rejected, but me, I felt fire. I hated it because rejection was my soundtrack since I was a kid.

There was a time when I had asked my high school football coaches for playing time. I went through four years of hell. I was made fun of, the seniors told me I wasn't good enough, I was a tackling dummy on the scout team, and finally, I got my chance to start as a senior. But that year, the coaches recruited two other kids for my position, placing them right in front of me and, without a shot, placed me back on the scout team as a senior.

After a meeting, I tracked down my position coaches and I asked them, "What do I have to do? I went through four years of hell, and you guys aren't giving me a chance. How do I get in the game?" I was practically begging.

All they said was, "The other athletes just have something you don't have and won't ever have. At this point in the season, we aren't changing anything." I was crushed.

It felt like they had a natural gift – a God-given ability that granted them exceptional talents that ate other men alive. Like them, Jay had a natural and charismatic instinct with women, and – as my coaches said – I just didn't. But I couldn't let that be the truth all over again. I felt like I'd never had any special instinct or natural ability, and it only reflected that I'd never be 'good enough.'

Rejection was the story of my life. Ever since I was young, people told me that I wasn't special, and I was treated like I wasn't wanted.

Over time, I began to believe they were right.

But in a matter of sixty minutes, Jay shattered my perception of reality. One hour was all it took to shatter more than twenty years of belief systems that existed only in my head. Women craved him, desired him. Through Jay, I saw a different life.

I first met Jay when I lived by the trainyard. He was one of the few I mentioned that, in my school, suffered just as badly financially as mine. His family members were immigrants, and they came to America with only the clothes on their backs – and Jay. With our similar situations, he still managed to come this far in such a short amount of time.

It reminded me of a story I once heard highlighting my situation.

A man was passing some elephants. He suddenly stopped, confused by the fact that these huge creatures were being held by only a small rope tied to their front legs. No chains, no cages. It was obvious that the elephants could, at any time, break away from the ropes, but for some reason, they did not. The man saw a trainer nearby and asked why these beautiful, magnificent animals just stood there and made no attempt to get away.

"Well," he said, "when they are very young and much smaller, we use a chain to tie them, and at that age, it's enough to hold them. As they grow up, they are conditioned to believe they cannot break away. They believe the rope can still hold them, so they never try to break free." My friend was amazed. These animals could at any time break free from their bonds, but because they believed they couldn't, they were stuck right where they were.

I knew these ropes that held me back were my beliefs, and Jay only solidified it.

"She didn't reject you, but you rejected yourself," he told me. "That's why you couldn't seal the deal."

"You think I could've?"

"She was straddling you, asked if you had a condom, and told you to touch her? How do you fuck that up?"

He was right. It was time for a change. I wanted to be desired. I wanted to be obsessed about and giggled about at the bar. So, I had to become Jay.

The Weeds of Scarcity

"The soul becomes dyed with the color of its thoughts." – Marcus Aurelius

I was just supposed to be a regular student who went to university, graduated, found a wife, and had children.

I went to a private university in Indianapolis. My parents thought I was an angel and, even behind my hidden lust for power, I considered myself a deep person. I never showed emotion and bottled everything up. To me, emotion meant weakness, weakness meant vulnerability, and vulnerability meant potential prey for the predators.

I loved quotes on pain, life, and emotion because I was very emotional internally. I just never let it escape externally.

At the university, I took a philosophy class because I was already spending my free time reading quotes by Seneca, Marcus Aurelius, and other stoics, or the texts of various religions and philosophies. I thought in that class we'd talk about deep shit, like the meaning of life or something, but instead, we just talked about shit – a total snoozefest.

Quickly, I lost interest in university classes and put most of my free time into the class of the wicked. The studies of the forbidden art of seduction. What I didn't realize was that when you shut the door, it locked from the outside. I became addicted and obsessed with this knowledge.

There are those like me who had zero ability with women. Then there were the naturals who seemed to 'just have it' like Jay. Finally, in the darkest part of the world, there were the 'unnaturals' – those who possessed abilities that were beyond anything I'd ever heard of. They were people who could own the world because they could own a mind. They had the classified information that I needed. Jay told me about his idols who had so much money and houses just for their women.

When they would go to the house, they all made love together.

In order to become an unnatural, I needed to become a natural first.

I tended to think in a straight line, asking a question, and then figuring out the answer.

My first question was, *Where do I start?*

I learned about this idea known as 'The Law of Duality.' To summarize it, everything has two parts – for example, if there is an up then there is a down. If there is an in, there is also an out. If there is strength, there is weakness. But the one I wanted to focus on is that our internal beliefs equal our external results.

Specifically, what is felt on the inside is what is reflected on the outside, typically through our bodies. My family would tell me, "To get the girl, all you need is to have confidence." I had no idea what the fuck that even meant. How do you just do confidence?

Strangers analyze hundreds of tiny details in seconds. From clothes all the way to body language. Our bodies communicate to others how we truly feel about ourselves. The mind and the body are connected. I tried to change my unconfident thoughts by thinking, which never worked. Instead, I copied the movements of Jay. When the body is moving comfortably then the mind tends to have more confident thoughts.

For example, when one is moving the body in an unconfident and desperate way such as leaning in, fidgeting, cracking knuckles, talking too quickly or softly, or chasing the girl heavily throughout the interaction, the brain thinks of itself as either lower value or in danger. In that state of mind, getting the girl is almost impossible. You will only have fearful thoughts or low-value thoughts, making flirting out of the question based on what you're communicating to the brain.

I noticed this when I watched a man named Adonis.

I had a group of three, outside of Jay, who I bonded with deeply.

Ace was the definition of cool. He was from the Philippines and the only person in our group who could potentially compete with Jay. He wore darker colors, gelled his hair straight up in spikes, and told us stories about how his mom got a contract to be a singer and how his dad was recruited to play professional basketball.

The day our bond solidified was when I went with him so he could fight a kid who was making fun of him back in high school. They both went at it for about five minutes, getting hits on hits on each other.

Then, Ace absorbed one hit that made his nose bleed like a faucet all over his blue shirt. I stepped in and took some hits, but I got one clean hit on him right in his jaw. Then the cops came, and we scattered like cockroaches when you turn on the kitchen lights.

On our walk home, I gave him my blue shirt so his mother wouldn't question him because his was full of blood. "Thanks for being there," he said.

"I'm always there." We fist-bumped.

It was hard for me to make friends, and that meant I would cherish a friendship more than most would.

Then there was Adonis and me.

Adonis also had a unique personality. He wore a lot of athletic clothing. He tended to dye his curly hair blond, and when he told stories about how he would kiss a girl, he would leave you hanging on the best parts by saying, "That's classified information, baby." His gift was his laugh; when he laughed, you couldn't help but find yourself laughing with him.

One night, the three of us were hanging out with a girl Adonis was obsessed with.

However, when Ace asked her, "How do you feel about Adonis?" she replied, "We are best friends – he's like a little brother to me." He was crushed.

That's how it normally went. Adonis never got the girl, and the girl he wanted was interested in Ace, and then I was stuck somewhere in the middle. On the outside, Adonis looked confident, but as soon as he stepped around a girl, he melted like butter in her presence. He couldn't make eye contact, and then when he spoke, his voice would betray him.

It was true: Women don't usually reject the man; the man usually rejects himself. It reminds me of the anonymous quote: "The world will always accept the judgment you place on yourself."

Pain Period

People believe that success is adding more to your life when real success usually comes from what you cut out of your life.

This was one of the first lessons I ever learned from Jay.

Specifically, eliminate all of the things that are holding you back, he said, like self-esteem-draining thoughts, negative people, and negative habits.

He tended to work out consistently in the gym and could have snapped me in half like a toothpick.

I weighed a weak 135 pounds.

He told me about the pain period for bodybuilders. They tend to put out ten times the effort but get back little to barely any results, but over time, if they could get through that period, they start to see incredible results. But only the toughest get through the first phase. I was going through my own form of the pain period.

When I first met Jay in my old neighborhood by the train tracks, we bonded through the hunger of having no money. That was until he went from being one of the poorest kids around to one of the wealthiest because of two things – his seduction skills and his network.

He weaseled his way into the club promoters' laps, and as soon as he got there, his life changed. They loved him, the clubs loved him, and he got paid for this skill. By fate, I had become best friends with him and got to experience this world firsthand.

The way he talked about seduction seemed so simple, but as soon as I stepped into the club he was promoting in Broad Ripple, all of that hope drained out of me.

Clubs intimidated me, and that's what they are supposed to do, according to Jay. They're designed to expose the desperate and weak-minded. There's always a huge guy at the front door looking down on you, it's dark and full of people creating claustrophobia, and the music is so loud that you can't even hear yourself scream.

Alcohol numbs pain and specifically the pain of rejection. It's a short-term solution, and that's why men crowd the bar area.

"Do the opposite of what every other guy is doing, and you'll get success," Jay told me as we walked past the bar to the dancefloor.

I wanted to numb myself because rejection was always hard on me, but the truth is that it's supposed to be at first. It's only when you can face those fears when you truly grow.

Jay had already gone to work within minutes, pulling a stunning five-foot-two brunette into what the club called the 'lights out room' where people tended to go to make out and grope each other.

Then there was Ace, who showed up with me and within minutes was pulled away by a gorgeous Hispanic girl for whom I would sacrifice almost anything for just one date. Within minutes, I was all alone in the club even though I was surrounded by loads of people.

Jay came up to me reeking of sweat and confidence.

"Remember when you challenged me to talk to the hottest girl in the club?" he asked.

My heart began to pound; I knew what he was getting at.

"Your turn," he continued, eyeing around the club.

He pointed to a group of four girls dancing, laughing, and radiating. Forcing my legs to step one at a time, it felt like they turned to jello. I thought I could ease my way into their group by dancing, but when I started to awkwardly dance next to them, they started to walk away. I grabbed the hand of the redhead who was wearing a tight white tank top and distressed blue jeans. She turned around and slapped my hand away while rolling her eyes.

My face burned crimson.

"Touch is something that's earned," Jay told me. "Never force yourself onto a girl; you want her to force herself onto you. When she does, you want to act like she is the one who is hitting on you because men are usually taking on the role that they are hitting on her."

He told me to say lines such as:

"Do you flirt with every guy like this?"

"I know what you're trying to do to me, but it's not going to work."

The hottest girls never came alone. They came in herds of two or more. I couldn't even talk to one, but I realized to get the hottest girl you needed to simultaneously win all of them over.

That's when I saw a golden opportunity to make a comeback and prove to Jay that I could be one of them.

A woman with jet-black curly hair offset by pale skin was walking alone to the bar. I accidentally bumped into her and applied the idea that she did that to hit on me.

"So that's how you do it?" I asked.

"What?"

"How you hit on guys," I said. I hesitated to say the last part, but I forced it out in a stutter. "It starts with light contact; what comes next?"

She laughed. It was a risky line, but it worked. She was interested and began talking to me. It could work.

"You have nice style," she told me, grabbing the collar of my leather jacket.

"Thanks," I replied. "I like your eyes."

I felt a connection until I realized I didn't know what to do or say after this.

Ten seconds of awkward silence passed before she said, "I have to go, but it was nice talking to you."

I walked back to Jay. "You gave into her. She wanted you until you gave yourself to her practically for free. You have to make her work for you."

Jay always emphasized what a high-value man tends to do versus a low-value man.

"Do you know the kid at lunch who doesn't want to eat his apple but as soon as you ask for it, he says, 'No, I want it. It's mine.' You need to be the apple and put value on yourself. People tend to take for granted what's easily obtained but value more what they have to work for."

"Okay…"

"Socially prove yourself," he told me. "When you tell a girl a story, indirectly imply that you hang around cool people, like models, and tell stories that show that others tend to want to be around you. People tend to want what others want."

"What would you have done?"

"When she touches me, I make her work for me. I'll say something like, 'I like you, but let's just take it slow' while casually removing her hand, implying that she's coming on way too fast like most guys do."

Even Ace was killing it.

He was making out in the dark room with the girl who pulled him away earlier. I was always jealous of him. He had parents who were married, they had money, but I was dealt a really bad hand in life. It was like the horse that nobody tends to bet on in the race or even the underdog. Compared to these two, I wasn't close.

Another night of failure was on the horizon if I couldn't figure something out.

Nobody wants something everyone can have, so I needed to be something nobody had that everyone wanted. That's when it happened. My potential finally awakened.

Part

Rodeo

Green stood for 'single,' red for 'taken,' and yellow for 'it's complicated' (whatever that meant).

This was apparently a special night planned by Jay. He gave the club this idea to pass out these colored bracelets, and it was a huge hit. Now I had the targets, eliminating the obstacles I shouldn't go for and focusing on the singles.

In the club, there's always one girl who guys can't keep their eyes off of. For me, it was a girl with tanned skin colored to perfection like burnt butter. She had straight, dirty blonde hair with highlights in it that danced on her shoulders with every move. She wore light-blue jeans that were so tight it was as if they were painted on her. I could see every perfect curve as smooth as a raindrop. Then she finished it off with a white T-shirt with the letters 'XO' on it.

When she tied her hair into a ponytail, I noticed a yellow bracelet on her wrist.

When the song ended, she started walking towards me. I had to make a move. For the first time in my life, my brain turned off.

One second goes by... She looked me in the eye, and I looked back.

Two seconds go by... I reached out my left hand to her, and she grabbed mine back. It was as if my body had a mind of its own.

Three seconds go by... Holding her left hand, I spun around 180 degrees. We were now walking in the same direction without missing a beat. Her hand, you ask? Wrapped around my side with mine on her lower hip. We continued walking.

"I was just looking for you," I greeted her. My eyes were gentle but strongly pierced hers. I had a slight smirk.

"Well, here I am," she smiled with perfect teeth. She was lighting up.

"Come with me really quick," I told her, changing our direction. I was making this up on the spot.

"Where are we going?" she giggled.

I noticed they were wrapping bracelets around people's wrists at the front door.

"To get you a new bracelet, obviously," I responded. "Yellow is so not your color." My mouth seemed to have a mind of its own.

When we got to the entrance, I told her to close her eyes. She did.

I picked up the green bracelet, looked at it, and thought, "No." I pulled out the red one instead. She's taken now. I put it on her wrist, simultaneously pulling off the 'it's complicated' one.

"Open your eyes now," I told her.

She laughed, hard, when she saw her wrist. "Red?!" she spouted. "Taken by who?"

"Let's go find out." I turned, walking to the dance floor.

"Wait!" she gasped, grabbing my arm. "Close your eyes."

A red bracelet appeared on my wrist…interesting.

"Good, let's go," I said, smiling ear to ear.

Because Jay was one of the promoters, he had special access to the VIP lounge. Inside were the DJ and some booths. Jay stood on the table above everyone, and I noticed that a hot blonde with Timberland boots, black spandex pants, and a cutoff shirt that showed off her belly-button ring was grinding all over him. They were the highlight of the scene.

I signaled to Jay, and he lifted the red velvet rope for us. It was the first time I had ever been inside of a VIP area. All eyes were on us.

The feeling was addictive.

I went over to the table next to Jay and his girl, and that's when she started to grind on me.

She took her left hand and put it on the back of my neck, getting into it. I moved my hips with hers. It was so steamy in there that her clothes began to stick to her body.

46

She turned around and breathed into my ear. "Let me give you a lap dance."

It was so loud that I thought she said, "Let me give your car a wax."

"As long as you do it in a bikini," I replied. At this point, she could have whatever she wanted from me, and she could wash my car whenever she wanted.

"You're so bad!" she gasped teasingly, hitting my arm.

She sat me down in the actual booth. I had no idea what she was planning to do to me, but she straddled me, then turned around and bent over, and finally, when the song ended, she turned around and sat on my lap facing me.

I froze.

She cupped my cheek and said, "You have a nice smile." She wanted a kiss, but I didn't go for it. I didn't know how to go for it.

I tried to play it cool, asking for her number instead since it was the last song of the night. She wrote down her number on a napkin and gave it to me.

"Text me," she insisted, kissing my cheek. I melted. Then she ran off.

I felt like the king, the alpha, the silverback gorilla, but Jay wasn't impressed.

"You didn't kiss her because…?"

"Um… I don't know."

"Look her in the eyes and say, 'You're making me want to kiss you right now,' which blames your feelings on her. Then lean in, and right before your lips touch, say, 'Nice try.' It's called the 'almost kiss.' Do that until the tension has risen so high, you can't take it anymore. It's an age-old concept known as 'pushing and pulling.'"

When Jay went over to talk to the club's manager, I pulled out the phone number and stared at it. To me, it felt like success, but it was barely anything to Jay.

I neglected to mention that Jay was the definition of a perfectionist. He had standards beyond that of the Queen of England.

When I made fun of him for it, he responded, "Everything can always be better."

I've noticed in my life that people tended to fade away. It was like I was looked at as something that couldn't be fixed. Whenever I made a friend as a kid, over time, they started making excuses as to why they couldn't hang out anymore. I saw Jay looking at me and then back to the owner, and I felt he was going to make an excuse like most people did. I wanted to do this again, but I was clearly holding him back. He'd say something like, "I can't let you in tonight," starting the fading process of eventually cutting me out completely so he could live this life.

It was the opposite, however, when he came up to me and said, "My partner was transferred to Kentucky, and in four weeks I'll be hosting a DJ for an event at Skateland. Since he's not going to be with me, I want you to be him."

He was always businesslike, speaking in a strong and clear voice.

I withheld my excitement. "I should be able to do that."

Escalate & Release

I needed an extra edge.

I had years of beliefs that I had to get rid of within a few weeks.

Jay explained that it was four weeks until one of Indianapolis's biggest events including a foam concert, neon rollerblading rink, and contests. I was going to be his partner.

First, I started to learn about attraction triggers and signs that she's interested. I designed a chart that listed every possible thing to look for to know if she thinks you're cute.

Attraction is expressed through the body.

In poker, there is something called a 'tell,' which is a hint in the body that the opponent is bluffing. When someone is interested in you and finds you attractive, there will be a tell in their body language.

One of my biggest fears was reading the signs wrong because if I escalated on the wrong ones, it was almost sure rejection.

It took several days to scrounge up categories and what happens in each one based on a scale from whether she's desiring me deeply to not interested at all.

It's all based on the three primary colors from art class: red, yellow, and blue.

The primary color *red* represents those women we should focus our energy towards. Red is usually a symbol for heat. Red means she is hot for you, she wants you, she is chasing you, and she has fallen in love with you.

In the beginning, she shows signs of interest. It's similar to what happens when a female cat is in heat. It will walk around with its behind raised higher, and it will meow a lot.

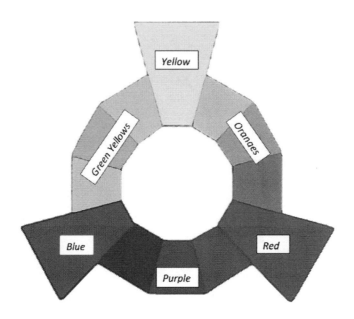

When a girl is interested in you, she will do the same by sticking her chest or butt out more in hopes you'll notice. Also, she may laugh more and look like she's having fun in hopes that you'll notice her and join the fun.

When a bird cleans itself or if you plant it on your shoulder, it will play with your hair. It's called preening, and women tend to preen or comb their fingers through their hair, and while they do this, they will glance at you. Women understand men, and they know men are visual creatures, so they try to look appealing to them.

Their body language will be more open and facing you, and they'll hit you or touch you every chance they get. Just like a magnet in a way, where it's always pulling the other magnet in because there's a strong connection. You are her magnet, and her body is being pulled in by you.

The primary color *blue* represents the women we should remove our energy from. Blue usually symbolizes cold. These are women who aren't that interested in you, ignore you, and never seem to reciprocate the effort you make. A lot of the problems that both men and women have with love and attraction are rooted in chasing people who aren't good for us, don't want us, or won't invest in or give back to us as much as we give.

When you try to pursue those in the blue section, you will feel like a hamster on a wheel. You'll feel like you're getting nowhere, that you're stuck, and it burns energy you could be putting into those who are interested.

I realized that most of the people I interact with at first are not going to be directly in the red or blue category. They will be somewhere in between, and the objective is to move them into the red section. This zone is the third and final primary color, *yellow*.

When you mix the primary colors red and yellow, they create orange. Orange is the state right after yellow where the person is starting to show you that they are becoming more interested in you and more attracted. It takes patience for someone to grow into orange and eventually into red.

It could be the reverse, though. When you mix the primary colors yellow and blue, they create green. They start displaying subtler levels of disinterest. A woman who has a high level of attraction in the oranges isn't going to let anything stop her from seeing you. A woman with a lower level in the greens makes a lot of excuses as to why they can't hang out with you.

High value actions and push-pull flirting move her towards the red while needy or clingy actions move her towards the blue.

Finally, the primary colors red and blue mixed together will create purple. These are also people you should avoid. This includes the 'hot and cold' types who get mad when you don't reply to them in a few minutes, who are all over the place, and the very insecure women who lash out at you but then become sweet a few minutes later.

An example is a story my dad once told me about the love of his life in high school. She was a cheerleader and everything he wanted, but every day when he tried to talk to her, she brushed him off and gave him little to no attention. He worked hard and accumulated enough money to eventually buy a Corvette, and as soon as he did, she ran down the hallway to walk with him. "Are you the guy with the Corvette?" she asked.

I wanted deep desire that was for me, not for what I owned.

Meanwhile, I wanted Jay to have some sort of faith in me, to know that he could rely on me. It was like he was constantly waiting for me.

I realized that I was getting 'alright' interactions, but I wanted hot interactions that would make her want to go out with me later. For that, I needed to add extreme value. I needed to change who I was around women and get rid of the old me who was too nice.

The common advice I heard from people who didn't know anything about women consisted of two ideas:

1. Be nice to her.
2. Be an asshole to her.

The balance between those two approaches is where attraction tends to grow through the 'push-pull' process of building energy and releasing it, which Jay briefly told me about.

The nice guy tends to pull too much with too many compliments, too many gifts, and he chases her validation constantly. The mean guy pushes her away to the point where she feels like she is being used.

When I listened to Ace interact with women, he was constantly applying this technique with slight teases and then used his body to pull her back in.

When she said something a little weird or outlandish (which happened a lot), he would say, "That's, uh…a little weird, but…" Then he looked off into the distance, and she slapped his arm playfully. When she slapped his arm, he tended to pull her back in, and it would escalate the attraction.

As I mentioned earlier, success comes more from what we cut out of our lives than from what we add. I needed to cut back on the 'nice guy' tendencies and replace them with more teasing and pushing to balance myself out.

Women want a high-value man, at least that's what Jay told me.

What makes someone different from the last hundred men who talked to her?

I read books by Anthony Robbins that explained the idea that what we say and how we act is a direct reflection of how we feel about ourselves.

Some guys will buy things (cars, flowers, and jewelry) hoping that they will attract her. However, when we buy things to impress a woman, it simultaneously lowers our confidence around her. Our brain will tell itself, "I need to impress her; therefore, she is of higher value than I am." When you place a higher value on something, you'll usually never reach it. Seeking validation externally shows that we don't believe that who we are is enough for someone.

I changed my body language by breathing deeper, sticking my chest out, and holding my head high like Conor McGregor. I realized that our eyes are invaluable assets that can communicate confidence. Most other men seemed to have little to no confidence and could barely hold eye contact, but I could only imagine how attractive it is to a woman when a man can look into her eyes as if it's no challenge at all.

I also took private singing and speaking courses to train my voice.

The unconfident voice will stutter, talk too fast, sound nasally, and raise the pitch near the end.

I began to understand different mindsets that included abundance, the idea that you have plenty of options, and scarcity, the idea that you must make yourself scarce and give her a feeling that she's never felt with any other man.

Then there's the mindset of believing that you are the prize and that she's constantly hitting on you, which produces lines such as: "If you were a man, I bet you would have the worst game with girls ever." Then she argues this, and you challenge her. "Okay, you have five minutes to seduce me – give me your best shot. How would you start off?"

Then Jay told me to pull back from the kiss and say: "Hey! Knock it off. You know what this does to me."

Even after knowing all of these tricks, lines, and mindsets, I still found the hardest part to be just going up and talking to her.

Magnetic

Pushing, or teasing, was my biggest challenge.

I had heard stories about a guy who flirted with a girl in the club who took it the wrong way and had her boyfriend come over and kick his teeth in. Then there was a guy who whipped his dick out in the middle of class because a girl apparently told him that she believed his penis was small. He barely escaped harassment charges.

I also heard about a classmate who was arrested in a club in front of everyone because he read the signs wrong, escalating on a girl who got creeped out. She had her friends call the cops without him knowing.

Hopefully, they were just unlucky, but I couldn't help but think about these stories when I was trying to dig up the courage to banter with a woman. Perhaps the worst that I'd get was slapped, or she would splash a drink in my face, or maybe I was overthinking. I hoped it was the latter.

I had three other fears besides approaching women.

I used to have a massive fear of bees and wasps. I was stung three times on my wrist, causing my hand to swell up to the point it looked like a rubber glove filled with water.

My second fear was being in ocean water where I can't see the bottom, fearing that a shark was beneath me at all times.

My third fear was in the clubs when they would form those dancing circles. One person was pushed to the middle, and if that happened to me, I didn't want to look like one of those inflatable air-tube dancers in front of auto dealerships.

I partook in the studies that showed one must be the cause and not the effect of their environment.

When fear would take control of my mind, it came out in my body, and I crumbled like sand in front of a beautiful woman.

I felt like I needed to face *some* of these fears to have some sort of mastery over my mind.

It was a purple sea full of lilacs. I could see other people in the distance swatting and running around, panicked because they didn't want to get stung by the bees. I've heard they will only sting you if they sense you have fear. When I was making sudden movements, it showed the bees that I wasn't friendly and could be a threat. I correlated that to talking to a girl because if I was constantly fearful around them, they would constantly be on the defense.

I picked a lilac flower and held it in my hands. My bright-red shirt had attracted bees already, but the deep purple in my hands attracted the insects more. I knelt in the flower patch and waited calmly as I held the flower by the stem. My mother had always said to be calm with nature, to mean no harm.

Bees flew around me, but I didn't waver. Instead, I was inviting.

Eventually, one landed on the flower.

It began to crawl around through the purple and dug into it. A second one flew onto it after it saw the first one. They were only inches from my fingers that held the stem. My heart began to beat a little faster as one of the bees changed its direction. Its little legs crawled down the flower, onto the stem, and onto my thumb. The other one began to follow. It tickled as they moved onto the back of my hand.

My breathing stopped when they walked over the scar from when I was stung years ago. I had a rush of adrenaline because at any moment they wanted to, they could really rough up my hand.

I forced myself to breathe and relax. I even smiled a little bit.

There was adrenaline, and it felt the same as when I went up to talk to a beautiful woman, but I also had a sense of peace. Slowing down my movements was becoming natural.

I also started taking cold showers, which was the closest thing to fearing water that I could think of, but I made myself stay relaxed in the water for two minutes. If I could do that then I should be able to maintain some level of internal calmness when I was in front of beauty.

I decided to save the fear of dancing for later. I wasn't ready to step into the club and look like an idiot.

I needed to start with just light conversation, so I went out by myself to the Keystone mall. This was where all of the wealthiest and prettiest women in Indiana tended to shop.

For five hours straight, I would see a girl, walk towards her, and then eject because I was absolutely terrified. I had snorkeled with barracudas in South America and didn't feel a drop of fear, but this was incomparable.

I noticed a woman with red glasses that matched her red lipstick eating at Chipotle. She had olive skin and brown frizzy hair that was held back in a ponytail. She wore aggressive ripped blue jeans that were just tight enough around her legs to connect the curves.

For two whole steps, I became a heat-seeking missile, and then it all drained out of me. She was a perfect specimen of femininity.

She would never want a man like me, I told myself.

When I began to walk away, I stopped. Life is about taking a chance. I could have left, which was preferable, but I had to push myself. I had to gain something.

I once heard that when trying to break habits, your mind will tell you anything to prevent change.

I felt the reason it was so difficult to just go up and say words to a girl was because I had many years of wiring to do the opposite. Don't take risks, don't talk to others, and don't do anything that's risky because bankruptcy scared my mom so bad it traumatized us and prevented us from taking any risk for years.

The best way to convince the mind is just to prove it wrong.

I turned around, walked through the food court, and went up next to her table. When I got closer, she looked like somebody who was a librarian by day but the girl in the front row of a rock concert at night.

She looked up at me, smiling. I had to do it now, so I went with a push-pull line.

"I always was told to stay away from a woman with red glasses…" I told her, "but damn, I cannot help myself."

I had to balance out the comment with something to pull her back in and gauge the rest on her reaction. Maybe I needed glasses because now that I was close, I realized she was way hotter than I thought.

Her face turned as red as her glasses. "Oh my gosh, are they too much?"

"Well, they look really good now," I told her, pulling her in. "Because they blend in with your blushing." A perfect tease to end it with.

I needed to separate myself from the other guys and show some sort of value, something to spark curiosity about me. Fortunately, I had a passion for science and interesting facts, and it eventually became one of my go-to lines.

She fanned herself off, and I said, "They say that the eyes tell a lot about someone. Yours are blue, and they say that blue-eyed people are more closed off at first, but after you open them up, they have a wild side you wouldn't expect."

"My friends have noticed that about me!" I had to keep my cool and continue to move her into the orange zone of the chart.

"I told you something interesting about the eyes; now it's your turn to share." This line was powerful. If someone starts trying to persuade you about something that's cool then they are telling themselves, 'I'm trying for his attention; he must be valuable.'

I couldn't believe that my anxiety completely evaporated after a few sentences. She was just a regular person named Heather, I thought, until she pointed to a poster outside of H&M. She was the girl on the poster, and she apparently modeled for them.

Luckily, I had done my homework and could counter this.

"Besides looks, what are two things that you think would make a guy want to get to know you more?"

She told me about her dog, which I teased her about because that wasn't really about her, and then she told me she could make a great fettuccini alfredo.

While I noticed this conversation was moving along nicely, I couldn't believe it was actually working. People around the mall were staring at me as they walked by. I started to blush.

"I have to meet someone for dinner," I said, pulling out my phone. "But let's get together sometime."

She put her number in, and I scurried off. I realized that interacting with a woman fit perfectly with a quote I read by Seneca: "We suffer more in imagination than in reality."

Refinement

What makes someone better or worse?

I realized that one tiny thought is the difference between success and failure. Just the thought of placing her above him causes a man to fall apart in front of her.

I heard a story when I was younger that my grandparents told me, and it stuck with me for life. Here's how the story goes:

One day, a disabled man stepped into an elevator with a woman. He thought that she was the most beautiful woman he'd ever seen. "Hello," he told her, tilting his hat. He wanted to talk further but stopped himself. He was partially deaf, and thought to himself, 'I want to say something, but I'm deaf. I know she would never want to go out with a man like me.' What the man didn't know is that the woman was disabled herself; she was blind. 'He sounds like such a nice guy; should I talk to him some more?' she thought. But she didn't say a word either. 'He wouldn't like me. I'm just a liability because no man would want to be with a blind woman.' Their hearts were reaching for each other, but their minds held them back. The elevator door opened, and they went their separate ways, never to cross paths again. Without giving each other a chance, they wrote a love story that would never be published.

It seemed like one simple thought was all it takes. I felt that I needed to change, and Jay thought the same, but it was not what I expected.

We were walking around in Keystone looking for girls, and I was telling him my thoughts about this and the elevator story.

"You think high-quality thoughts, but your looks say otherwise," he said.

"What?"

"Look at yourself. You look like a wannabe Justin Bieber. You wear sweatpants and the same blue Nike jacket. My 10-year-old niece might like you, but not a '10' model. You got lucky at the club because you're smarter than most people, but that won't last if you can't improve yourself."

I scanned Jay up and down. He dressed like an asshole. Ripped jeans as if he was attacked by a tiger and a designer hoodie.

"But I like my long hair," I told him.

"You're not an emo teenager anymore. If you want a high-quality woman then you need to dress like a high-quality man. Respect yourself and join a gym."

He was an asshole, but a persuasive one.

I was six-foot-two and only 135 pounds. I was basically skin and bone and looked malnourished, so I tended to cover up my skinniness by wearing baggier clothing that gave the illusion I was bigger than I was. It probably didn't fool anybody.

So, we went to a barber who sheared my golden strands like I was a sheep. To which I got my sides faded into a permed top. When it was all over, I opened my eyes and saw a golden Chia Pet staring back at me.

Jay also dyed his brown curls blond, but it turned out copper, so I called him a dirty Q-tip and he replied, "Your jaw is so sharp, it looks like you chew five pieces of gum at a time."

"Think so?" I asked, checking out my L-shaped cheeks in the mirror. I'd heard that girls liked jawlines. I guess this was his way of complimenting me.

For the first time, I left a barber confident in the way I looked.

I also picked up some pinstripe pants and a blazer to wear to a club that night, and the brand-new me had quite the effect on the girls. My wishy-washy charisma had come back when I was talking to a short but sassy Hispanic girl from Chicago. She had a city accent, and when

I teased her a little bit, she laughed and replied, "This white boy has no ass, but he's got game."

So, I took up Jay's advice and joined a gym the next day.

Overcoming Obstacles

"She was testing you."

That's what Jay tried to explain to me about the girl who teased me about my skinny body.

A test is something a woman throws at a man to see how he responds. His response determines whether he deserves her interest and keeps the interaction going.

When first meeting, he continued, she wants to make sure you're not some creep. After she realizes you aren't, she will test you to see if you're as cool as you seem, and then in relationships, she wants to test a man to make sure he can be a good protector, provider, and lover. Sometimes she will test, if she wants a relationship, to make sure a man isn't a player.

It's a little like boxing. She will throw minor jabs at first, and how he responds to these test blows are what causes her to open up and move along the color spectrum.

Some examples:

Her: "Buy me a drink."

If you buy her a drink then she sees that she can walk all over you, so the trick is to make her invest just as much. "You get the first round; I'll get the second one."

Her: "You probably say that to every girl."

Me: Describe her indirectly. For example, if she's sassy, say, "Only the semi-cute girls who tend to have sassy personalities." (Input an indirect tease about who she is to indirectly say you're hitting on her.)

Her: "You're so cocky."

Me: "That's funny because when a girl has said that to me before, she always fell in love with me." Or turn it back on her: "Says the girl who is doing [X and Y]." Then this will turn into a play fight.

Girls tended to direct a few tests towards me, including this one:

Her: "You look like you're 18." Or: "You look like a little kid." (I have always tended to look younger than my age.)

Me: Before, I would try to fight this logically by saying, "I'm 22." But that didn't turn her on. Instead, I had to say, "I know you're worried that when you kiss me you'll get in trouble, but I never said you could kiss me either, so let's not worry about it until you can persuade me." Then I'd wink.

I realized that attraction already existed within her, for us, from the start. With women, their attraction is revealed, not built, when she throws jabs like these.

You need her to challenge you for her to feel desire, and it's almost like a game in a way where if you pass her test, she opens up more, and her attraction for you is uncovered more. This causes her to move deeper into the orange part of the chart.

However, if you don't pass her tests then her attraction is covered up and this causes her to retract into the green area of the chart.

Her tests are a chance to power up and gain leverage. Fortunately, I learned this just in time for my big debut with Jay. It was the start to a lifetime career.

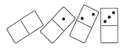

Chapter III

The Mind's Eye

The Magic in Your Reality

[The Mind's Eye – The power in the mind's ability to visualize and the scene it creates.]

The *quality* of a man's life is directly correlated to *how much stress, pressure, and anxiety he can handle* before coming unglued.

There were two points in an interaction with a woman that I felt my heart rate peak.

The first was in the moments right before I attempted to talk to her. The second was the moment right before I had to go for a kiss.

I thought men were supposed to automatically know how to kiss a woman, so I felt like half of a man because I never knew how to just do it.

Logically, it's simple. Pull her in, close eyes, and touch lips. But I couldn't get past step one of just pulling her in or having the balls to do that, or even knowing if she wanted to.

I also didn't want to experience her rejecting the kiss and the awkwardness that came afterward. Even if I had all the recourses, I couldn't get past that hump.

It was like a Scantron for a test where every answer was correct if you knew how and when to pull it off.

You had answer (A), the 'Almost Kiss' where you say (at some point in the interaction after you've made her laugh or at some emotional high point), "Let's do the 'almost kiss,' but promise me that you won't kiss me because I'm not going to kiss you." You get in super-close like you're going to kiss, hold the tension, and then back away. Do that a few more times until the kiss actually happens.

You had answer (B), the '1-to-10' where you simply ask her, "How good of a kisser are you on a scale of one to ten?" If she says, "Seven [or below]" then tell her, "You should be more confident; let's find out" and pull her in for a kiss. If she says, "Eight [or above]" then you say, "Wow, you're cocky; I'll be the judge of that" before pulling her in for a kiss.

You had answer (C), the triangular gaze where you simply build sexual tension while staring into her eyes and then at her lips, and back to her eyes, and if she wants a kiss then she will look at your lips.

You had answer (D), a romantic routine where you lean in close and look into her eyes. You then say, "If we stare into each other's left eye for thirty seconds, our hearts will beat at the same pace and our breathing will become in sync." Hopefully, she will want to try it, and then you pull her in for a kiss.

But even with line after line and act after act, it didn't matter if I couldn't apply it. That's what they say about knowledge – that it isn't actually powerful until you can apply it.

Of all the stones on Thanos's gauntlet in the *Avenger* movies, the stone that I most wanted to have was the reality stone, which let you literally change reality in an instant.

I wanted complete control over my sex life, and over the past couple of months of learning, I was slowly taking control of my own reality.

I knew the next level was a kiss that I had to initiate to be the alpha male I never learned how to be. My kisses from the past usually happened because the girl initiated it, but I wanted to feel more control.

After talking to her and establishing some form of attraction, eventually a kiss would have to happen. The hardest part was just saying the actual words to see if she would take me up on the challenges. It isn't the actual kiss that scares a man but what would happen if she rejects it.

In the movies, whenever the man goes in for the kiss, it seems to just happen, but the last time I followed Hollywood's advice, I got fucked – and not in the fun way.

I wanted to prove to myself that I could, and I finally would that night.

Green Lights

Sometimes in a game, you get a hot streak. Tonight, I'd win the game.

This was the big event that I was preparing weeks for. My arsenal was packed with everything I could stuff into my brain. The lines, the quick responses, the moves, the body language, and the mindset. I just needed the man to come out.

I used to believe that the strongest and tallest man got the hottest girls. The football players or the bodybuilders, because even Jay had muscle and some height. If you put those two together then I felt it would be unstoppable. I remember when I didn't talk to my first girlfriend for two days because she called Taylor Lautner from *Twilight* "hot." I was jealous as fuck because I thought muscles equals a woman desiring you, and I had no muscles, so I believed that was holding me back from success.

I knew that looks mattered to some extent. If we aren't physically attracted, it'll never work. A girl will be stuck in the blue zone on the scale forever.

Therefore, I had to dress myself according to the crowd in order to amplify scarcity.

Scarcity is something that we can use to our advantage. For example, if you see ten girls in the club and nine of them are all wearing the same skintight black dress – but then there's one girl who's wearing a bright red dress – subconsciously your mind puts more value on the object that is scarcer – the red-dress girl.

So, to offset my insecurity, I put on the pinstripe outfit because I figured most people would be wearing T-shirts and jeans. I wanted to be out there, but not an eyesore. Quickly, my belief about the strongest man prevailing would be exterminated from my mind.

I wasn't wrong; the strongest man will get the woman, but not physically. The mentally strongest man will win her heart because limits exist mostly in the mind.

Walking into Skateland, I expected maybe a number – if I was lucky – or maybe a kiss.

In line to get skates, both girls and guys kept turning around and whispering. They were side-eyeing Jay and me. I didn't say anything, but I wondered if Jay felt it too.

I thought the clothes I was wearing would bring attention, but dozens of people took notice. At the front of the line, we got our skates, and the worker behind the desk kept darting his eyes to mine, then looked off into the distance behind me and then back into my eyes.

With warm and partially damp skates – probably from the person before me – we turned around to put our stuff in the locker bay.

"Holy shit," Jay whispered.

It all connected. The worker and the people in line weren't looking at me, they were looking at who was behind me.

She was sparkling.

Her golden-blonde hair gleamed as if she had the starring role in a shampoo ad. Her body language oozed confidence like the female boss of some big corporation who's used to telling men what to do. She casually held one hand on her hip that was wrapped in bright blue denim jeans that stretched to the max around her curves. You could see every detail. A robin's-egg-blue cotton hoodie with the DJ's logo on it that matched her blue eyes completed her wardrobe. But it was her perfect smile that was the cherry on top. This was what pierced hearts like a dagger.

She was like a Picasso but, you know, better.

The men stared at her and melted in her presence while the women in line uncomfortably side-eyed her. It broke the scale of beauty. There is hot, and then there is so hot that other girls are uncomfortable around her.

I felt the power behind her gaze that could split a man in two when I walked past her. She was talking to the security guards, the apparent manager of the place, and two friends, including the DJ who Jay was promoting.

The DJ was a mixed-race girl who looked like she should have been born in the Eighties wearing cuffed jeans and bright neon colors.

That's when her blue eyes and mine connected like a Lego piece.

I had to hold it.

I once heard a quote, "Beauty lies like the sparkling sea." Tests don't only come in words but also in beauty and what isn't said. Beauty itself is a test. It separates those who are hypnotized by it and melt under its pressure from those who are able to keep their cool. I kept my cool, slowly looking away with a smirk on my face.

There were three hours before the foam concert – the main event – and during that time, the girls danced inside the DJ booth. The guys were like zombies lining up outside the red velvet ropes trying to strike up conversations with the girls. One kind soul tried to get the blonde's attention, and she shook her head at him. He walked away red-faced and embarrassed.

But it wasn't until she put on her skates and went out into the whirlpool of skaters that men really crashed and burned.

Dozens of men tried anything to get her to notice them. Just to have a chance at the plate.

They would skate next to her and talk, but she ignored them like there was an invisible glass wall separating them. One brought her a slushie and she said, "No thanks." It was like watching a tiger versus a house cat every time.

Nobody could break her walls.

At the end of the event, it was time for the foam concert. It took fifteen minutes to move the DJ equipment outside. I went to the locker bay to collect my stuff. I didn't really want to do the foam, but Jay did. We argued about it while the locker bays filled with more people. More people meant louder noise, so our argument grew louder until an instant silence took over the locker bay for a few seconds.

I noticed someone at the locker right next to mine on my left. It's like when you're driving and every time you pull up next to someone, you have to look at them. I turned and looked at who was right next to me. I couldn't believe it. It was her – the blonde.

Was this called fate?

I looked at Jay, who was to my right, wide-eyed. He made a gun with his pointer finger and thumb signaling to pull the trigger and go for it.

I gulped.

Fear takes control of your chest and your knees first. It feels like you have no strength as your stomach does loop-the-loops inside. You sweat, but you feel cold, and then you feel nothing until you notice your heart beating at the pace of a galloping gazelle fleeing from a predator. I was no match for this perfect specimen of femininity, so I had to be an incredible actor.

To be successful is to be the opposite of what everyone else is. Attention seemed to equal rejection with her. Every man who gave her some was nothing less than annihilated. I had to get her to 'open' me somehow to get a massive edge. I heard that women don't want to open the man though. They want the right man to open them and take charge. According to the chart, girls will act differently around a man they find attractive. In my peripheral, I analyzed every detail.

She flipped her hair and laughed loudly with her friend as if she wanted to be noticed.

Her laughing might have been my signal to break the ice and shoot my shot. But after a few moments, she broke it instead.

I was looking at my phone and something of hers dropped by my feet. She knelt, picked it up, and on her way back up, 'accidentally' bumped her elbow against my ass.

"Oh my gosh!" she blurted. "I'm so sorry!"

This was her way of breaking the ice…by abusing me.

I knew in this moment that I had to commit to believing in myself fully because women are apparently three times more 'sensory aware' than men. She would recognize insecurity, manipulation, or insincerity in a microsecond. I'm sure that she had witnessed every single small detail of low-value men. She would instantly pick up on one sniff of fear, one bluff in my eyes, one slight fidget, deflating her curiosity.

This was pressure, but I loved it.

I gave her a surprised look. "How forward of you," I insisted. "This is how you flirt with someone?"

Over time, I began to get better at assessing reality. In every moment, we are in control of two things: the way we interpret our reality and our reactions to it. For example, an unconfident man subconsciously communicates, 'She'd never want me...' while a man who views himself as the prize communicates, 'She wants me so bad that she would touch my ass while acting like it was an accident.'

Maybe it was an accident, but either way, it was an opportunity. It was time to upgrade my operating system to compete in the big leagues.

She chuckled. "You think *I'm* flirting with *you*?" Her sarcastic huffing implied that I was crazy to make this assumption. But it wasn't crazy...she literally touched my ass, and that's the game – whose reality is stronger? The game had begun.

Luckily, she reacted emotionally, which was what I needed to spark desire.

Her response – a test – was designed to throw a weak man off his center, but I knew the secret.

I had to use it to gain leverage.

I disconnected our eye contact and smirked. "Well, flirting starts with words, and touching usually comes later..." I took a slight pause before continuing. "Slow down, babe, you're rushing me a little bit."

She bit her lip, and a smile grew slightly.

"Oh my gosh, shut up!" Her face reddened, just like every guy she'd rejected before me.

Most men hit on her, and that was the frame of their conversation – that she was being rushed and hit on. I reengineered that idea and accidentally stumbled upon something that's absolutely intoxicating to a woman, implying that not only was she the one who was hitting on me but that she was rushing me. It was a lethal card to play.

"Tell me something interesting about you," I said, positioning my body away from her so it looked like I could walk away at any moment if she couldn't keep me interested. I was doing and saying everything I could to make her chase me.

She told me she was a model, which was obvious. But I remembered a line from Neil Strauss, author of *The Game,* and used it when I saw this opportunity.

"A hand model?" I asked, slowly looking down at her hands. A mischievous smirk formed as I looked back into her eyes.

"A hand model?" she retorted, and then caught on to the tease. She gasped and slapped my chest teasingly. "Wow!"

I chuckled.

"Oh, ha-ha," she fake-laughed. "So funny. No. I'm actually a model for the Colgate toothpaste commercials."

Jay wheeled around us and began to flirt with her friend – a girl with blonde hair but skin that reminded me of a redhead I knew. My peripheral noticed that everyone around us was listening to our conversation. I was so nervous that my sweat was sweating. Every guy there wanted her, and every person there could clearly see how she was reacting to me. Not a single man that night had gotten more than seven seconds with her. These guys wanted me to join the rejection club with them, but I'd paid my time in that club far too long. Just a second in that club was a second too long because...I chose that. It was my belief and my commitment.

Now I chose to be a winner.

"Sure, you're pretty okay," I said, reciting a push-pull line, "but in my experience, the prettier the girl, the more boring she usually is."

She scanned me slowly from my shoes up to my eyes. "You're so confident," she replied.

I copied her, scanning her from her boots, up her skintight jeans, and all the way to her eyes. "Go on," I whispered, "I love being sweet-talked." I smiled ear to ear.

She started laughing. "No!" she snapped. "The way you act... You're the kind of guy who talks to lots of girls." She paused, staring into my eyes. "Or a lot of girls fall for you."

"But that doesn't mean I like them back," I countered instantly.

"I don't like guys like that." Her tone completely changed. She was pulling away as a test to see if I would chase. It's not what she says but what the message is behind what she says.

I had to assess my options in a split second. Logically, I wanted to respond, "I'm not that type of guy" because logically this made sense.

She said she didn't like that type of guy, so if I told her I'm not, then she would like me more.

But it's actually the opposite.

She'd lose interest because she'd know I would only say that to prove myself to her. She was playing emotionally, so I had to play her game. I had to do what's called a pattern interrupt to break this negative state she was in.

My heart raced because I was risking the entire conversation.

"Oh, really?" I responded. "I can tell how much you don't like me, you know, by the way you grabbed me from behind earlier." I looked away, or rather, pulled away because I had set the bait for her. I exaggerated because she hadn't grabbed my ass, but if she was going to argue about it then I'd win this.

She broke out in laughter. "What?! That's not true!" She kicked me with her skate. "You know I didn't grab it! Besides, there's nothing to grab."

I looked at her, offended at first, and then I thought about it. She had just indirectly said that she was checking me out. I just stared into her eyes as if I was onto her.

"What?!" she said again.

I shut my locker as if I was about to leave.

"What's your name?" she asked. I told her and then realized it was a slight loss in opportunity. I could have made her guess so it felt like she was working for me, but no problem. I found out her name was Caitlyn.

"Well, Connor, will I see you at the foam concert?"

I held out my hand. "Only if you take me there."

Caitlyn grabbed my hand, and all four of us walked outside to the VIP area of the concert. Me, Caitlyn, Jay, and his newfound girl, Becky.

Part

Misdirection

Some people are car geeks, some are video-game geeks, and I happen to be an anime geek.

Misdirection, a term coined from *Kuroko No Basket*, is a technique that diverts the opponent's attention, allowing its user to vanish. Commonly, misdirection is seen in magic tricks, specifically sleight-of-hand tricks, in order to manipulate what the attention is on.

The game of flirting is won by how well a man can handle pressure, and misdirection was my newfound ability to counter a test.

I realized I did have something special.

I could process quickly, and when I figured out how to use that, it created a huge advantage.

Attraction builds by how well a man is able to handle the emotion of the interaction. Usually, it comes from tests to see if a man emotionally reacts. For example, if she says, "I don't like that shirt on you," maybe she doesn't, but if you change your shirt to please her then she disrespects you because you're giving in to her test by attempting to please her. Also, if you react to her test by saying, "I paid $70 for this shirt," she sees she can throw you off your center.

Instead, to pass a test, misdirection is key. Also known as a playful interpretation or reframing, the key is to reflect her test back onto her.

In that example, she is bringing the attention to your shirt, attempting to throw you off of your center, but you misdirect it back onto her by saying, "Please stop sweet-talking me, you know it's my weakness. I know what you're trying to do." Or, "You just can't keep your eyes off of me, can you?"

You take the attention away from your shirt and redirect it back onto her as if she is the one hitting on you.

No matter what she is saying, you play the role that she is hitting on you. She will test again, and you will say, "Stop, it's not going to work. Like you're cute and everything, but pretty words aren't enough to get me into bed."

This is addicting for a woman because if she can't get you to emotionally react then it indirectly implies that you are strong – that she can trust you and that you could protect her because she can't have her way with you emotionally as she does with every other guy. It's about what her actions are saying because 93 percent of communication is nonverbal.

You shouldn't reply logically to her words because this game isn't logical. It's about how a man can make her feel. Supplication, changing your answers to match hers, and logic will make her feel bored. Never try to convince her on why she should go out with you, but create a strong frame and interpretation that will make her feel excitement and passion, and leave her wondering what's going to happen next like a good love story.

She told me she wouldn't like a man like me, but *she's* the one who touched my ass. *She's* the one whose full attention is on me.

Hidden in people's words are always signs that tell you what they are really thinking. She put the attention on me by saying she'd never like me, but I mirrored that attention back onto the flawed contradictions in her actions.

Also, contradictions are one of the best ways to flirt with a girl. If she's eating candy, for example, but says that health is important to her, you can pull away like Ace by saying, "Yeah, I can really tell" in a sarcastic tone.

I still had a problem, however.

I could carry a conversation, and I could potentially trigger some desire and flirt when months ago I could barely talk to a girl. I felt like a man of the world with Caitlyn dancing on me and the crowd staring at us, but when she turned around and moved her face to within inches of mine, she stared into my eyes. I needed to kiss her. But my body wouldn't move the few inches to do it.

I feared rejection – sexual rejection, just like it was with the softball player.

If she said "no" then I didn't know how to bounce back from that, and everything I'd built would disappear with one word.

Life is about choice. If I didn't go for it then she would most likely view me as timid and I'd lose. She'd see the real me that I was trying to hide. If I went for it and she declined the kiss then I'd also lose. There was a chance I'd get it, though, and I had to figure out a way.

I remembered watching *Titanic* when Jack kisses Rose for the first time in that famous scene where she said "I'm flying," and even though she was married (unhappily), he went for the kiss, and she kissed him back. From that point, she was hooked on him. She was obsessed to the point where she let him draw her naked. I wanted to feel what it felt like to be obsessed over, so I had to take the risk, like Jack, and expand my comfort zone.

I mustered up the courage when I saw Jay also take a risk. He asked Becky to go somewhere alone, and when she said, "I should stay with my friends," he still walked away. She hesitated and then followed him. In order to get success, you must risk failure.

I grabbed Caitlyn's hand and led her back to the rollerblading alley so we could have some quiet alone time. We sat at a table, and the black light from the alley lit up each of my pinstripes in a purple glow.

We flirted and bantered for a few minutes, but she was right next to me, and she was close.

I had to say it. I'd heard another way besides options A to D from earlier – option E – but it required two sentences that I had to force out.

"Let's play a game," I said, reciting the first line.

"What game?"

All I had to say was eight words that I'd heard from the dating coach Jason Capital. My hands were cold but sweating. Butterflies flapped around in my stomach. I was so nervous, but I spit them out in a stutter.

"If I... If I win, you have to kiss me."

She stared at me for a moment. Fuck. Fuck. She had to be on to me. This was a bad decision. I was like a little kid trying to play a game with her. I should've just gone for it when I had the chance.

"Okay," she said, smirking. "You're on."

Relief.

The game consisted of five simple questions – at least that's what I told her.

I redesigned the questions to my liking, the first being, "What's your favorite song out right now?" She told me it was a song by The Weeknd. The second question was: "If you could be anywhere on vacation right now, where would you be?" She said she would be in Cancun to party. The third question was: "What's your favorite thing to eat all time." She told me it was Chinese food. Question 4 is where the kiss happens.

We were sitting together on a bench, and our legs were touching.

I held up one finger and told her to watch it.

I moved it in close, right between her eyes, and touched her nose.

Then I backed it a hair away. She was cross-eyed.

"Am I touching you right now?" I asked, saying the final question.

"Um, no."

"Bésame," I told her, using one of the only two words I remembered from Spanish class. (The other was "Té amo," which means "I love you.")

"What?"

"That's 'kiss me' in Spanish," I whispered, leaning in. I pointed to our legs, showing her that we were in fact touching the entire time.

Her mouth dropped, and she let out a laugh right before we finally kissed. It was the best kiss I'd ever had. Her lips locked perfectly with mine.

"You're an asshole," she whispered between kisses.

"I don't like losing," I whispered back, bringing her in to kiss some more. Right before we kissed again, Jay and Becky walked in.

"What's going on in here?" Becky said, implying that sparks were flying.

Becky explained that her friend Stacy, the DJ, needed their help. I gave Caitlyn my phone to put her number in, but they were in a rush.

I didn't see her the rest of the night.

I felt so good until I realized on the drive back that night that she put in nine digits and accidentally forgot the tenth digit in the cellphone number. This meant I couldn't contact her.

Dammit.

I didn't know if she did that on purpose, or maybe it was the fact that she was being rushed, or maybe it was the opinion I've heard about models being brainless.

Part

Insider

While waiting to see if Caitlyn would call, I received a call from Noah, an old university mate of mine before he transferred to Indiana University to enter the Kelley School of Business.

He also had a dream to be a fraternity boy. Breaking 'code,' he showed me some of the things he had to do to even be considered a part of the 'family.' This is known as 'hazing.'

I remembered two videos that were in a deep chat archive. One of the newbies took a doll, put it in a stroller, and pushed the stroller into oncoming traffic. The cars slammed on their brakes or swerved around the stroller. The other started with a student walking down a hallway. I didn't know what his plan was, but I covered my mouth when I found out. He walked into the middle of a class that was in session. The teacher was lecturing about forty students. He then yelled in a monotone voice, "I. Have. Hemorrhoids." The professor turned to him, staring, and the two kids (the one with hemorrhoids and the videographer) ran off before he could say anything.

Noah was born into an upper-class family, kind of like mine at first, but the only difference was that his family was still together.

Raised by Christians, he was shunned away from any talk about sex and had been programmed to target one special girl who he could marry after college. Growing up, he and I were put into the same crib together when we were babies, but then his family drifted away from ours after the divorce until we reunited in college and stayed in contact.

"The reason I called was that I saw you at the foam concert," he told me on the phone, "but I saw you with a girl, and I didn't want to interrupt."

I updated him on Jay, the community, and Caitlyn. We bonded over talking about girls.

He said that he made a mental note to call me later to invite me to a special event at IU called 'Little 5.'

Noah told me that IU is one of the biggest party schools in the country, and this event went for days on end and was known worldwide. More than 25,000 people traveled from across the country to attend, including professional athletes, famous DJs, models, and more. The parties never stopped, all day and all night for an entire week. The way he described it as alcohol, foam, and mascara-covered girls giggling up and down the streets of Bloomington. It didn't take much convincing for me to agree to attend it with him.

When I thought of partying with girls like this before, my heart started to race just thinking about it because I didn't have the ability to make a girl like me. Now, I couldn't wait to test out this newfound power I had adopted. If for some reason I get rejected, I could just turn around and probably see a new girl to try the techniques on again and keep doing that until I win.

"It's in fourteen days, but one more thing," Noah said. "I've been dating a girl for the past month and she's the girl who I want to settle down with, so if you and Jay decide to come, make sure not to hit on Selena."

Noah was a virgin, claiming to be waiting for the right one, but I felt that deep down that wasn't the truth. I think he wanted to be the Jay or the Ace. One of the major reasons he left my university was because he was messaging girls left and right looking for dates, and when he finally got one after dozens of tries, they went out. After treating her like a gentleman – buying flowers, opening the door for her in the Porsche his parents bought him – she still called him after three weeks to say, "Let's just be friends."

A week later, he migrated to IU, running into Selena at some fraternity party, but the only thing that changed was the environment, not him.

"So, have you, like, slept with her yet?" I asked.

"She let me kiss her once," he snapped. Every time that I asked him about his experience with women, he tended to get awkward or would retaliate as if I was saying it to attack his ego.

"She's different from the girls you and Jay tend to go after," he continued. "Selena doesn't want sex; she's not into that stuff."

One of the things I was beginning to understand was that women want sex just as much as men do, if not more, but when I tried to give him advice to seduce her, he went back to his old self.

"You need to romance her, tease her, and be bold by going for the kiss with her," I said, revealing some of the tricks I discovered on how to go for the kiss. "Women want a man who will take the lead, the high-value man who will bring out her wild side."

"Well," he responded, "that stuff works on easy women. So, when you guys come, don't do any of that and mess it up between me and her."

We had bonded through the pain of rejections, but when I felt like I finally had a fresh start and could move both of our lives in a different and better direction with girls, he was resistant to it. I couldn't tell if he craved power like Jay, if he was in denial, or if maybe he was actually right that a man should focus on finding someone different like Selena.

Maybe I was wrong because I felt different about Caitlyn, but I couldn't deny that what Jay had taught me yielded huge results. Part of me was like Noah because 'the one' was an idea that my parents pushed when I was younger.

Even Casanova, arguably the world's most famous charmer, had one special woman he fell in love with – Lucia. However, she disappeared, and it was said that his hundreds of love affairs were an effort to evade the pain of the one who got away.

Maybe Caitlyn was different just as Noah had described Selena being. Maybe she was my Lucia. Or maybe I was letting old habits take over.

I realized that Caitlyn was truly different when I went out with her for the first time.

True Colors

I had two sides to me.

There were two places I loved most on this earth that represented these sides: the isolated mountains and the populated city. My dad tended to take my brother and me on vacation to the mountains – the Smoky Mountains and the Rockies in Wyoming and Montana, while my mom took us to beach cities – Cancun, Miami, and cruises with stops at big cities.

It seemed like my mother always saw me as the extroverted flirtatious guy because when I went out to the clubs or on cruises, I talked to everybody. But with my dad, I rarely talked and tended to isolate myself and go into deep thought. People typically only saw one side of me and believed that was the true me.

I was like the moon. One side lit up and glowed, but the other side remained cold and dark. Depending on which side you saw, that was who you believed I was.

I always felt like my dad wouldn't like the extroverted wild side to me, so I tended to stay quiet, but then my mom never liked it when I was quiet. I was constantly changing who I was around other people like an actor.

I found out that Caitlyn was much deeper than my surface interpretation of her when we finally went out on the next weekend.

On the outside, I saw her as perfect.

She probably had a great family with few issues. I thought her dad probably spoiled her like Noah's parents did for him. She had guys hitting on her constantly because of her beauty, and her confidence most likely stemmed from that. Quickly, however, I realized that the opposite was true.

She had tracked down my number from Becky, who got it from Jay.

"So, you just weren't going to contact me ever again?" she asked.

"Um, you only gave me part of your number, so what did you want me to do? Fill in the numbers and text each one until I finally stumbled upon you?"

"That would have been so sweet if you did that."

I guess I could have done that.

"How did you forget to put your number in my phone?"

"I don't know! I was being rushed, I guess."

She lived forty-five minutes away from me, and the gentleman in me decided to see if this Noah tactic really worked. I drove over to her place, and by the time I reached her house, it was dark. It was in the middle of nowhere in the boonies of Indiana, and according to the Google Maps, it was in a dense forest.

"All I see is a cobblestone driveway leading into complete darkness," I told her on the phone when I got close to the house.

"Yes," she said. "Drive into that."

So, I drove into the dark forest to a medium-sized log cabin that looked like it was made in the 1800s. Bugs flew around the lights and buzzed passed my ear.

When I raised my fist to knock on the door, she opened it before my knuckles could strike the heavy wood.

Eye-catching as usual, she wore a skintight metallic red dress and wore her blonde hair in a bun with zigzag bangs.

"Come in," she said, hugging me. She smelled like a flower-filled meadow. "Someone wants to meet you."

The room was dimly lit with a crackling fire burning in the chimney. The shadows danced off an old man in a wheelchair. He had clear plastic tubes leading from a tank to his nose. His handshake was weak, and his body might have been giving up on him, but his spirit seemed to make up for it.

He nudged me with his elbow. "Caitlyn has never had a boy over before."

Caitlyn embarrassingly bantered with him. We talked, he asked me questions about my intentions and how Caitlyn and I met, and we finally left.

"Your grandfather seems like such a ladies' man," I told her.

As we talked in the car, she slowly opened up about her past. Her mother died when she was young, and she was sexually abused by her father after her mother's death. He was eventually thrown in jail. After her grandparents found out, they took her in. Her grandmother had passed a couple of months before, and her grandfather was going to be going soon as well.

He had lung cancer, hence the breathing device in his nose. So, she took care of him.

Men just saw her as a piece of meat they could stick their meat into. Not her soul, her heart, and what made her who she was. I liked connecting with people and hearing their stories because ever since I was young, connection was the thing I lacked. Connection was my greatest asset but my greatest curse as well.

I had an ability that allowed people to believe they could trust me, that they could tell me anything.

It was because of my past. When I felt alone as a child I craved a connection. What aroused me most was the feeling that they were showing me a side of themselves that they kept locked away – their true colors. If they felt they could show me that, then they must trust me.

I had to make sure I didn't abuse that gift, but it was intoxicating to know you're someone's escape – that you are priceless in someone's life.

As she told me about her life, I listened, but I also *felt* what she was saying. I listened deeply to what her heart and soul were truly saying. I realized that when I told her about my past, I was showing her my true colors too. It was like our souls were intertwining. I wanted her to be obsessed with me, but perhaps she already was.

I led her into Kumo, a Japanese hibachi restaurant. As we were being escorted to our table, every eye was on her.

I noticed a husband with his wife as we walked by their table; he was checking her out, and the wife caught him, provoking a scolding look.

"Everyone is looking at me," she whispered to me as we sat down.

"You think so?" I asked. "Because I was going to say the same thing to you about me."

She rolled her eyes. "You're so confident."

After we ate, I took her to a park nearby, and we talked for hours.

When I took her home, I walked her up to her doorstep like a gentleman, as Noah would call it. We began to kiss passionately. The unromantic sound of bugs flying in our ears and swatting them with our hands as we kissed caused her to say: "I can't stand this. Do you want to come in?" Of course, I did.

We snuck past her grandfather sleeping in his chair and went upstairs. Each wooden stair creaked. She led me to her room, and then went down to check on her grandfather. I couldn't help but notice some pictures on her desk. I picked up the pile and started to sort through them. It was her and another guy. He had black hair, a smile that looked as though it was a stick-on, and reddened eyes as if he'd been smoking. The last picture showed them kissing. On the back, she wrote, "Mitch and I" with a date that was from a month and a half ago.

I heard the stairs creaking. She was coming back up.

I put the pictures back and hopped on the bed.

She had changed her clothes while she was downstairs into a T-shirt and shorts. She fell on me, and we instantly started to make out. I forgot about the other guy in those pictures as my hand felt what had teased my eyes earlier. I began to take her clothes off. She stopped me.

"I've never had sex with a guy before," she said. I stood up because I was shocked.

"We're so similar," I told her.

"What do you mean?"

"I've never had sex with a guy before either," I said, smiling. I leaned in to kiss her some more.

She pushed me away, laughing. "No, seriously, Connor."

I hadn't been trained or studied for what I needed to do when she rejected a kiss. I thought it would be a nightmare, but I found the resistance to be arousing.

I knew that patience was key in this situation.

When a man tries to pressure, chase, or rush to try to get a kiss or a date from a woman, she becomes extremely uncomfortable. Nowadays, we hear sickening things about rapes and other fucked-up things that happen to women. When a man tries to force or pressure instead of letting a woman come to him, she subconsciously categorizes him in that creeper zone, hoping that she doesn't become the next story that makes the news.

There is this idea in the pickup world that sex was based on survival back in the Stone Age – that women wanted to mate with the alpha male because of his genes. If they could produce the strongest offspring, they could survive and reproduce, keeping their genes in existence.

But I realized that this is no longer the truth of relationships.

Women respond to alpha-male characteristics, but women don't need a man anymore to pay the bills or provide food for her like in the old days. She is fully capable of doing that herself. Also, men don't need a woman to clean the house or prepare the food. These gender role ideas are dying.

Relationships now are based on the connection.

As we sat there, Caitlyn looked at me so innocent and pure. "I don't want to lose it to someone and then regret it later," she whispered.

Under all of that beauty and the tough act was just a fragile and caring girl.

I leaned in closer to her, resting my arm on the side of the bed.

"The last thing I want to do is make you uncomfortable," I said, reassuring her. "I'm enjoying what we have going on right now. When you're ready, and when I'm ready, that's when it will happen." I took a big inhale and smirked. "I can't help but notice that you talk about your virginity and sex a lot around me."

She blushed and dug her face into the pillow. "I can't help it," she whined into the pillow. "I want you, and I think you might be that person."

"Then show me how much you want me," I whispered, reciting a line I heard from a movie. I looked into her eyes and at her lips, exercising the triangular gaze.

It started with a slow kiss and grew in heat and passion after each second like an oven that was on preheat.

I read in Robert Greene's *The Art of Seduction* that being a great seducer involves bringing all of your passion into the moment with her. For that brief moment, it's as if you are madly in love with her, and you kiss her as if you are. I also heard that women will infer what sex will be like with you based on the first kiss, so I had to make it passionate.

I took my shirt off. I put her on her back.

"Put your hands above your head," I whispered into her ear. They went up like a draw gate. I slid her shirt up. She had goosebumps. I kissed her starting above her pelvis bone and, in a line, all the way up to her sternum and in between the black Calvin Klein bra she was wearing. Her back arched. I took the shirt and continued past her head.

As her head popped out, her hair was tattered up.

She thought I was taking her shirt off, but I wasn't. I decided to release a small portion of *50 Shades of Grey*. I had witnessed time and time again how Jay tended to dominate his girls in the bedroom, and now I needed to be that man I never knew how to be. I put her wrists together, and right when the shirt reached her palms, I wrapped it around them. Her hands were now tied together as if in handcuffs.

I acted like I was going to kiss her; she closed her eyes.

I moved my head to the side of hers and used the front of my jaw to turn her head.

Her sternocleidomastoid popped out of her neck. I never thought I'd use anatomy in this book, but besides all of the cheating I did off my neighbor's tests in that class, I knew what this muscle was – my ace in the hole for a turn on.

It runs from the bottom of the ear to the center of the collar bone.

Lip-biting and kissing it, I was an educated young man applying school for once.

It was as if I was playing a DJ board. Every part of her body that I licked, bit, or sucked caused a different noise to come out.

She put her hand over my jeans and rubbed my dick. I took off her shorts and saw the matching Calvin Klein underwear. She was soaking through them. I rubbed her clitoris over the underwear and then moved her panties down, slipping a finger in.

Commotion came from downstairs.

"Caitlyn?" her grandfather yelled. "Come down here, hurry."

Of all the times, it had to be right then. Just like that, the moment evaporated. It took hours to build and only one sentence to blow away.

She put her wrinkled shirt back down and ran her fingers through her hair as she left the room.

When she came back upstairs, she told me that her grandfather was having health issues. She needed to take him to the hospital.

"Do you want me to take you guys to the hospital?" I asked, putting my clothes on.

"No!" she hissed. "Are you crazy? I don't want him to see you're still here."

"Well, I'm kind of in the driveway."

She pondered that for a moment. "We are going to sneak you out."

Somehow, I snuck past the old man when he wasn't looking, opened the door leading into the garage, and shut it too. Then, in the garage, I went out through the back door and snuck around her house to the driveway. Finally, I got into my car and somehow pulled out of that pitch-black driveway with very little light. I got home around 3:30 in the morning.

I knew the next time I was with her, it would happen.

Part

Calm Before the Storm

I had exactly seven days until Little 5.

This was when I received a phone call from Adonis describing his first sexual experience.

Adonis had his own version of value.

He was the guy who you would beat twenty times in a video game, and as soon as he beat you once, he would say, "I'm retired, man."

Then you wanted to play him again. This was especially true for Ace.

"I'm better than you!" he would argue. "I beat you every single time."

Then Adonis would pull out his unique voice. "Whatever you want to think, man," he would say as if he was stretching and then moved his shoulders acting as if he was walking away even though he was sitting down. "But we both know who number-one is." Finally, he moved his shoulders up and down, holding up one finger.

He had his own way of capturing your attention, and it was intoxicating to me how he told a story, leaving me in tears of laughter practically every time. It wasn't flashy nor was it magnetic to women, but to Ace and me, it connected everyone.

"I have to tell you about this experience," he said.

He had this slow, deep storytelling voice and threw in extremely long and dramatic pauses. I couldn't ever describe it, but I could do it.

If you asked a question, he would look at you slowly, then go "humph" as if he was snickering, and then say, "Duh."

"I go over there, and I'm being all sweet and nice to her mom. But she's foreign from somewhere in Asia. I couldn't understand a word she was saying. Eventually, my girl says we are going to the basement, and I was like, 'uh-oh,' that's when you know it's on."

"She took you downstairs?" I commented.

"Hell yeah, baby, and we started watching a movie on Netflix. You know, Netflix and chill, right? We were spooning on the couch, and my dick was hard as fuck. She had to have felt that shit. It was like stabbing into her back. Like *boom!* Right there."

He paused to go into a separate room to finish the story.

"I offered to give her a massage," he said. "The dirty masseuse."

"That's like the oldest trick in the book!"

"Yes," he said. "She looked in my eyes during it, and I looked into her eyes. I know she wanted the D. I started making out with her. I felt her everywhere. Then I started sucking on her titties. She had those Asian boobs, the ones that are pointed."

I had never been with an Asian girl before, but I made a mental note to perhaps see for myself at IU.

"Then I went into her pants," he continued. "And I literally gave her the ultimate technique."

"What's that?" I asked.

"The finger-blaster 9000, baby," he answered in 'the voice.'

All I could picture in my head was a jackhammer or a nail gun.

"Well," I said, "I'm glad you had fun."

Even if the dirty masseuse was the oldest trick in the book to turn her on, it worked. I wasn't sure about the finger-blaster 9000, however.

The next person to call me was Jay.

"What do you mean we can't go to IU on Saturday?" he asked.

"Caitlyn and I are supposed to go out Saturday, but after we go out you and I can stay down there the whole rest of the week."

She had asked me to hang out on the following Saturday, and I wanted to, so I postponed the IU trip for the next day.

"This is why," Jay huffed, "you have to be able to say no. We have stuff to do, which is why we can't be close if you bail on plans."

He was going to be promoting a club in Bloomington on the last night of Little 5, and he wanted me to attend it with him.

Over time as I watched Jay interact with women, he tended to have his own style that worked, and I finally began to see how it worked.

He would flirt with them, but somewhere in the interaction he would say, "It's too bad it would never work between us." Or, "You're awesome, we will make great friends." Or, "Blonde girls are my favorite" when he was talking to a brunette.

I realized that his style was disqualifying the girl to make her desire him more. Hot girls are usually lusted after by men. To them, men like that are abundant, but Jay did the exact opposite. He would in essence imply that he was interested, but verbally say he wasn't. It kept her guessing. When she has men asking her out on dates all the time or buying her things but then a man tells her, "We will make great friends," she tends to respond, "Ha-ha, definitely…wait, friends?" Because she's used to men hitting on her, when he did the opposite, it created scarcity.

All of a sudden, she would try to persuade him why he should sleep with her.

He was using a similar tactic on me and, even though I knew what he was doing, it still managed to work on me.

"Let me see what I can do," I responded.

The next call was from Caitlyn.

"I won't be able to go out this weekend," she said. "I know I said we could, but I'm going to be at home taking care of my grandfather. Can we reschedule?"

I guess it all worked itself out. I called Jay back and told him that I canceled on Caitlyn, which was a lie, but he didn't need to know that.

I wanted to be in peak performance form for Little 5. Even if there were thousands of options, I wanted to be so much in sync that I could win on my first try.

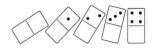

Chapter IV

La Douleur Exquise

Wanting Someone You Can Never Have

[La Douleur Exquise: A French term defined as "The pain of feeling like you found your soulmate but realizing you aren't theirs."]

This university was a spawning ground.

Every time I walked out of a party, club, house, or fraternity and then went back in, it seemed that the room had completely refreshed.

Hotter women appeared out of thin air every minute.

It was perfect for gaining experience at a lightspeed pace.

"My fraternity is starting its party tonight at 11," Noah said as we walked around the campus. "And we are all on the guest list. I had to jump through hoops to get you on it, but it's going to be packed with IU's hottest girls."

Noah dressed like a fraternity boy now. Khaki pants, loafers, and an unfitted burgundy button-down shirt. He had tan skin, messy black hair, and his best attributes, hazel eyes and a winning smile. Even though he was five-foot-six, I felt that if he knew how to sell himself then he would be a total monster, but he was still in denial. In contrast, I came dressed in plaid grey pants, suede tan boots, and a dark-blue long-fit T-shirt.

"Is Selena joining us?" I asked.

"No, she isn't really into the partying thing," he said. "I promised her I wouldn't be drinking or talking to any girls."

Jay snickered.

"What?!" Noah snapped.

"If you don't just fuck that girl already," he said.

"We are waiting; it's what you do when two people respect each other."

I thought they would bash heads like rams. We had the preppy boy from the suburbs who was raised by a nice family versus the city boy who practically raised himself and focused only on getting results.

It looked like the White House with a huge flag hung in front with random letters that apparently were Greek. When I asked Noah what the name of it was, he said what sounded like "Phi Grammar Zelda."

So, that's what I called it.

"You live here?" I asked.

"Well," he hesitated, "not yet. They didn't let me in, but I helped them with the guest list so hopefully, that will get me in."

"So, you're being used?" I asked.

"It takes time," he assured me.

It sounded bogus. I had never been a fan of fraternities or sororities. I really didn't see the point. My image of a fraternity was a bunch of rich, spoiled kids who did an unreasonably large amount of cocaine. I asked Noah the positives of being in one, and the only one he could think of was "networking." I still saw no point in paying that much money and being bullied to 'network.' And network with whom? I wasn't there to network, I was there for one reason – to sharpen my skills.

I tried to be sincere and understanding, but I could only reply with one word because I just wasn't interested. "Cool," I said, faking a positive tone.

When we walked in, I did see one positive sign. It was packed to the walls with girls I wanted to meet. There were also a lot of people doing lines of cocaine off a glass table in the basement, solidifying my image of frat boys.

It was Jay and me. This time, I believed that I could be his equal and bring the heat. Noah checked people in at the back door, and Jay was already hunting. I guess it was just me then. I saw Jay once throughout the next hour, and he was walking down a dark hallway with a girl.

Dancing and stumbling around was a possibly drunk but attractive girl with curly dark-brown hair. She wore jeans with holes all over, and specifically on her behind that showed the crease where her ass met her hamstring. The grey turtleneck she wore made her look business professional at the top, but the jeans made her look like a teasing stripper from the waist down.

When the song ended, she sat down on a black sofa next to a girl who looked pissed off and didn't want to be there. The girl with a touch of annoyance or anger in her look folded her arms, and brushed her blonde hair behind her shoulder. She wore black glasses and reminded me of someone who taught a science class. I needed to win over the entire group of girls in order to get the one I wanted. But I didn't know which one I wanted. They were both cute.

My heart began to race again because opening a girl was still nerve-racking to me. Once I got the conversation going and actually saw them becoming interested was when I tended to relax and make great things happen.

I had to say something. Anything.

The opening line is the first impression, so I tried to figure out what could set me apart.

Something that showed I was socially 'proofed' – the idea that if it's shown that other girls like you then your targets most likely will too. I also needed to apply the idea that I wasn't needy or clingy like most guys. Perhaps I was overthinking it and just needed to say anything.

Maybe the words didn't matter that much, and it was about how I presented myself.

I acted like I was casually walking past the pair.

"No way," I said, backing up and pointing at the two of them. "You two *have* to be twins."

They looked absolutely nothing alike.

"You think so?" the brunette who was dancing earlier said. I had commandeered their attention; now it was time to reel them in. "We actually get that a lot!" she chirped.

She was the talkative, energetic one of the group.

"I can already tell that you and I are going to be great friends," I said, reciting a disqualifier for the heck of it. "You're very energetic like I am."

After a few moments of fluffing, I noticed the blonde was side-eyeing me.

"You know," I said addressing the blonde, "if you're going to look at me like that, you should at least talk to me."

She smirked. I had broken through.

"You know your outfit is pretty cool," I said, baiting her. "My biology professor literally has the same one."

Her jaw dropped, and she couldn't help but start laughing. She kicked me under the table.

"Whoa, my love language is physical touch," I told her, exercising a line that indirectly said she was coming on to me. "So please try to control yourself."

The blonde perked up. "I've read that book!"

Now I felt I was finally getting somewhere. I'd found out that her love language was words of affirmation, so I told her that she was the cutest biology teacher I had ever seen. She argued back that she wasn't a biology teacher.

"This is why we could never be together," I said, conjuring up the disqualifier. But before I could finish the sentence, something caught my eye. I saw the back of a girl who looked exactly like Caitlyn.

"Why couldn't we work out?" the blonde asked.

"Because, um, never mind." I couldn't believe what I was seeing. "Something just came up," I told the girls. "I'll be back shortly."

"You'd better," the brunette said.

I was in the basement of the fraternity, full of people and loud music. I snaked through, undetected, to the side of this girl who looked like Caitlyn's twin to see if it was really her. When I could see her face, there wasn't any doubt about it.

I was about to walk up and say hi when a man walked over to her, gave her a drink, they kissed, and started walking upstairs. It was the guy I saw in the pictures when I was in her room.

I followed, and they turned a corner into a dark hallway. When I thought the coast was clear, I was about to turn the corner when Jay ran right into me.

"I've been looking for you everywhere," he said. "Made any progress?"

"Dude," I angrily whispered. "That girl!"

"What? Who?"

"That girl who just walked past you was Caitlyn!"

"Where?"

I took him around the corner, and right in our face, she was making out with this guy. My jaw dropped. They stopped and noticed us.

My eyes and Caitlyn's locked. Then she glanced away.

"Excuse us," I said, walking away.

As we walked back to the party, I looked at Jay. "She told me she was at home taking care of her grandfather tonight."

"I thought you cancelled on her."

Oh, fuck. That's right. "Yeah, she actually canceled on me," I admitted.

He burst out into laughter, but then he stopped abruptly. "Oh man, she really played you."

I tried to bounce back, but it really got to me. That night, and for the next two days, it reminded me of that one scene in *The Mummy Returns* where the chariot came through and took all of The Mummy's special powers away. Every time I tried to talk to a girl or flirt, I was shot down. I was clearly in a slump that I couldn't figure out how to get out of.

"You got played, man," Jay sympathized. "You got played."

"You think she lied to me about being a virgin too? And everything else?"

"Probably," he said. "It's the game. Everyone is trying to win, which means someone has to lose. You're the loser this time."

Something that was inspiring to me about Jay was his ability to bounce back from hardship and rejection. When his family moved here as immigrants, they got played by a scammer and lost $10,000 of hard-earned money. Jay said, "It happened. We have to work even harder and focus on how we can make it back." He never believed in basking in one's own misery; he only focused on action.

I remember a story my dad told me about a professional baseball player who was one of the best batters in his time. One season, he went into a slump, becoming one of the worst. Everyone thought his career was over, but the season after that he shot right back up, better than he ever had been before. The press asked him how he did that, and his only answer was, "I just stopped caring."

I didn't think that not caring could be my answer, but I searched for one.

I decided to return to Indianapolis the next morning to give myself a mental break from striking out. Jay stayed behind. He was tireless.

Falling

"I think I owe you an explanation," Caitlyn said on the phone.

She had called me while I was on driving home on the third day of Little 5.

"Mitch and I have been on and off since last October," she said. "I know it was wrong to lie to you, and I should've been honest."

"I appreciate that," I replied. I could have been angry, but I was there doing exactly what she was doing to me.

"So, what now?" she asked.

"What's your choice?" I said.

"Choice?"

"Are we going to continue, or are you getting back with him?"

"Why do I have to make a choice? I still love him, but I want to be friends with you at least."

I couldn't be around her and not be able to touch her. Or to flirt with her. Deep down, it brought those feelings back to the surface. It was like life was telling me once again, "You just aren't good enough." This time, another man had something that I didn't to keep Caitlyn, and I was left in second place.

"I can't be friends with you," I told her.

"What? Why? That's so selfish," she snapped.

"What's more selfish? Asking me to be something for you that I don't want to be, or me doing what's best for me?"

It basically ended on that note. I was fuming after I hung up.

Jay's words echoed around in my head: "Everyone is trying to win, which means someone has to lose. You're the loser this time."

But I was always the loser. Even if I won, I eventually lost.

My father once told me, "Second place is only the first loser."

I wondered why I cared so much. Perhaps it was because I still had that part of me that wanted marriage, that wanted one woman, while the other part of me wanted results. The unnatural abilities. Maybe it was just because she was the girl I worked my hardest for, only to have her leave me.

Over time, I felt I was being too nice and let myself become attached. After this moment, I realized that it truly is just a game. The strongest make it to the final round. I was only on the first few rounds, and every round had some form of sacrifice or lesson that nearly wiped me out every single time.

I wondered who had made it to the final round. Who were these people? I wondered what they had to sacrifice. I could only imagine how cold they were.

If I was worth it, and if I truly meant something to her, I believe she wouldn't have done that. It wasn't her words but what I saw in her actions. Her actions said that I was a piece worth sacrificing. I was the pawn, and it made me feel so worthless to be so easily tossed to the side.

It reminded me of why I started. I wanted the ability to break hearts. I wanted to feel what it felt like to be obsessed about. I had to put my pride aside and leave my emotions out of it.

I needed to create a style that was virtually impenetrable. A monopoly of seduction. A technique that included a high probability of success and an unnaturally low probability of rejection.

I woke up again. The nice guy in me found his way back to the surface, but I had to kill him off. This game played me when I played it as him. I wanted to be the player, the user, and the favored. I was distracted, but I'd leave my emotions behind, and I would come back colder.

Emotions & Their Meanings

"Never let success get to your head and never let failure get to your heart." These are the words of Drake – the perfect lesson for people dealing with love.

Remember the lesson, not the disappointment. If it consumes you, it will grow your attachment and you will suffer ever deeper until you stop it.

The struggle with my emotions always felt like it was a part of my life. Depression felt like it was in my life frequently, and the same with stress, anxiety, and other taxing emotions.

I grew colder, but that meant the loving and caring parts of me were extremely warm. I felt that most people experienced the cold, heartless side to me, but one thing that reached me every time and brought real tears to my eyes were those who struggled with severe depression, anxiety, and overwhelming sadness.

On my way back from IU, which was about a one-hour drive, I stopped at a diner that Noah told me about. After I was seated, I saw from the window a semi-truck parked across the street. The back half of it I could see, but the rest was behind a small shop. The half I could see read, "Life will never give you…" I couldn't read the rest. I thought that it was probably something useless anyway.

When I left, the warmth of the morning sun refreshed me. Maybe this was a good omen; maybe something good was coming. I got in my car, drove off, and got pulled over by a cop.

Maybe not.

I was speeding a little bit. Sixty in a thirty to be exact. I saw the cop; it was too late. The red and blue lights flickered behind me. We went through the typical routine. He told me how fast I was going and asked for my information. I give it to him, and he walked back to his patrol car to scan it. Then, during the few minutes he was back there, I flipped a coin to see whether I would get a ticket this time. Tails meant 'ticket,' heads meant 'how did I not?'

I flipped it. It landed. Tails it showed.

I looked at my mirror, waiting for him to step out with the ticket.

I stared out the window, and I noticed the drivers watching me as they passed by.

Two lanes over were for the cars turning left. The green arrow lit up, and they all proceeded to turn left. One after another until a semi-truck caught my eye.

It was the one from earlier at the diner.

My eyes widened as I read the rest of the quote: *"Life will never give you more than you can handle."* It seemed to drive by in slow motion.

In that moment, I realized something. I truly believe that life gives its toughest battles to its strongest soldiers, and the battle with my emotions was one that I struggled with almost my entire life.

Those kids from early in my life always told me that I was useless.

I was treated like I was a germ. When I was younger, I was always picked last for kickball or any sporting thing because nobody wanted me on their team. Caitlyn was the first time I ever felt like I connected with someone deep down. It felt like I was picked first for her kickball team because she wanted me. But when it was taken away from me, even if I was hurt or upset, I never would admit it.

I'm the type of person who bottles up their emotions.

Some of us tend to avoid our negative emotions, some endure them, and others fight them. I was more of the enduring type.

After enduring mine for so long, I came to the conclusion that if you try to run from them, they will give chase. If you try to endure them, they will erode you, and when you try to fight them, they will fight you back.

From what I have found, pain is a tool used to help promote personal growth.

We view pain as negative, but perhaps there are no such things as negative emotions because every emotion we have is really just a message telling us to change something or grow past something.

Life gives you obstacles that you can handle, but it challenges you to find a way through them. Life will throw obstacles in our way to challenge us to grow and to let us see how we react to them.

"Any painful circumstance that you have to endure in life is like a call to attention. Life is pointing out something that you need to learn. Anything that no longer serves you in life – whether it's a relationship that must end, a friendship that no longer serves you, or a job that runs its course – all these difficult changes need to be understood in that light. Pain is life's way of telling you that you're doing something wrong – you're stuck, and you need to grow past it before the pain goes away. The more you ignore the pain, or try to suck it up – the more life brings it up in front of you to deal with. It's only when you consciously face up to the truth that you can overcome those things."
- Corey Wayne, *Mastering Yourself.*

It's all in our mind's eye as to how we decide to perceive a situation. Each situation we're in is neither negative nor positive, but it can turn into a negative or a positive based on how we label it.

Here's a story I once heard:

A man was riding a bus. Two children ran around inside the bus, causing commotion and bumping into the man every couple of minutes. The man began to get angry. The kids then bumped into him so hard that he spilled some of his drink on his outfit. He turned to the father of the children and spat, "Could you please control your children?" The father looked at him and said with a hurt in his voice, "I'm sorry. Their mother passed away a few nights ago while we were away, and they haven't been handling it too well." In an instant, the man's anger turned to sorrow. "I'm so sorry to hear that. That must be devastating." At first, he was mad, but in an instant, his anger had transformed into sorrow. We can change our perspective instantly; we just have to change the way we communicate to ourselves and the way we interpret a situation.

I believe that when we are feeling an emotion like anger or hurt then we aren't seeing the bigger picture. We have incorrectly interpreted the situation that we must change. In order to grow, I needed to let go.

All negative emotions exist either in the past or the future. If one is feeling sad, heartbreak, and depression then they are held up in the past. Anxiety and stress arise within us from thinking about the past or future. In reality, fear, anger, depression, and pain are all messages. Sadness is communicating to you that you are living too much in the past. It is trying to help you to find a way to let go of whatever it is that is weighing you down. Anxiety and stress are communicating to you to let go of worrying about the future.

Pain is life's way of telling us that we need to let go of something.

Dwelling on the past only hurts us more because it's something we can never change, and worrying about the future is harmful because it hasn't happened yet. The only moment that counts is the present moment because that's the only moment we have control over.

Anger, depression, stress, anxiety, etc., are all found in those who feel like they need something in order to be fulfilled and happy. I'm not saying it's wrong to feel these emotions. It's natural. But to let them control you instead of using them to help you grow is a conscious choice. If we use them correctly, they are among our greatest allies, but they can instead be our biggest enemies if we let them take us over and control our actions.

Sit back and listen to why you are angry, hurt, sad, or frustrated. What are you seeking? Why? Do you not feel enough? Significant enough? Are you not fulfilled without the thing you crave? *The emotions we feel are messages that challenge us to grow to a point where we aren't in need of the something that we believe will fulfill us. To find a way to be happy without it.*

104

"What you are is what you have been. What you will be is what you do now." – Buddha

Presence is what you experience when you're completely at peace in this moment. You're accepting how you feel right now – the good and the bad. We must let emotions be our guides but never decide our actions. It's all about how we choose to see it. I could sit here and continue to be upset, or I could change my perspective and ask myself:

"What is good from this?"

"How can I use this to become better?"

"What is life trying to tell me by throwing this in my way?"

Our problems and obstacles cause emotions we perceive as being bad, but these emotions are life's way of challenging you and trying to tell you that there is always a way through it, under it, over it, or around it.

That is the very core of life's testing is for us to find a way to overcome our problems. Life doesn't give you obstacles that you can't handle; life doesn't want you to run away. It gives you a situation to help you grow and become more than what you currently are. The toughest battles are the ones that we don't know are going on within us.

Emotions are usually calling us to learn more patience and ask better questions to find a solution to the problems within ourselves.

The battles within are what create battles on the outside.

Negative emotions are a call to action. You're supposed to do something differently or think a different way than you are now. As Einstein said, "We cannot solve our problems with the same thinking we used when we created them."

Positive emotions are rewards for taking the proper actions, but pain serves a purpose.

Without our struggles or bad times, we would never know what the word 'good' even means or is. It is what has made the current you 'you.'

105

Life will throw obstacles at you to see how you respond to them. Especially if you really want something.

If you want a woman or a date, life might take that possibility away to see what your response is. Instead of reacting, realize that life is trying to teach you a lesson. Instead of falling into negativity, challenge yourself to find an answer, and take a different action.

Many people believe that a great life or relationship consists of no bad days, but that is only an illusion. Think of it this way: Every year, winter comes with heavy snow (at least in Indiana). Spring comes with a lot of rain. Summer comes with hot temperatures. There are rarely days where the temperature is perfect, and there are rarely days when everything goes just the way you want it to.

Knowing this, I had to leave my emotions out of my game. I needed to learn how to manage surprises and hone my skills for 'the comeback.'

Now it was time for me to take action and perfect my technique.

Oh, and I forgot to mention, that cop who pulled me over didn't give me a ticket.

The Deal

It was the final night of Little 5 when the wildest parties occurred.

Every day, the parties grew in every way: speaker loudness, number of attractive girls, and cocaine, marijuana, and alcohol consumption.

Jay was hired on to promote multiple clubs in Bloomington, and that was how the night started. We roamed the strip of clubs on Walnut Street, but when we took a side detour into BlueBird, the night took a wild turn.

One of the girls who had too much of some substance decided to get up on one of the tables during a song. She proceeded to take off all of her clothing for the whole club. Phones started recording when she had stripped all the way down to her bra and panties. The club cheered her on as the security guards and her boyfriend tried to awkwardly get her down.

"Don't touch me!" she snapped in a drunken babble. "I'll call the police."

"We are the police!" the guards argued back.

She then took off her bra and threw it into the crowd of people.

The crowd went wild as if it was a Lady Gaga concert.

This is when Noah and I witnessed one of Jay's greatest pickups of all time. He was on fire.

Amy was a typical party girl who liked to dance, get drunk, make out with random people, and then demand to be treated like a princess (not necessarily in that order). Jay won her over in about twelve minutes.

He hit her with push-pulls and disqualifiers one after another, and before she knew it, she was hooked.

He would pull her in by pouring a bottle of tequila in her mouth.

Then he pushed her away. "That's all you get," he told her. She slapped his arm.

"Give me some more!" she whined.

"It would never work between us," he said, exercising a disqualifier. "You're too demanding."

"I would make the perfect girlfriend!"

"You're probably a mediocre kisser anyways," he said.

"I give the best kisses," she argued.

"Prove it."

"No."

"Bad!" he said while lightly pushing her away with his hand. "Go to timeout!"

She held onto him when he tried to unwrap her arms.

"Alright, here's some more," he told her, acting like he was going to give her a drink. When she opened her mouth, he said, "Just kidding!"

He fluttered around like a butterfly, unable to be caught until he wanted to be.

When he looked deep into her eyes, he blamed her for turning him on. "Stop it!" he told her. "I know what you're trying to get from me, but it's not going to work."

Her brain was fried.

Then they kissed, and right before he left with her, he told me – slightly intoxicated – "I have a room a few blocks away at SpringHill Suites." He tried to enunciate the best he could. "If you can get a girl to the suite by midnight then I think you have what it takes to join our team."

Without waiting for my response, he turned around and walked out with Amy wrapped around his arm. Jay hated waiting. He stressed consistently that time is a person's most valuable asset; no amount of begging or money can give back time.

I was left with Noah, who had invited Selena to the club, and I finally got to see him interact with her for the first time.

It was a train wreck. Selena was completely different than how he made her out to be.

She was shy, but I could tell deep down that she liked to let loose and have some fun. She looked similar to Selena Gomez but tended to be unsure about everything she said until she got alcohol in her. She was just a regular girl who wanted to have fun, but it was Noah who didn't.

"Gentlemen don't get drunk in front of a girl," he said, spouting nonsense as usual.

I didn't have time for their awkward relationship, so I practically tore the place apart opening group after group. Attraction was flying, but nothing was sparking. I would grab girls and spin them around.

Eventually, a slightly tipsy Selena walked up to me on the dance floor and stood there staring into my eyes.

I was having fun as Noah stood in the back of the club.

I took her hand and spun her around as well, but it was code to never flirt with, hit on, or date one of the pack's girls – *ever*. Basically, it was an unwritten rule that she has to be dead to you.

Selena wanted to be dated, romanced, and swept off of her feet, but Noah wouldn't do that for her. For a moment, I considered taking her back to the suite so I could win Jay's challenge.

I shook my head. I couldn't do that to Noah. I wasn't going to break the pack's rules, but I had to ask: "You have a wild side to you, don't you?"

"Is that hot to a guy?"

There was no doubt about it. She was interested in me, but luckily Noah pulled her away. Then I awkwardly dismissed myself as I stepped outside to the sidewalk for a last-resort game.

12 A.M. Hustle

She stood by herself, leaning against a telephone pole on the corner of North Walnut Street.

She had the confident body language of Caitlyn and wore a skintight plaid grey dress and high heels. Her blonde hair was held back in a ponytail and she had high cheekbones. For some reason, every girl at IU who I'd talked to had more attitude than the average girl, and this one proved to be no exception when I opened her.

"I was about to head out, but you have a classier look than most girls around here, so I would hate myself for the next fourteen minutes if I didn't at least say hi."

Expecting a laugh, I received the opposite. Sometimes it takes a few attempts to light a fire. I'd witnessed that with her. On the scale, she was in the green section because she was off-put immediately.

"Oh, am I like the last resort?"

I chuckled. "What?"

"The girl you go for when there's no other option."

"Well, there are plenty of girls around here, but none that have overly excited me."

She had up what pickup artists call the 'Bitch Shield,' always ready with a defensive response to shoo away strangers. It didn't mean she was rude. It just meant it would take some ability to slowly break through the barriers to her true self.

"Well, I appreciate the effort, but I'm not available for anything," she said. Her assumption was that I was hitting on her – which I was, but it was a huge assumption.

"Um," I said in a sarcastic tone, "available for what?"

"Well…" She paused.

"*Well?*" I interrupted, extending my hand. "How about we agree to take things slow, starting with our names, and leave labels out of it for now."

I casually threw in the frame that she was hitting on me and rushing me.

She giggled, taking my hand.

"I'm Connor," I told her.

"Paige."

"I mean, we just met."

"Yeah, but you met me on your way home, so…"

She was subtly testing me with the fact that I would only talk to her this late at night because I was trying to get into her pants.

I had to flip that emotion into attraction.

"Ah, I see what you mean," I replied. "If I really wanted to find someone to take home, don't you think I'd be in there?" I pointed to the clubs.

"I guess you do have a point."

Finally, I was getting somewhere.

"I'm not from around here," I told her, "but I can definitely see where you would be closed off. Guys out here are very direct."

"You're not from around here?" she asked.

I told her I was from Indianapolis about an hour away, and then she asked what I was doing up there. I told her this was my first time at Little 5, and I was staying in a suite with some of the promoters for the clubs. It implied some sort of social proof.

"What are you up to tonight?" I asked.

"Well, I was about to catch a lift back to campus because my friend left with a guy," she said. "What are you doing?"

"I was on my way to The Chocolate Moose to get some ice cream…"

"I love that place!" she gasped.

"I've never been, but it's the closest spot for ice cream, so if you're in the mood, you're welcome to join me – but on one condition."

"What's that?"

It was time to pull out the tease, creating an inside joke from earlier. "If we do eat together, I don't want you to have any expectations because you keep wanting to label us."

She started laughing and teasingly pushed me.

"So, if we go to eat together then that determines our label?" she asked.

"Um, we don't *have* to talk about that," I emphasized. "We can talk about normal things."

She laughed again.

I had to implement a technique to make her feel special because I was on a time crunch. The technique had the formula of 'Most girls are X, but you are Y'.

"Well, most girls around here are sloppy," I told her. "But you are interesting, and if I eat with you then I'd most likely have a good time."

"You're interesting too," she said.

"Good, we're perfect for each other." I held out my hand for her to take. "Wait," I added, pushing the pull. "Let's not talk about 'us' just yet."

She giggled and told me to shut up as we walked down the streets to get some ice cream. After forty-five minutes of conversation and fluffing, she told me she had never been in a suite before when I told her where I was headed. (I never had been either, but I didn't tell her that.)

"I can show you really quick, and we can hang out for thirty minutes or so, but not for too long because I do have some work to do."

I wanted to make it seem low-pressure, so I threw in some constraints such as 'really quick' and 'not for too long.' It's a great way to get someone to commit because an obstacle in someone's head when invited is, 'What if it's weird and I have to find a way to leave?' By mentioning those constraints, you eliminate the red lights.

I arrived at 11:56, and Jay let us in wearing a white fluffy bathrobe. The suite was decked out with multiple bedrooms, a kitchen packed with fruits, popcorn, Fiji water bottles, and a balcony that looked over the strip of clubs in the town.

In that moment, I decided that I wanted this lifestyle. I needed to be in this business no matter what.

Jay went back to his room with his party girl, and I was left alone in the kitchen with Paige.

I discovered her wild side when she challenged me to a drinking contest of green apple vodka that Jay left out on the counter.

After six shots, I was well on my way to buzzed and she found her way to the bathroom, throwing up and passing out on the floor.

Part

Jump Start

My tactics would never work on a 'good' girl like Selena.

At least, that's what Noah thought. He was going to go through his own realization soon enough, just as I did, that it not only works but that the impact it has is frightening.

Because Noah let us stay with him on the first night, Jay allowed Selena and him to crash in the suite with us on the final night. I had carried Paige to the bed, wrapping her up in the blanket, and then answered the door to let Noah and Selena in.

She immediately noticed the vodka on the counter, went over, and took a shot of it.

Noah seemed annoyed and told her that she was already too drunk.

He pulled her to the closest bedroom, shut the door, and left me alone. I had a couple of options. I could go back out to the club and keep practicing, or I could just stay in and watch the flat-screen hanging on the wall and sit on the balcony watching the town alone.

I decided to go with the latter. The town's lights and the sound of the city oddly put me in a trance. I made some popcorn I found in a cabinet, pulled a Fiji bottle out, and stood against the railing listening to the after-hours of the night.

The door behind me slid open, and I assumed that it was Jay coming outside to scold me for drinking his bottle of alcohol.

Without looking, I said, "I know I drank half of your bottle of vodka, but just know that it wasn't my idea. I'll get you some more."

A gentle touch wrapped around my stomach.

"I'm not worried about the alcohol," Selena whispered. My heart raced. Sure, I was tipsy, and clearly, she was too, but that wouldn't be a good enough excuse to break the pack's code. Alcohol is a truth liquid that brings out what people's secret desires are when they are sober. Right now, it had turned a shy and chaste Christian girl into a direct and horny party girl.

She sat me down on the balcony's couch, straddling me.

"Selena, we can't do this."

"Oh, we can't?" she asked, beginning to kiss down my neck. "I'm sure that we can."

My dick started to bulge through my pants, as Adonis would say.

That's when the door slid open – again.

"What is this?!" Noah steamed.

I pushed her off me. "Dude!" I tried to sympathize. "This is not what it looks like."

While he argued with her on the balcony, I slipped inside and laid on the opposite side of the bed from puke-breath Paige. After fifteen minutes, I peeked through the crack of the door to see Noah stomp across the family room with Selena. He opened the front door, they walked out, and then he slammed it in a bang.

The next morning at 8:00, I woke up to the buzzing of my phone. Noah's angry screeching left my ear ringing. "What the fuck did you do to Selena?"

"I promise you she completely came on to me," I told him. "I told her we can't, and she still escalated on me."

"I'm breaking up with her because of you."

"I'm sorry. I know I look like an asshole, but I hope that we can make things right."

He hung up on me, but within hours he reached out again.

"Clearly, I'm doing something wrong," he texted me. "Let's forget about this whole thing, but I want to start going out with you guys and learning this stuff."

Noah had tasted the sweetness of the possibilities in seduction. It was like the fruit that Eve ate that God told her not to. Seduction was the forbidden fruit, and when he witnessed its potential, he couldn't help but want its power as well. Little did I know, because I consumed the entire thing, that my life was about to change in drastic ways.

115

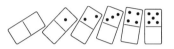

Chapter V

Hotwired

Sparks of Attraction

A year later... It was the dead of night.

Driving at 45 miles per hour. The white speed-limit sign reflected my headlights in my pupils. I squinted. The arrow on my dashboard kept slowly growing.

It read 50...75...90...110 miles per hour... The engine purred louder and louder.

I couldn't believe my storm-grey little Mitsubishi Eclipse could be pushed to this extreme. I didn't care if I crashed. Dying seemed better right now anyway. I couldn't believe that this would ever happen to me. We talked about marriage, children, and everything in between. I was blinded by rage. I needed to take my mind off of life, and I took my emotions out on the road at the time.

My headlights lit up far down the road. There's a certain peace about the dead of night. In the distance, a bird poked its head up from the side of the road. It was a mother goose and her babies. They began to cross the road, and my car was coming in hot.

Could I stop in time? Sweat rolled off my jawline and dropped onto my black sport jacket, absorbing into the fabric. I slammed on the brakes. My car began to skid into a halting stop. My head jerked forward, and the smell of burnt rubber filled the car like a hotbox.

I slowly raised my head fearing that I'd see goose remains and feathers scattered all over.

Nothing. I saw nothing.

I opened my door to see if I had hit any of them. My boot clunked onto the asphalt. I could hear the open-door alarm as I walked to the front of my car. Right before I reached the front, I heard the goose honk.

It poked its head up, sideways, and stared me right in the eye.

Then she and her four baby geese scurried to the other side of the road. They stopped and looked back at me.

Another honk. Maybe she was thanking me.

I wanted to make sure I didn't hit any, so I knelt in front of the car and pulled my phone out of my pocket to use it as a light. *Nothing under it and nothing stuck in it*, I thought. I hadn't hit any of them. I stood up, and with all of the adrenaline pulsing through my body, I subconsciously realized there was something on my knee.

I moved my hand mindlessly to wipe it away. But it didn't wipe away. It just stuck to my fingers. *What the hell is this?* I thought, angling my hand in the beam of the headlight. As the light showed my hand, my eyes narrowed. Then I picked up my leg in the angle of the beam. I couldn't believe it. The geese had taken a shit, and I'd knelt in it. I guess it wasn't thanking me earlier, it was laughing at me.

"I should've just run them over," I swore to myself. "All they do is just shit all over the place and attack you." I sat in my car and opened my glove compartment to see if I had any wet wipes to clean myself up with.

I continued to grumble. "Charging at people, flapping their wings, and hissing."

I continued babbling to myself as I pulled out a wipe from its container. I looked out the window. A couple hundred meters from the road, beyond the fireflies, the full moon reflected on a pond. That's where they must be going. I'm guessing their nest must be there. "Unbelievable," I huffed, letting out a noise almost resembling a balloon releasing air.

The goose and her babies had slowly walked off the road and into the tall grass. Just like that, they were gone. This was the perfect metaphor for the position I was in. My life was falling to pieces right now, but no matter what I was going through, life didn't wait for me. Reality kept cruelly moving forward.

The orange glow of the clock in the dash of my car reflected off my face.

I watched it as it clicked to exactly 12 a.m.

I didn't know what to do, so I sat there and breathed. I raised my hand, adjusting my rearview mirror. I moved it to the point where I was staring into my own eyes.

The orange glow masked my face. Orange is my favorite color.

It cloaked my eyes, my hair, and my skin. Everything was orange.

If I turned off the ignition and let the regular lights turn on then I'd see a completely different image. In the mirror, the orange glow hid my emotion. I couldn't see the color of my eyes, how puffed up they were, or how red my face was.

When you take off the mask you wear, you see what's truly underneath.

I couldn't deny it; I had been crying.

I shifted the gear into 'Drive' and sped off again. "Where should I go now?" I asked myself. I pulled into my former elementary school and sat on the swing set. One blinking light shined on me. I stared at it and watched the bugs cluelessly fly into it.

This place was the first one that came to mind. On the basketball court during the summer, my friends Ace and Adonis would come here and shoot hoops until the lights turned off at midnight. When the lights turned off, they only left one small light illuminating the playground.

It was this light that I was staring at that reminded me of my youth.

The other lights left this one alone to glow all by itself. I felt all alone in this moment.

I needed someone to talk to. I unlocked my phone and searched my contacts. My phone was getting a barrage of texts from her. The newest message popped up at the top of my phone screen: "Connor, I'm so sorry, please just respond to…" I couldn't read the rest without clicking on it. I scrolled up and ignored the message.

I found my dad's contact and began to call him. One ring…two rings… "He's not going to pick up," I told myself. Three rings…

"Hello?" he yawned loudly. "It's late. Is everything okay?"

"No," I let out. "Melanie…"

"Yeah?" he questioned. "What about her?"

This has happened to others, and when it did, I couldn't understand what they were going through. She texted me again, and I went back to read what I didn't want to be real. Every time I checked, I thought it would change, but it didn't, and it was cemented.

This was real, and it was happening to me.

I let out a big puff of air. "She's been cheating on me."

Prior to this event, a lot had happened. I'll have to go back to post-Little 5 to explain.

Turning Points

[Hotwired: An English term meaning, "To bypass the ignition system in order to steal it."]

I received a letter within seven days with a request:

> *Dear C,*
> *I would like to personally invite you to a private luncheon May 14, 12:30 P.M EDT located in the Marriott Downtown Indianapolis. (The shiny blue one.) If you are interested in preparing some of the best nightclubs in the world and have experience, then you could have what it takes. You will be joining a few other handpicked candidates. Come prepared.*
> *P.S. Keep this letter in absolute secrecy or you will be automatically terminated from the selection.*
> *Best,*
> *Gary*

I wrote down the time and place on the letter, burning the rest so that I could erase all of the evidence. I couldn't let this chance be blown by some dumb mistake.

According to Jay, this was going to be my 'in.' If I was truly interested in being involved with this society and becoming a master of my social life, this would be my opportunity.

I knew that Gary was the next person that would take me from natural to unnatural. I had no idea what the stakes would be or who I would be placed with inside the room. The letter stated "handpicked," and part of me in my current state wouldn't be able to last against the pros.

However, Noah claimed that he had someone who could help us advance our game by the name of Alexander.

He was around five-foot-ten with a very muscular face. His body shape was awkward as if he had back problems. But probably his biggest characteristic was his mouth. Not the fact that he never really brushed his teeth, but the fact that he was like a mixture of Adonis and Jay. He tended to yell every other sentence like Jay, but the words that came out of his mouth were like the ones Adonis told me in private. The word he used the most, at least once every four sentences, was "top," which was apparently a New York term for 'blowjob.' He was originally from New York before moving to Indianapolis after his mother passed away.

His mother had left him a large inheritance, which he tended to blow on alcohol and bribes to people to let him into parties. He was the type of guy who had all the information on what parties were happening and when.

He somehow made a connection with a girl who lived in a mansion thirty minutes west of the city where high-status people tended to go to party, and he put us all on the guest list that weekend to attend with him.

However, when I asked Jay to join us, he claimed that he knew of Alexander already and wanted nothing to do with him, so I had the original team get back together: Ace, Adonis, and me. It would be a night that we would call 'House Party, Part 1' and what Adonis would label as 'classified information.'

Part

Sun-Kissed Peaks

There was still somebody I wanted to not only learn from but model.

Ace was the definition of a pure natural. We hadn't been to a party together in months because I was so involved in my own journey, but he had developed an even stronger game since I had been out with him last.

When we arrived at the mansion, it was magnificent. It reminded me of the houses my mom would drive by and say to me, "One day, when you graduate college and get a good job, you may be able to buy one of these."

There were multiple Mercedes, Jaguars, and other luxury cars parked in the circular driveway with a fountain in the center. The house was white bricked with ivory posts on the front porch, like the White House. It had a gated entrance, and to me, entering it felt like I was walking into Mt. Olympus (the home of the gods) that I read about when I was younger in Percy Jackson books.

When I first met Alexander, he was doused in the smell of cheap – I think it was Axe – body spray. He wore a loose-fitted grey dress shirt that looked to be a hand-me-down from his dad. Also, khaki pants that led down to untied, worn-down Nike shoes. His style was in desperate need of a makeover.

He scanned me from head to toe. I wore fitted pinstripe pants, Chelsea boots, and a Hugo Boss pinstripe jacket.

"Just make sure you don't get in my way around Stephanie," he said as he rang the doorbell.

"So, she's off-limits?" Adonis asked.

"Yes!" he hissed.

Stephanie answered the door. She was the owner, a big girl with attitude. Her dad was a business owner who trust-funded her with $20,000 a month until the day she dies.

Perhaps Alexander was a male version of a gold digger.

Alexander treated Stephanie like a queen. He brought her roses, and he said that she looked beautiful in a robotic and shy voice as if he had been rehearsing it in the mirror. He was at her entire beck and call like a servant. He was trying very hard. She was stuck up and controlling, and took pride in her property, probably because she threw all kinds of parties with high-class models, athletes, and more almost weekly.

"My dad told me that Larry Bird used to own this house."

"That's nice," I replied nonchalantly.

"You bet your ass it's nice."

It just took one sentence to understand someone's way of thinking. I processed things quickly.

Stephanie took pride in her house, and it was her weakness because this house fueled her confidence. If she were without it, she would have no confidence. According to self-help experts, you should never base your inner happiness and confidence on external things such as girls, money, cars, or in her case, a house (and a monthly check). If you lose that source, you lose everything.

Living room 'A' was in the shape of an octagon with windows that stretched from floor to ceiling with no wall. Bleach-white carpeting and red sofas were in front of a bar stocked with tiered shelves of alcoholic beverages. One hallway from there led to living room 'B,' dominated by a pool table. The other hallway led to a spiral staircase that ascended to Stephanie's extra-large bedroom. Multiple bedrooms connected to both hallways.

Despite all that luxury, the treasure of the house was outside: a sunken hot tub, a saltwater infinity pool lined with black tile, and pathways that led to a pond that Stephanie's room balcony overlooked.

The feature I liked best was how secluded it was. It was in one of the only locations around Indianapolis where there was little light pollution. You could see the stars light up the sky like little diamonds.

Noah claimed that Alexander was the best with the girls, but Alexander was also the definition of two-faced. When talking to Stephanie, he was a sweetheart, but when talking to me behind her back, he used his favorite word in every other sentence as he repeatedly talked about how he wanted 'top' from her.

"Stephanie is looking so good tonight," Alex said in private. "I'm going to definitely get her into bed."

"How are you going to go about doing that?" I asked, trying to sap his style.

He grinned. "Get her a little drunk, give her a little massage, and then start kissing her."

There's no way this guy was serious.

"You know," I said as if I'd just come to a realization, "that could actually work."

"You think so?" Hope filled his voice.

"Fuck no," I said.

I believed that he must have been kidding and that it was all an act. I was waiting for the other side of him to come out. The one that was a Casanova. The one that truly could sing the love song of a woman's heart. I was hovering around him waiting to see what I could steal and copy for my own use. It aroused my curiosity but quickly deflated into amusement and embarrassment.

Ace gasped, "Oh my God," clasping his hands over his face.

Adonis laughed as if it was a comedy club.

I just sat with my mouth open because I couldn't believe it.

In living room "B" was the dancing area. The house was packed with people including models and professional athletes. I felt slightly out of place like I didn't deserve to be there, but I kept my cool. It was Alexander who was out of place.

Stephanie joined two girls moving their hips to the music. One of them was a girl who wore a cowboy hat, and if she was a professional something, I would guess an equestrian trainer. Ace told me that she eyed me when I wasn't looking at her with her emerald-green eyes.

The other girl was one who Ace had already been with, a shorter girl with bleach-blonde hair and a skinny body. He said that when she was riding him, she asked him, "Do you love me?"

He responded: "Um, we can talk about that later."

Alexander watched Stephanie. It was like watching a crocodile stalk its prey. Rarely did it ever catch it, but when it did, it was satisfied for a while.

He swam with his head up in the water, got right behind his target, and decided to put his hand right on her hip. From there, he moved right behind her, putting his crotch on her tailbone.

She was supposed to start grinding on him and dancing, however, she turned around, and with a look of disgust, she yelled, "Ew!" Then she and her friends fled.

In this moment, I realized a few things.

First, I watch too much *Animal Planet* episodes because I use a lot of animal references, but all I saw right then was a gazelle gallop away from the crocodile thrashing itself out of the water with its gaping mouth.

This guy was a woman-repellant, but I had to give credit where it's due. At least he had the guts to go up there and try. If only he had some social awareness and could calibrate the situation, he could be really good. There are those who come on way too strong and those who come on way too weak. Starting right in the middle, also known as 'pace and lead,' it's best to let the woman tell you through her body language whether you should be more direct or to slow down. This gives you an insight into how much you can risk.

The girls immediately ran over to Ace. Like a flock of geese, they migrated. Lexi, the skinny blonde, clung onto Ace.

"Hi Ace," she cooed.

Ace was also like Jay except a little more easy-going. He wasn't a stone-cold wall like Jay. Ace was more of a player while Jay tended to lead, but deep down, I connected with both of them. Ace always had a girl. Even if he walked in with no one, he'd leave with one, but this time he didn't need to try.

We moved back to living room 'A' where Adonis sat to my left at a circular glass table. Noah was beside him, Ace was to my right, Lexi was standing right next to his chair clinging onto his arm, and Stephanie with her country friend was across from us. Alex quickly sat down next to Stephanie.

I watched Ace. There was something that made girls respect him but also crave his attention. When Lexi would touch his shoulder, he would smack his lip and look at her as if she was disrespecting him by touching him. Then he would take his hand, grab her hand, and take it off his shoulder, which made her want it more. Then he wiped his shoulder off as if her hand was dirty. When she would pout, he would laugh as if he was joking the whole time.

The guy was an M-Fer. (Translation: Master Flirter.)

It was all a playful vibe, though, and I think that's what hooked them. He was authentic and would tease her with perfect timing. He treated these girls as an older brother treats his little sister. If she asked him if he had any gum, he would reply, "Yeah, you need it." She would whine, "Ace!" He wasn't afraid to push her away because he viewed the situation as if he was the prize. She would be back.

Probably the greatest takeaway that I got from observing Ace was something he did that was like the trap card of flirting. It completely put him in the position to win her over. It was simple.

Here's how it went. Lexi was telling a story to him, and her last line was, "Isn't that funny?!" He fake-laughed – "ha-ha" – while simultaneously acting like he was scooting away. "Yeah, that's so funny," he said in a this-is-so-awkward-hopefully-she-leaves-soon kind of tone. He smiled at her, but then turned his head to us and shook his head. He put his hand over his mouth acting like he was talking about her. The purpose was a huge push-pull. She would see him doing this and slap his arm.

"Stop!" she laughed.

I can't even put into words how effective this was. He did it to both guys and girls. You had to watch yourself around him because without knowing it, soon you would be validating your entire existence to him. When the guys did or said something weird, he would scoot away, making sure they saw, and before you knew it, you were his pet.

His personality was just so unique.

He expected others to be curious about him, and when they asked, he said, "Don't worry about it." Which made people even more curious. When Lexi said something that was obvious – for example, "I'm feeling a little tipsy" – he would sarcastically respond, "Clearly" while rolling his eyes and looking away. If somebody tried to tell a joke, he would say, "Cut," gesturing scissors with his fingers.

Stephanie decided to change the subject to herself. She was talking about guys who wouldn't stop messaging her and how tired of it she was.

All I was thinking was, "What guy would ever want you?" I once heard a quote by Helena Rubinstein: "There aren't ugly women, only lazy ones." Stephanie was one of the lazy ones – borderline obese, acne, and she was too loud. She was like the song that made my ears feel like they were bleeding.

On the scale, I was blue for her but colder than the color when she tried to test me.

As she talked, Adonis tapped my shoulder and leaned in to whisper in my ear, "Bro, that's one of those 49ers."

"That team sucks," I whispered back.

"No," he insisted. "A girl who is a four-out-of-ten attractive who thinks she's a nine." This self-illusion was caused by her association with men who validated her so much from their weak behaviors that she felt entitled to a great man without actually having anything to truly give. I sighed. Sometimes it's not always the men. When did these girls become so entitled?

She saw us look at her at one point while we whispered. "What are you two whispering about?" she interrupted us. "Are you talking about me?"

"Don't worry about it," I chuckled, copying Ace.

She smacked her lips at me. "I've heard about you."

"Heard about me?"

"Yeah." She took a sip from her red Solo cup. "Your friends say you're the guy who's really good with girls." She let out a laugh. "But I'd never date you."

I raised my eyebrows and let out a soft laugh.

"That's interesting." I looked away, and then I looked right back in her eyes. "But you're missing one thing," I pointed out.

"Oh yeah?" she barked. "What's that?"

"Who said I wanted you?" I smirked at her, holding eye contact for a second.

Alex covered his mouth, and with him, everyone laughed.

She was speechless.

It was carefree, and it came from the fact that I couldn't care less how I looked to her. Whether I was good-looking to her or not, it didn't matter because the end result was the same – she'd never have me, and she knew it, but someone had to put her in her place. She could get her way with all these other guys, and her daddy may spoil her rotten, but she wasn't going to get that treatment from me. She wasn't going to walk all over me.

I guess university was good for something. In one of my business classes, my professor told us that when we are negotiating salary and the boss asks, "How much do you want?", usually the opposing side will answer, "Between [this figure] and [that figure]." But if you tell them a minimum, you are going to be given the minimum.

Instead, you tell them one figure. You tell them your desired salary, and you believe in it fully.

They will test you and say, "That's a lot!" In which case you're supposed to hold that tension or say the word 'Yeah' like it's not a big deal.

At the end of the semester, I had a D+ in the class. I went into the instructor's office during the last week and said, "I want an 'A.'"

"An 'A?!'" he gasped. "You have a 'D.'"

"Yeah," I replied as he taught us to do.

"I'll see what I can do," he told me.

I ended the semester with an 'A.'

It was a lesson on valuing oneself. Alexander would have given in to her tests, but the strong man is willing to walk away. I essentially told Stephanie through my actions and belief in myself that she needed more than her dad's money to win me over. It's a risky move, but you have to risk in order to gain.

Part

Fire & Ice

It was only supposed to be a small kick-back at Stephanie's mansion.

It ended up with two people in the shower, me throwing up on the bed from so much alcohol, naked lap dancing, and worse.

It all started when a guy by the name of Hakan showed up. I never thought that I'd reunite with old friends from high school. I was there when the love of his life broke up with him, and it turned him into a cold womanizer. I witnessed the rise and fall of his character.

His name meant "fire," apparently, but his features reminded me of Jack Frost. His bleached hair was solidly gelled up in the front, he had blue eyes, and a lot of people said we could be brothers. He was known for getting women, and the girl he brought was actually my ex-girlfriend's best friend, Holly, a short brunette with a free spirit and chiseled curves.

She hugged me as if we were best friends. "Hi, Connor." Her breath smelled like hand sanitizer. She was definitely drunk.

He pulled a bottle of Bombay out of Stephanie's bar. "This will make you very horny," he told us.

Drinking had never been my thing. I had certainly tried it before, but I had never been drunk. The girls were quick to seize on the opportunity to consume free alcohol and ran over there like a buffalo stampede with Alex following.

To every negative, there's a positive. When it was awkward or quiet, Alex tended to be the entertainment. He started dancing and was able to let everyone loosen up.

Ace and I took a shot of the Bombay. It smelled like a pine tree and tasted just like I was swallowing one. "This tastes like shit," I told Ace.

He looked at me and changed the subject. "Ava, the girl with the cowboy hat, has been talking to me about how she thinks you're really cute." I nodded. I guess it was time to clock in.

Lexi and Ava were sitting on barstools at the kitchen counter. She called Ace over, and I followed. Lexi and Ace began to talk, and I noticed Ava giving me the eyes. We stood awkwardly behind them. I needed to take that seat because with them sitting there, it made Ace and I look like we were chasing them.

"Listen, you guys need to see my new magic trick," I told them as if it was the coolest thing in the world. "Hold out your hands, and stand up for a second." I threw in a time constraint for good measure. If your audience thinks that something will only take a second, most people will comply and go along with it.

They stood up. "Now close your eyes," I smiled. It was as if Ace and I were communicating telepathically because once they closed their eyes, he took Lexi's seat immediately. "Are you ready?" I asked them. They both agreed simultaneously. I slid onto the barstool. "Now open them." They turned around to see us in their seats. "Thanks for the seat," I laughed. Now they were on the outside awkwardly standing over us.

They pestered us, trying to get their seats back.

Lexi and Ace continued to talk. I moved on to the marble countertop with my feet on the seat. I looked at Ava. "How big are your hands?" I asked. I held up my hand as if I was looking for a high five. Our hands gently kissed as she placed it against mine to compare. "Your hand is small." I mentioned, which could have been either a compliment or an insult. I wrapped my fingers between hers and squeezed as I continued to talk to her, and she wrapped back. This was a sign that she was interested. We were basically holding hands.

I was setting up for a technique that I learned on how to escalate physical touch.

"They say that couples who hold their hands like this with the fingers locked symbolizes a strong connection between two people who seek a stronger bond the more they hold. But couples who hold their hands like this…" I said, repositioning our hands so they resembled a handshake in which the hands are clasped instead, "these are couples who are secretive, but when they are together, they are very intimate and passionate, and they know each other very well."

"I think I'm more of the hand-clasping kind of girl," she chirped.

When she got excited, as she did right then, she had a country accent that came out. I repeated what she said with an exaggerated country twang. It was a tease, and it was playful. She let go of my hand and slapped my leg.

Ace poured a couple more shots of alcohol.

One shot turned into three, and three shots turned into six.

I discovered that when I get drunk, I lose the feeling in my fingers and lips. Ava poured me my seventh shot, and I already couldn't feel my face.

"You're just getting me drunk so you can take advantage of me," I said, reciting a playful interpretation, "but I'm not that easy, babe."

I forced down the shot.

"How did you know?" she flirted back.

"Because I'm as sharp as a papercut."

Alex came over and took another shot. He made us take another with him. I lost count after that one.

I looked at Alex. "Watch this," I insisted.

I took Ava's hand, placing it on my inner thigh. I was exercising the frame that she was the one coming onto me. "Watch it," I said, removing her hand and looking her in the eyes. "I need trust, comfort, and care before we do those kinds of things." A line I had once heard from Todd Valentine.

She giggled.

I looked at Alex. "Did you just see her try to do that?" She was laughing hysterically, and so was Alex. I etched this technique into my intoxicated cerebral cortex. I had to remember this so I could use it again.

"That was you!" she exclaimed, bumping into me.

I was very drunk.

I didn't know where Hakan was, or Holly. Some guys were sitting with us on the couch who I had never met before. Somewhere in my mind, I came up with an idea.

"Let's go to a private room," I called to Ace and the group.

In the room, I connected to the Bluetooth speakers and laid in the middle of the floor with Ava. I told Ace to lay down next to me, and Alex laid down on the other side of Ace. I put Ava on top of me, and she began to grind on me to the music.

Lexi hopped on Ace, and Stephanie hopped on Alex. We started to make out, and she put my hands on her body so I could feel it. I took her shirt off. I wanted to make it even more interesting. I wanted a rotation going.

I switched the song, and yelled, "Next!" I moved Ava off of me and moved Lexi from Ace onto me. Stephanie moved to Ace, and Ava moved down to Alex. Lexi and I began to make out. Ace kissed Stephanie. Ava wouldn't kiss Alex. This is when I realized that my plan had backfired. The next person up was who I didn't want at all, but my fate was sealed. If I switched the song, Stephanie moved to me. If I waited, eventually the song would end, and she would still move onto me.

I couldn't win. Each second that went by, my fate grew closer.

I don't think Ace wanted Stephanie either, but she was going to town on him. I stalled for time because I didn't want her on me.

However, in my final moments of thinking through the dilemma, Ace interjected. "Switch the song already." I did.

Oh no, I thought as she positioned herself on me. I had to endure this.

I was trying to enjoy it, but even while intoxicated, I was disgusted. She leaned in to kiss me, and I turned my head. I dodged a bullet there. She was on top of me for a total of nine seconds before I yelled, "Switch!" Then I changed the song.

"I missed you," I told Ava as she climbed on top of me. I eventually got up because my head was spinning, and I stumbled to a bed. I needed to lay down.

The last thing I remember is laying on that bed, and when I closed my eyes, it felt like I was floating in outer space. I was spinning around and around. I couldn't help it; I threw up all over the side of the bed.

Then I went to sleep.

I woke up the next day and felt like shit. I rolled myself from the bed and crawled on the floor because when I stood up, I'd felt a throbbing heartbeat in my head. I found Ace in a different bedroom. He woke up when I pulled the blanket off him and curled up on the floor in it.

"What happened last night?" I moaned.

He didn't answer. I think he fell back asleep.

Where were the girls, where is everyone, and, more importantly, where were my pants?

I must have drifted back to sleep because I woke up to Ace saying, "It's four o'clock."

"A.M. or P.M.?" I asked him with my eyes still shut.

It was bad that I was hoping it was the afternoon and not the morning. If it was the morning, that meant I was asleep for a whole 24 hours. Luckily, it was the afternoon. He told me all of what he could remember. He remembered the rotation, and he remembered that he apparently told the girls that he would take them home if they flashed their boobs.

They did, but he realized he was too drunk to drive, so apparently, they either walked or passed out there.

"That walk would take like three-and-a-half hours," I said to him.

He nodded. "At least."

According to him, I sat down next to Ava at some point and she said, "Connor, make out with me right now." Apparently, I turned my head, looked her in the face, and said, "No." Then I got up and walked away. She chased me around the house. Memories in the form of short clips started to comeback.

Then I remembered that Hakan's girlfriend, Holly, and I kissed.

Guilt took over my body as I remembered. I felt awful about it. I remember Holly telling me, "I used to not like you, but you've grown on me." The bad part about it was that he was right there when it happened.

Before Ace and I left, I saw Hakan asleep in his bed. I wanted to apologize, but I couldn't work up the nerve to wake him up and say it.

When I saw Hakan, I remembered one conversation I had with him and Stephanie when we were well into the tipsy range. I overheard them discussing someone by the name of Gary. When I heard about club promoting, I jumped into the conversation.

"You were invited too?" I asked Hakan.

"No way," Stephanie said. "Have you been chosen by Gary too?"

I tried to drunkenly get intel from them.

"My father used to do business with him," Stephanie said. "He is big-time, and I know he's looking for talent. You two are going to be great fits for him."

I couldn't believe Hakan was one of the handpicked.

"However," she paused, "since both of you are meeting with him, act like you do not know each other. He is very secretive. He will probably kick both of you out on the spot because he wants the individuals in this position to have no relation with the others."

"But why?" I asked.

"For multiple reasons. You will all be his right-hand men. You could easily work together and form a company to take out his business. You guys will be the oxygen of his work."

"The oxygen?"

"You'll see."

Mastermind

May 14, 12:15 p.m. I arrived at the Marriott. I walked into the hotel and already felt out of place. A neon-orange Lamborghini was parked in front of the hotel. The people were dressed in high fashion that went beyond business professional. Even though I wore my fitted pinstripe suit, this was beyond me. I had known nothing but poverty my whole life. I worked in a warehouse making $13 an hour, and as a university student, I had little to no spending cash.

When I walked in, I was stopped immediately.

"Excuse me," an older man said who I'm assuming was a butler. "Can I help you?"

I acted like I was high-class and belonged here. "I'm looking for Gary."

I was taken up an elevator where a shorter man wearing a black suit guarded a conference room.

"What letter are you?" he asked.

"Letter?"

"On your invitation, who were you addressed as?"

"Oh, I'm C."

I was the third of eight people to arrive. Inside was a long glass table with soft chairs that made a swishing sound when you raised and lowered them. It overlooked the northwest portion of the city. Suited men stood in the corners of the room, and two other individuals sat at the table. The feeling in the room was grim. Not a word was said, so I decided to speak up.

"So, what's your guys' name?" I asked the two people seated at the table with me. They were both clearly older than me. They looked to be around 30 and had great style.

One was dressed like a greaser from the book, *The Outsiders.* He had jet-black hair, slicked back with what looked like a gallon of gel. He had a toothpick in his mouth and wore a black leather jacket.

The other man had messy brown hair that was also gelled. He had a warmer feel to him when he gave me an inviting smile. He wore a grey suit, wore a Rolex, and had the top two buttons of his dress shirt unbuttoned to achieve a casual look that showed off part of his tanned chest.

"I'm sorry, but Gary has requested that you are not allowed to share information," one of the cornermen said. "We ask that you sit silently until everyone has arrived."

The next to arrive was a shorter man who had muscles that popped out of his grey T-shirt and a cross tattoo on his forearm. It looked like he laser-whitened his teeth and buzzed his hair to the skull as if he was in the military.

The fifth person to walk in was Hakan. We followed Stephanie's advice and acted like we didn't know each other. He sat a couple of chairs down from me. Little did we know that she'd really saved our asses.

The sixth person was an energetic guy with red hair and a beard to match. He looked like a ginger version of Ryan Reynolds, wore black jeans with holes in them, a large silver chain wrapped around his neck, and a ring on each finger. He was told to stop talking by one of the cornermen when he began an open conversation with all of us. He gave the cornerman a surprised look when he was told to keep quiet.

The seventh person to enter the room was a guy who had a face that resembled Jesus. He had a slight beard and long brown hair. But what stood out most was that he was six-foot-five with tattoos all the way up his neck and on his hands. He smelled like he had just finished smoking a cigarette when he sat next to me. He wore a long trench coat even though it was hot as fuck outside, but it was his dark-brown eyes that captured people, I realized, when he looked into mine and smiled.

"Everyone except one is here," one of the cornermen said. "We will call in the boss."

When I scanned everyone in the room, I realized that I was not only the youngest but the outlier. Some of these guys looked to be in their thirties and had full careers. Even Hakan was older than me by two years at 24.

Everyone in the room gave off the same vibe that Jay did: a 'don't fuck with me' vibe. I wondered if they felt the same vibe from me.

Everyone here thought they were the best. This was the room I needed to be in. They could grow my skills exponentially if I learned from each one.

The eighth and final person walked in, and it was Gary.

I was expecting him to be in a suit and to convey a professional personality. I was expecting a man in his forties or fifties who had to have owned the world based on the dramatic setup he had given us.

Instead, a five-foot-five man walked in wearing flip-flops, pink swim trunks, a white tank top, and a cigar in his mouth that he put out in an ashtray. I only got one of my three guesses right. He was in his forties. He lifted the sunglasses to the top of his shiny bald head. His hazel eyes were bloodshot as if he was either smoking too much or had jetlag.

"Let's get started!" he beamed as the blinds began to dim the room. "I'm sorry, I am the one called Gary by the way." He looked around the room. "Is letter-X not here?" he asked one of the guards.

"He didn't show."

Gary sighed and pinched the bridge of his nose for a few moments.

I didn't know who Letter-X was, but he must have been somewhat important.

He signaled the workers to pass out two things to us: a Fiji water bottle and an iPad.

"While they are passing these out," Gary said, "allow me to share who I am in a sentence or two... I love clubs, and I love money. I graduated from Stanford with a master's in business. I created this business when I was 24. One of my best friends bought a club with his parents' trust fund in Ohio, and I was the one who put the people in the club. From there, I blew up in a year taking my business from six figures to nine figures in less than two years. It was because of one simple psychological trick."

He raised his finger.

"I took advantage of the male mind. I hired some of the world's best pickup artists and masters of social situations to get the hottest girls in the club – because what happens when rumors start to spread that one specific club is a hotspot for women? Men tend to fill those clubs. So, I was hired to turn clubs from piss-poor to regional hotspots."

As I listened, I realized that Gary loved to talk. Each time he'd say a sentence or two, it packed the wallop of ten or more sentences. But nobody seemed to mind.

"This is what you guys will be doing if you would unlock your iPads," he said. "By the way, don't try to peek at your neighbor's screen. Each iPad was made with a privacy screen so you won't be able to see a word of your neighbors."

He was right. I looked at my neighbor's screens.

First, the guy who looked like Jesus, and his screen looked black. Then to my left at the man in the grey suit; it was the same.

"On the first page, you see a date, a time, and a location. Everyone's is different. This is your 'tryout,'" he said, using air quotes. "We are not affiliated with these clubs, but someone will be there to watch how you operate in the setting to see if you're a fit for ours."

Mine was May 24 at 10 p.m. EDT at a club called Revel in Indianapolis.

Our tryout was basically to see how well we worked in social settings. Before we even got into the business, he wanted to see how we handled pressure, how we acted inside the club's walls, and how we tended to network with people such as managers, women, and even high-status men.

But what worried me was the tryout he talked about.

"On the second page, you will see a list of requirements," he told us. The requirements listed were as follows:

1. *The abilities of a pickup artist including taking a girl from street to club, and club to home. Then getting her friends into the club.*
2. *Understand social dynamics, social media, and owning the ability to manipulate human psychology, and have a huge awareness of it.*
3. *Stay in the shadows.*
4. *Know how to network and influence others – specifically those who have power.*

The buzz-cut muscle man cut in. "These requirements are so simple."

My palms began to sweat. Was this really simple to him?

I could barely get past requirement number two without my heart racing. I kept a poker face, but I was only able to take a girl from club to home on the first night once.

I only witnessed Jay do that twice.

"Business is simple," Gary responded. "Make people feel like they need something, and then fulfill that need beyond the expectation."

"What's in it for us?" Buzz-cut asked.

"Our clients need people to fill their clubs. People are their oxygen. You fill the clubs to max capacity then you will be given multiple things. I realize that some of you live in different cities. Each one of you will be given a hotel suite within walking distance of your tryout location. Food and other necessities as well. You guys are like my children. I will treat you as such because you will bring significant value to my business. If any of you don't want to do this or aren't interested, please turn in your iPad and leave."

Nobody stood up.

"What's the tryout?" the greaser asked, taking his toothpick out of his mouth.

"I will decide based on multiple things on the day of. Show up, beat the challenge I provide, and you're in. In the next two weeks, this room will be reduced to half as many people. I'm looking not only for the most talented but the most talented of the talented," he smiled. "I need the top one percent of social masters."

I could barely even breathe correctly, I was so nervous.

I looked over to Hakan. I couldn't read his body language. I couldn't tell if he, or anyone else, was as nervous as I was. Maybe this was just business to them. I didn't know how I matched up against anyone in this room.

"One more thing," Gary said, focusing his gaze on us. He looked in my eyes. "All of you are not to talk to each other. Your identities remain a secret to each other. If you share this with anyone, you will be permanently banned from this opportunity. We will dismiss each of you in one-minute increments so that you remain out of contact with one another."

I didn't really see the point of that. I could just wait outside the building for Hakan and then talk to him.

"Don't try it," Gary said. "If you're thinking of meeting up outside of this building with each other, I will know. I have watchers throughout this building who will make sure each of you leaves without a word to each other."

Fuck. It's like he could read my mind.

"If you share this information with anyone else in the room, you are out. If I find you at the same place at the same time as the others, then you are out because I'll assume you exchanged information," he told us. "Ha-ha-HA-HA-heh-heh," he laughed as if he was joking. Everyone else laughed, and then he switched to full seriousness in a snap. "I'm only serious."

We stopped laughing. When it was my turn to leave, the greaser asked him, "Was that your orange Lambo outside?"

"No," he responded, "I have someone drive me around in my Rolls, my Ferrari, or my McLaren."

I was in a different world.

Time Under Tension

Time under tension.

Muscle is built by pressure from the weight and by how long you are able to keep the muscle under that pressure. At least that's what Jay shared with me.

I needed to put myself under pressure.

I was once told that to become great, you must take most people's extreme and make it your average. To be prepared, I needed to sharpen my skills and, more specifically, constantly pressure myself. I once heard that a diamond cannot be made without extreme pressure.

I wanted to talk to Hakan about this. I needed to because the tension was killing me. I didn't want to be the first to reach out to him, though, because it was dangerous.

Fortunately, he reached out to me.

"Soooo," he texted. "What's your date?"

We exchanged dates and times and discussed how we felt during the meeting. We agreed to keep our relationship a complete secret but would communicate outside of the events.

His date happened to be the Friday right before mine in Broad Ripple. I made a mental note to attend his to see what the challenge was so I could strategize.

I had exactly ten days to prepare for my big debut. For a week straight, I was in downtown Indianapolis, the Broad Ripple district, or the Keystone mall. These three places were where the most beautiful women tended to spawn in the city.

I must have spent more than five hours each day talking to women for seven days straight. On the second to last day, I probably had a bag as big as Santa's present sack but full of phone numbers.

Two nights before my tryout happened to be a Thursday; downtown calls it "Thirsty Thursdays" with specials usually offered in the clubs.

I invited Noah to come out and develop himself a little more and we found ourselves in the Sky Bar nightclub on Indianapolis's most popular strip.

We were on a schedule. We took a free shuttle from my university, and the last stop it made, to pick us up, was at 2:30 in the morning.

College kids don't want to pay for anything, so we had to make that shuttle. We arrived at around 12:30 a.m., and it was packed. It probably had 300 to 400 people in the club, and maybe 150 of them were women.

When I talked to people, Noah stood right behind me, listening awkwardly.

"Dude." I glared at him. "You have to go talk to someone."

"I want to watch you do it," he argued back.

"I've noticed," I said sarcastically, implying that he'd been on me this whole time.

A group of five girls walked by. I noticed one of the girls was a petite blonde. I'm guessing five-foot-two. She had a touch of baby fat, but it was under a skintight avocado-green sparkling dress. It was her peppiness that I found interesting, but also her shyness around her friends as she smiled but stood distant from the other girls. She dressed to be noticed but acted shy. It was like a female example of push-pull.

She and I made eye contact, and I got a feeling that she was interested. She looked down as soon as we made eye contact, and then she darted them back up at my eyes once again, then looked away.

When I wasn't watching her, I could feel her staring at me, but when I looked, she was looking somewhere else. Either I was imagining things, or she was fast.

When you make eye contact with someone and they look away but then look back at you within the next thirty seconds, then chances are they are interested. I've noticed that if you lock eyes with a girl and she looks down and away, then she's probably a little shy. Shyness means that she cares about how you perceive her, which means she's attracted to you. The eyes can't lie. They will look at what they desire.

When she and her friends came near us, she stood close to me and danced by herself. When I spun around abruptly, I caught her staring at me. She was hitting all of the checkpoints on the scale for me to open. I was about to make a move when a guy came over and started talking to one of her friends. I knew his face; it was the same guy Caitlyn chose over me. The same guy that I saw in the pictures on her desk that night. It was Mitch.

He put his arms around a different girl in the group. Either he was cheating on Caitlyn, or that didn't work out very well. Either way, I had a new target.

I could see her staring at me again out of the corner of my eye. I chuckled to myself.

I told Noah, "Go up to those two girls, my target and the friend who's with her, and say, 'Holy shit!' Hold your finger out at them, and pause to get their attention. Then ask, 'Are you two twins?' because they kind of look alike."

He grumbled, but he did it and I saw them giving him laughs and signs that they thought he was attractive. He was improving. Then my target in the green looked at me.

There were two guys between me and her. One of them was Mitch, and I'm guessing the other was his friend. His friend tried to dance with my target and pull the moves on her. As Mitch held his new girl, I reached out. These two beta males had to move. Mitch gave me a dirty look as he saw my arm pass in between him and his friend's heads. They were in the way of what I wanted.

I tapped her shoulder and reached out my hand.

She looked at me with a shocked look on her face. A test. I continued to hold out my hand unfazed with strong eye contact. I motioned 'come here' with my fingers.

She pointed to herself and mouthed the word, "Me?"

I nodded, took her hand, and when she started to come to me, the two guys moved aside like a gate. I bumped Mitch hard in his arm with my elbow on the way back, which was a dick move. "Sorry, man," I told him, but I'd lied. It was intentional, and I wanted him to feel it.

My opening line was: "I saw you checking me out a few times, so I thought you might as well come and introduce yourself." She laughed.

I reached out my hand and asked what her name was.

"Laura," she chimed. "What's yours?" I tend to keep my name out of the conversation until a girl asks. If she asks, it's a sign that she's interested.

"Guess," I said, smirking. "It starts with the letter 'C.'" I wanted to be a challenge and be playful.

"Um, is it Connor?"

I shook my head in surprise. "That's actually my name. How did you know?"

She jumped in excitement. "Is it really?"

"Oh my gosh," I said, grabbing her hand. "It's like we were meant for each other."

"I know." She smiled ear to ear.

"This is so romantic." I put my hand over my heart. "I bet I know something about you."

"What's that?"

I pointed at her. "You're a good dancer."

"I am!" She jumped again. I found it cute that she was so excited. "I'm actually on the dance team for the University of Michigan."

"Show me," I said, taking the hand I was holding and gently pulling her away.

She giggled.

While I led her through the crowd of people, I walked past Noah, who was with the girl I told him to talk to. It seemed they were hitting it off.

I wanted them to see us.

I stopped in the middle of the crowd, turning and facing her.

"Don't worry," I said. "I promise I won't be gentle."

She laughed.

We started dancing together, and we got into it.

She would grab my hands and guide them to feel her hips and her body. I put my hand on her back, and she bent over for me.

She was flexible, and it was hot.

Dancers do this one thing with their hair where they whip their head and all of their hair waves around and covers half of their face. She turned around and did the thing with her hair, then she looked at me with these eyes of desire.

I think I was falling in love…or maybe it was just infatuation.

She wrapped her arms around me and looked me in the eyes. We were so close, and she looked at my lips.

"You probably spent hours practicing that in front of the mirror in your bathroom," I said, holding her hips. I've tried to figure out where I come up with some of the things I say. I think that it's because everyone is actually very similar. If we all had cameras watching our inner lives, we would see stuff we all do, but if others knew, we would be embarrassed. Like performing in our own private mini-concerts or checking ourselves out in reflections.

The fact is that I'm able to joke about what most people don't want others to know. I tease others because we all do these things, but most are afraid to admit it. I tease them about things they probably do but never want to admit, and if you call them out on it, it brings a great reaction.

She probably did dance in front of the mirror, and if someone walked in on her, she would be embarrassed, and that's probably why she laughed melodically when I said that.

"Your friend even told me that you do that," I joked. Even though I never talked to her friend, it wasn't really lying but flirting.

"No, she didn't!" She jumped.

This was just mindless banter before a kiss that was about to happen. I was sweating, and she was sweating. Her hands were on my chest, and mine on her lower back. We stared deeply into each other's eyes. I couldn't hear the music.

I forgot about everyone around us. It was just us now.

I couldn't help myself. We started making out right there in the middle of the club.

She pulled back. "You know, I'm like the mother of my group, and I'm supposed to be watching over them," she claimed.

I brought her close and talked in her ear. "I have such a big thing for moms."

She laughed again, and I passed that test. Women like to blow up a situation, making it into a big deal to see how a man handles it. But it's really no big deal, and men need to take what she makes into a big deal and deflate it as if it's nothing at all. We started kissing again.

"Are you in love with me yet?" I asked, smirking.

"No," she chuckled.

We started to kiss again.

"How about now?" I asked.

"Shut up," she said, leaning in to kiss me some more.

These kinds of girls have men left and right hitting on them. Guys spend weeks trying to get a girl like this. They chase but get nowhere.

I had her in less than eight minutes.

Most women over their entire lives feel so judged and constrained by the expectations of society. Our society has been set up to make women feel like sluts if they are having fun with a guy. Some women feel suppressed because they are constantly worrying about what their friends or family will think of them.

They just want to have fun. They want to feel admired, be touched, and experience sexual tension with a guy – the right guy.

It's rare when they get to express the feminine side of their personality to a guy because either she will be judged or a guy could hurt her.

She takes a risk opening up to men.

The greatest gift you can ever give a woman is letting her feel free to show you who she really is without judgment. The freedom to open up and be vulnerable to you.

After she does, she feels as if the best place in the world is with you in your arms.

During these past eight days of seduction, I was asked a common question.

"What's your sign?" she asked.

When I was first asked that, I had no idea what that meant. I realized it was about your date of birth – I am a Cancer – but I also realized it was a perfect opportunity to flirt some more.

"If you were to guess, what would you say I am?" I asked her.

"Sagittarius!"

"Oh my God!" I gasped. I held it for a moment. "No."

She laughed and slapped my chest.

It has been advised never to just give information away but to instead have a girl work for it. If she works for it, not only is she interested, but when someone is working for something then they are subconsciously telling themselves, 'I'm working for him, so he must be worthwhile.'

Noah ran over by us. "It's 2:20!" he yelled. "We are going to miss the shuttle!" The bus stop was more than a mile away. We had to get moving.

I saw Laura's phone was in her front pocket. I reached down and pulled out her phone, handing it to her. I told her to put my number in and text me.

"We've run out of time tonight," I whispered, kissing her one last time. "But text me later, and I might have to come back for you."

I didn't come back.

Part

Leveling Up

Choose a technique and model it.

There was Letter-Jay, who had the natural abilities and leadership tactics that tended to make the room want to follow him. His certainty, tonality, body language, and charismatic disqualifiers tended to leave a woman's brain fried.

There was Ace, who had an extreme ability to push-pull anyone in an unnatural programmed way. His teasing remarks were able to get the woman uncontrollably aroused, unknowingly qualifying herself to him so that he only needed to deliver a simple sentence to lead her right into the bedroom: "Come with me really quick."

There was Alexander, who was a driver and heavy hitter. His style wasn't for everyone because it was extremely direct and only worked when the woman was already horny, looking for anyone to fuck. His gorilla-like instinct of physically escalating on a woman usually turned her off, but when it worked, it made her extremely aroused.

Then there was Hakan, who gave me my first-ever experience of witnessing the prowess of a real unnatural with the opposite sex. I felt like everyone had their own particular style or unique ability, but I was still yet to develop my own signature style or move. I was a natural at this point, which was more than I ever dreamed of being with a woman, but after sitting in that room, I knew that everyone had to have some special ability. I didn't know what mine was, but I finally awakened mine while watching Hakan perform.

Hakan had sent me a screenshot of the message he received from Gary. They sent him a picture of a single woman sitting alone at the bar.

The text read:

"A man by the name of Rover will be giving you directions to your hotel room, your suite number, and basic necessities are in the room. Your single challenge is to be able to get this lovely woman from this club to your hotel room (legally)."

He nerfed everything. He said that he couldn't use alcohol or force her to the room in any way, which I didn't think he would, but Gary had probably seen it all at this point. It had to be pure interaction mastery to make her want to come back to the room. Alexander wouldn't have been able to do this.

"This is a test of your social skills," he texted. "I want you to show me your capability with social awareness. You have from 10-2 A.M. and if you can't then you simply don't advance. What you do from there is up to you. Have fun, good luck! – Gary"

Advance? I thought. I didn't know that there were rounds to this.

This first round was already near impossible for me. I'd only pulled a girl on the same night twice. Once with Jay's help, which doesn't even count, and then again at IU.

I had to see if Hakan could pull this off, but I couldn't be seen by Gary or his squad. If I did, I'd be eliminated.

I had to completely change my appearance.

I swallowed my pride and asked Stephanie if she could put makeup on my face. We had a fiery start at first when we met at her mansion. We butted heads like rams, but when I got to talk to her one on one, she was actually cool.

She agreed to put makeup on me, and I told her that she wasn't allowed to speak of this to anyone. I wore eye shadow and foundation; I looked like a woman. I changed my eye color from blue to black with colored contact lenses. I wore a cowboy hat over a fake wig of dreadlocks and wore baggy jeans, cowboy boots, and a plaid long-sleeve shirt. I had no idea what the fuck you could call this style. It was a mix of Jack Sparrow from *Pirates of the Caribbean* and the cowboy from *Ghost Rider.*

My own mother probably wouldn't have recognized me.

My mind went through multiple scenarios. Like what if she is there with a man? What if there's only a one-percent chance of pulling her home. How do you do that? Unlike me, Hakan was always cool and calm. He probably felt like this would be a breeze.

I arrived in Broad Ripple early around 9:30, and I definitely got some strange looks from the people on the sidewalk. The tryout was in the Red Room. Coincidentally, his girl – the target – was wearing red. She had on a simple red cutoff T-shirt that showed her belly-button piercing and wore her long blonde hair in a ponytail. She wore light-blue jeans, I'm assuming stretchy, that curved around her legs as if they were painted on her. She had to be 24 at least, and she wore a black sparkling choker around her neck.

An idea popped into my head. If I convinced her to leave with me, Hakan would lose, and I'd have less competition.

I didn't go through with it. It would have been too risky because if I got caught, I would be out. Too much was on the table to lose.

That's when Hakan walked into the club.

I stayed far away in the shadows of the club. I hadn't seen Gary or anyone of his sort yet. I was nervous because maybe they were already on to me. That I was already eliminated. Maybe I was just overthinking it. Hakan had already gotten an envelope from one of them though. They were so slick that I didn't even see him take it.

I waited an hour and a half before Hakan made his approach at 11:30, and it didn't even happen in the Red Room. It happened after she left the club. When she left, he caught up to her on the sidewalk and started a conversation. I followed about fifty yards behind. Fortunately for him, it was an easy tryout. She was alone, and he had no obstacles to take out like a friend, or even worse, a boyfriend.

From there, he took her to Insomnia Cookies. About an hour after conversation there, he left with her to the closest hotel, which was about a mile away from Broad Ripple. It seemed to have gone smoothly, but I wanted to know what he did. What happened when he brought her inside the suite, and especially what was his technique – his power.

Hooking the Heart

The following afternoon, Hakan and I met up twenty minutes south of Broad Ripple at a China Buffet so we could stay far away from any of Gary's potential watchmen.

He pulled out his phone, showing me a message. "Well done," Gary texted him. "You are one of the few who are advancing. Stand by and wait for further instruction."

I wanted that same message. The only one I had received today was, "Revel @ 10 o'clock tonight." Saturdays were when clubs were usually the most packed but also the most dangerous.

I was so nervous. It could end any type of way. I could come out on top, or I could fail miserably. Before I asked him about the details, I wanted to see his true colors, and how he got involved with this clubbing business to begin with.

"How did you find this community?" I asked. "How did you even get here?"

"Well, my father left my brother, mom, and me when we were kids. He was an alcoholic, and he agreed to find help but never came back."

He paused and then continued. "I found out years later that he didn't leave for help; he left to marry another woman. I think that he's where I get a lot of my addictions from. I was in the clubs, month after month, talking to girls until I ran into one of Gary's partners; Letter-X. He moved to Chicago and recruited me to take his spot here in Indianapolis."

He showed me a picture of his father and they looked almost identical, but when I said that, he put his phone away and tried to change the subject.

"Did you see someone with dreadlocks last night?" I asked him.

"No," he replied. "Why?"

"I had Stephanie disguise me so I could watch you perform."

"You're an idiot! What if you got caught!"

"Um, then I would have been out."

"No shit!" he sarcastically intoned. "Well," he said with a complete change in tone, "I'm probably going to do the same for you tonight."

"So, what happened?" I asked him.

Here's what Hakan told me:

She was such a shy girl; I could tell. I love shy girls because I always know what to say to them. The emotional connection that I could create is always the cherry on top.

I don't remember what I said in the opening. To me, it's not important.

The interaction is like an art. Stories are my favorite form of art, and the buildup is what makes the ending. Keeping her constantly in a love story by keeping the mystery, the uncertainty, and the challenge.

You can ask questions, but then there's the man who makes assumptions and statements. For example, instead of asking where she was from because she looked like she was from the West Coast, I could say, "You aren't from around here, I can tell." It's a technique called the 'cold read' where people tell you insights about yourself without any prior information, and it captures their attention.

In that moment, she wants to know what makes you think that. It must be something about her looks, her personality, or just the way she walks. She wants to know, and you now have something she wants, so she works for you.

She told me that she was a model from Arizona when we sat down in Insomnia Cookies.

I told her a story of other models I was friends with. It was killing two birds with one stone. She would see that I'm social-proofed by telling her indirectly who I hang around, and then I would finish with,

"Most models are all over the place and kind of annoying, but you seem different. I feel like you are focused like you have a goal or an interesting story."

It made her feel special by gluing together the idea that she was different.

"Tell me," I said, "what happened in your past to make you motivated like this. Was it a guy who broke your heart? Family? Financial problems?"

It's almost a trap in a way. If she says she doesn't have a story then she would call herself uninteresting. Who would want to admit that? It also helps her open up and talk. While she's talking, and while she's telling you this, her brain is subconsciously telling itself: "I must like this guy because I'm sharing with him a lot about who I am."

While she was telling me about her life story, she would pause and turn red. "I don't know why I'm sharing this with you," she said, fanning herself. "We just met."

I read in her voice that she truly is shy and slightly insecure. One of the major hooking points with winning her heart is when she reveals some of her biggest insecurities to you. That's when you know she likes you, but the trick is how you compliment her.

She believes that her flaws are bad, and when they're shown to someone it would be a negative, but the romance happens when a man is able to find and then compliment her insecurities.

I told her that this insecurity is one of the two or three things I liked about her. I then told her the second thing. When she asked for the third thing, I said, "I like when you…well, never mind. I'll tell you later. It's too cute for me to say."

She bothered me all night to find out the third thing.

I always carry a few cheap hoodies in my bag. Women love wearing a man's clothes. I'll spray it with my Versace cologne and tell her to give it back to me the next time she sees me. Usually, she will wear it when she's not with you, and as soon as she puts it on, she's thinking about you. It's dangerous because when she's thinking about you, her desire for you is growing too.

To push that along, when we were coming down the elevator the next morning, I pinned her to the wall and made out with her aggressively. As soon as the doors opened, I walked out without looking back. This amplified her emotions before I left so she would think about me all day.

Part

Gateways of Desire

After Hakan and I left around 4 o'clock, I realized he was at a different level.

It was like he could hack into her mind and steal her heart. This was the style that I was waiting to perfect.

I learned from Jay that it takes confidence to approach, and I learned from Ace that it takes competence to spark interest and desire.

Part of competency includes the process of pulling her in and pushing her away. This is what sparks attraction and causes it to grow: pulling her in with indirect compliments, interesting tests, stories, and validation.

Every pull must be balanced with a push to keep the mystery including teases, sarcasm, or just turning away. However, these aren't cold, they are flirty because you do them implying the opposite of what you're saying.

Notice how women will do the same thing to men. They will say things and a lot of the times mean the opposite. You say these things to her, and you imply the opposite of what you're saying with a smirk or smile. For example, hugging her and then saying, "Okay that's enough" or "Okay, that will be five dollars."

Or, "You have something in your teeth [or hair]… It's, um, cute, but you might want to get it."

Or, "Get away from me" while you push her away and then add, "You're too cute for me to be around." With a wink.

If she says, "I need to shower," then you say, "Yeah you do" or "I'm glad you noticed too." As you cover your nose, roll your eyes, but smile.

We can compliment her only if it is balanced out with a push. You give her some validation, but men lose her when they give her all of their validation from the start.

Teasing and pushing her away are risky, so most revert to pulling her in with compliments, questions, and acting like they truly care about her.

It has to balance like a scale or otherwise one side will become heavier and fall. When you pull her in too much, it causes her to become bored and disinterested, and she'll walk away.

Only the men who realize they don't need her are able to tease her, and it shows that you believe you're on her level.

I was so focused on sparking attraction that I had hit a plateau, but the love story was my favorite theme.

I finally learned from Hakan that the true nature of a powerhouse seducer is his ability to create a great love story. It's addicting if done correctly.

This realization came just in time to use that night.

I got ready. I had a few people who would accompany me in the club. Gary never said if we could bring people, he just said to keep it an absolute secret.

Noah was the first to take me up on my offer. In the past two months, he had dropped out of the IU business program, which I didn't recommend, in order to learn more about the dating life. It was his all-time dream now to become a pickup artist and revolve a business around that.

He also had a friend to join him who came all the way from Dubai in order to get the full nightclub experience.

The next to come was Alexander, who I realized would be a major asset for the night, and finally, Jay decided to come because Gary knew that Jay was the one who recruited me.

I put on my lucky pinstripes and my suede Chelsea boots. Tonight was going to be a big night for me. One of the turning points of my entire life.

When I walked into Revel, a woman greeted me as if it was regular conversation. She was sly and handed me the envelope. Then walked away without a sound. I saw why I never noticed Hakan receive his envelope.

I opened the envelope to find a note, a key to a suite at the Holiday Inn a few blocks away, and $425 to cover food, drinks, etc.

The note read:

C,

Wait at the railing of the second floor for further instruction. I will be sending you a message here shortly on what you will be doing for your tryout. If you aren't able to complete the challenge, one of my people will find you and take the envelope back. The money is yours to keep, however.

Best,

Gary

Puppet Master

I've hated the word 'tryout' ever since I was cut from the high school baseball team.

In the past, whenever I was in sports and had to compete with others watching me, I usually choked. I never believed in myself and always tended to drop the easiest passes or flyballs. I let up because I felt like I had no chance.

Now whenever I was in front of others and walked into a club, I felt this charge of power as I pondered who I was going to make out with, dance with, or potentially take home? But it was on this night that I dove deeper into forbidden territory: the power of an emotional connection with a woman.

Tonight was my big debut. The gate that led me from a natural to an unnatural.

I stood at the railing on the top floor per Gary's instruction. As soon as she walked in, I knew what Gary was going to tell me to do.

She was stared at, purred at, and whistled at all night when she stepped foot into the VIP lounge of Revel's nightclub.

"Holy shit," Alex gasped. "That's a platinum blonde."

Her silver hair matched her silver silk skintight dress. It looked as though it compressed her spray-tanned fake breasts so much that one wrong move and they would rip through.

With all of that silver, she reminded me of the antagonist in *Terminator 2* who could turn his entire body into liquid steel. Of all of the women I had met, I failed to realize that 'platinum blonde' meant her hair. I had never heard that term before he said it. I thought the term meant five stars, a well-known supermodel, or something of that caliber. At least that's the description I saw in my head.

I didn't want to say that I was disappointed when I finally made the connection hours later, but I wasn't necessarily impressed.

I watched her as did the entire club.

My phone buzzed.

It included the picture of the platinum blonde sitting down. The challenge was the same as Hakan's – in short, win her heart.

Noah went in for her first, breaking the ice and attempting to tease her on her dress.

"Silver is usually for second place," he said. Before he could finish the line, she turned her back to him and shut him out. Then his friend, Oli, the visiting foreigner from Dubai, opened with an option. She shooed him off like he was a stray cat.

That's when Alex said, "I'm going in."

"Wait," I said, halting him with my hand. "Look."

A six-foot-five musclehead sat next to her at the bar.

No fucking way," Alex said. "That's a linebacker who is considering signing with the Colts." After he finished his beer, he took the can and crushed it into a refined disc. I didn't know who it was, but Alex studied fantasy football, so he knew about every player on every team.

It took every brain cell to create a strategy. This was life or death and would take a flawless seduction to win her not only from him, but for me.

In my head, I plotted three sacrifices that needed to happen to get her.

I began to move into position.

I told the DJ to play a certain mix of dancing songs that brought most of the club to the center-room dancefloor. From there, I had to get myself into 'state.' In pickup-artist lingo, this meant to bring my mental state to a place where I was feeling good and balanced. So, I wrapped myself in the power of social proof by taking the hand of a woman who, when I was 20, I would have given up anime for a year for and spun her around.

I glanced sideways to see if the platinum blonde noticed us as the center of attention on the dancefloor. She did, and that was all I needed for proof.

My dance partner was only a pawn piece to get to the blonde – my first sacrifice.

The football player left her alone for a few minutes, so that's when I saw the opportunity. I strutted up to her, first talking to a couple sitting next to her at the bar.

What I said was irrelevant. It was really all to get to her. Now was the time; I had to pull out the big guns on her in order to capture her attention.

I turned to the platinum blonde. "What's your problem?" I asked. "Why are you sitting here with all this fun going on but with that look on your face?"

I said it with a smirk, but she didn't take it that way.

She glared at me cold but came back with fire. "Excuse me?" she hissed, looking me hard in the eyes. "Why would you try to embarrass me like that?"

This wasn't playful. She was serious.

I realized that I was playing Russian Roulette with my words except with five bullets in the chamber, not just one. If by chance I pulled the trigger on the wrong words, she would overreact, and the linebacker – who was now on his way back from the bathroom – was going to do to me what he did to his beer can earlier.

My heart was beating. I was on the edge, and it inspired me to clutch up.

I realized that anger is the perfect terrain for my misdirection. If I could turn her anger around, I'd win her heart.

"I can tell you're not having a good time," I admitted. "But would you rather *I* be the friend who walks away and leaves you like this when I can clearly see you're not doing well or the friend who picks you up and wants more for *you*?"

Before she could respond, the hulk came over. "KT, is everything alright over here?" he asked, side-eyeing me.

I stood my ground. This was the moment of truth.

If she told him I was being a problem, I'm assuming he would have started an even bigger one.

"Yes," she said. "I'm just catching up with someone." I guess I had an effect on her, or maybe she just didn't want to start a fight.

He grabbed her hand and pulled her away to the opposite side of the bar. She looked back at me, and it reminded me of a child being pulled away from a candy store by a parent. When you take something away from somebody, they value it more.

It also reminded me of Romeo and Juliet. The parents of the families separated the two of them and said they were never allowed to be together, but it only amplified their love for each other. If the families just let them have sex or do whatever then they probably would've just dated for a few months and then broken up without having to kill themselves. It's simple psychology. Now, I was going to take advantage of Alex's psychology.

When I walked back to the group, Alex asked, "Well, how did it go?"

I told him that the linebacker was controlling, and she's been trying to get away from him all night, but she wants a man who can take her away – who can get rid of him. As I was telling him this, hope filled his chest and his eyes like a gas tank.

"Also," I added, "I think she was checking you out."

It was easy to manipulate Alex.

He only thought about two things: getting top from a girl and getting alcohol to help him get top from a girl who's drunk. So, when I told him a hot girl found him attractive, the beast in him came out. He thought he could be the knight in shining armor and fight this hulk-like figure away.

"Top time," he said as he stood from the seat. I followed him to the bar but hid behind a pillar so they couldn't notice me even though I was close enough to hear the conversation.

"So," he addressed the platinum blonde, "I have to know. Does the carpet match the drapes?"

Perfect, I thought.

162

"What the fuck is wrong with you," the blonde seethed.

"What?" Alex responded. "It's a compliment."

"You think you're funny?" the linebacker growled, grabbing him by his shirt collar.

Alexander never took provocation well. He was extremely hotheaded and especially competitive for a woman. He was also big enough to fend for himself for a few moments before he would get ripped apart.

I, on the other hand, wouldn't last a second, but I didn't have to.

Alex pushed him off and grabbed a knife from the bar counter.

The linebacker shattered a bottle.

The platinum blonde tried to get them to stop, but they both couldn't control themselves.

They stared into each other's eyes holding their weapons.

The entire club seemed to stop and watch this battle. The tension was killing me. I didn't know if I was going to see someone die in a fight.

"This is why!" Jay hissed into my ear. "This is why I don't like Alex!"

"This *is* why." I smiled ear to ear.

Security grabbed both of them, escorting them outside.

I said that I needed three sacrifices to get to the blonde, but I didn't address the last two – Alex and the linebacker. Yes, I sacrificed him, my friend, for what I wanted.

I pawned the entire club to get to her. With these two gone, I had a fair shot with the platinum blonde now.

She sat back down at the bar, sinking her face into her hands.

I slid next to her, signaling the bartender. "Two shots of tequila, please."

She lifted her face from her hands and looked at me. After he poured the shots in front of me, I placed one in front of her.

"It looks like you could use this," I told her.

I normally don't buy drinks for a girl unless she puts in something of equal value because they tend to lose respect when a man does that.

But this case was the exception because she needed somebody. And I needed her if I wanted to advance in Gary's competition.

I held out my shot for her to clink hers against. "To finding a good man," she said, clinking it against mine and downing it.

After a few moments of adjusting to the burn of the alcohol, I asked her, "How can you find something good when you're searching in all the wrong places?" A line I once heard in an anime, but I believed it.

"That sounds like such a line," she chuckled, testing me.

"If it was a line, I'd ask you if the carpets match the drapes," I responded with a smile.

"Oh my gosh," she laughed, signaling that I passed that test. "Did you hear him say that?"

"Sadly, I did."

I used to hate awkward silences when I was talking to a girl, especially in the moments when I couldn't think of anything to say.

But I realized over countless conversations that it's actually an advantage.

When a girl is interested in you and you decide to randomly go quiet, she will fill that silence with conversation. It was a subtle test to reveal her attraction for me. All I had to do was turn my head away and stare out the window.

"Are you from around here?" she asked.

"I am," I said, "but I can tell that you aren't." I was exercising the cold read.

"How can you tell?"

"You are so different from the people around here." It may have sounded like an autopilot response by me, but over time, I trained myself to stop asking boring questions and instead making short and interesting statements. Guessing instead of asking because the guesser leads the conversation; it's like bait.

"I'm different?" she asked.

"I can tell you've been through a lot and have so much to say," I told her. "But I feel like it's extremely difficult for you to open up to people." With every word and every assumption, her eyes dilated more and more, and her face blushed pinker and pinker.

She began to tell me about how she was a former model who moved from California. That the people there weren't her crowd and that she wanted something more real. I tended to wait until she asked for my name because when she's interested in you or reaches the point where she's attracted, she will want more information about you. She called herself KT. I don't know why it wasn't 'Katie,' but it was the letters 'K' and 'T.'

"You still wind up surrounded by the same people," I continued. "Tell me, KT, that guy who got escorted out – he doesn't get you, does he?" I began to go by my script of adding more truisms and reads after another attempt to destroy him while simultaneously showing her that I possessed what he lacked. "I feel like you really like someone at first, but over time you tend to lose interest, and you can never figure out why or when that man will come into your life who will sweep you off your feet and never gets old."

"Well, I, uh… He is…" she stuttered.

"You already told me everything I need to know," I said, holding up my hand to stop her. "You don't have to lie to me; I promise you can be open with me." I threw in those lines to lower her walls, implying that she wasn't able to be open with him or anyone else, but that I was different in a way that she could be with me unlike she was with anyone else. It was the ability of a hacker.

"It's funny the way you're resisting him but have so much in common," I added.

"No, we don't!" she snapped. "How?"

"You both get mad at me when I talk to you."

She laughed, slapping my shoulder. Touching, to me, was the window to escalate.

"C'mon," I said, attempting to get her alone, "you have to see this."

But she resisted. Perhaps because she felt it wouldn't be right to leave with me when she came here with another man.

My last resort was the false takeaway.

"I like that about you," I said, nodding approvingly. Then I got up to walk back to my friends. After two steps, she grabbed my wrist.

"We need two shots, please," she said to the bartender while holding my wrist. I gave her a confused look. She downed one and gave me the other.

"Alright," she said, "show me."

I took the shot then grabbed her hand, leading her out of another exit to avoid the crowd. Luckily, the Holiday Inn where Gary had reserved my suite was a few blocks from the strip of nightclubs because he wanted me to be fully equipped. I took her to the very top floor and opened the corridor to the rooftop where we could see the entire city and the dazzling city lights.

For a few minutes, a little girl came out. She danced around and pointed at random buildings that she said she wanted to visit. This was the side to her that I was waiting to see.

Eventually finding her way next to me, we leaned over the railing.

She looked into my eyes; her voice lowered to a whisper.

We kissed gently. At 1 a.m. in the suite, we made out and slowly removed our clothing, one at a time. By 1:45, she was blowing me. At 2:30, we took a shower together until our skin pruned. (For Alex: The carpets were red, not matching the drapes.) By 3:30, we fell asleep together, hair still damp.

In the morning when she left, she said to me, "You're different from the guys I typically date."

I responded with the line that my former coaches said to me: "I just have something that they don't."

I was becoming the cocky asshole. The Jay. The one who could not only talk the game but show it time and time again. The villain who was arrogant but had the credentials to back it up. Eventually, of course, he'd stumble upon the one to take him out.

I was transforming into an unnatural. I just didn't notice, or maybe I just didn't want to face, that I was diving deeper into a dark and lonely path, and if I sunk deep enough, I'd never be able to get out.

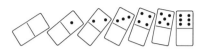

Chapter VI

Kilig

The Rush of Feeling from Achieving

[Kilig: A Philippine term meaning, "The feeling of achievement within romantic settings."]

"I think I'm done with clubbing, alcohol, and any other thing of that sort."

This was what Jay said after that night.

"How come?" I asked.

"Truth is, I found a great girl. I want to go work on being a great man, and this game gave me anxiety problems. I'm ready to reorganize my life. I want to start waking up earlier and not sleeping until noon. I want a family and children."

I guess it was his way of passing the torch to me.

I'd gladly accept. I loved this life, and I was having fun. I understood. I didn't like it, but I understood.

Jay was like a stem cell and adapted quickly.

Whatever he chose to be, he became fully. If he chose to be your wingman, he would be perfect. If he chose the party life, he embraced it fully.

Now he chose to leave the game for a relationship, and I'm sure he would figure out what that took.

I was on the opposite spectrum. A relationship is said to come when you're least expecting it and when you can tell yourself, 'I'm happy on my own' and truly feel that way. I felt that way right now but in a different way.

There were seven things that made me happy.

Five of the seven were hibachi grills, massages, anime, kittens, and occasionally tequila.

Especially massages by a lover because, to me, when someone touches you, that's how they show their affection and care for you.

Whenever I was talking to a woman and at some point in the interaction she slapped my arm or tried to touch me in some way, I got all aroused and worked up.

It's because humans are physical creatures, but it was even more than that for me because touch and connection was the thing I constantly wanted – the sixth thing to make me happy.

Prior to my parents' divorce, they tended to kiss me, tell me they loved me and tickled me, but then that physical connection abruptly stopped. After it was taken away from me, I missed it deeply. It still happened sometimes, but it was loose and it felt like there was a lack of effort. It wasn't that tight, warm, and fuzzy feeling that I felt when a woman would touch me.

When I was cut from the baseball team, it felt like further confirmation that I wasn't good enough, that I wasn't special. The seventh thing that I tended to love was hearing affirming words that showed that wasn't the case. Compliments were cool, but it was the indirect compliment that I craved. It was a feeling of belongingness – an acknowledgment that you have something someone else doesn't.

Gary fulfilled that need for me when he texted me: "7 P.M. Friday meet me at Circle Center Mall downtown for the final round. 3rd floor arcade center."

These were the texts that made me feel special. That I belonged and had some special talent that nobody else had. I was the person this time who 'just had it.'

Neon Lights

Gary was like a 10-year-old who won the lottery.

Everything you'd expect a kid to do with his money, he did.

When I walked into the arcade center on the third floor of the mall, he had four bodyguards huddled around an air hockey table. He spent the tickets he won at different games on the questionable multiple-year-old candy prizes.

He threw me an air hockey paddle. "In business and life, you have to risk something," he told me. "What are you risking for this game?"

"Fine," I smirked. Little did he know, I used to go to the arcade all the time when I was a kid. I faced everyone in air hockey and always won.

"If I beat you then I *automatically* advance," I said, "and I don't have to do this next challenge. If you win then what do you want?"

"If I win then you have to do this next round without being able to talk. If it was someone else, I would have bet your elimination on the spot, but your performance in the club impressed me so much that I want to see if it was a fluke or actual talent."

It was a huge risk. My heartbeat slowly picked up the pace.

If I won then I was automatically in with this business. I would move right to the top. But if I lost then my chances were that his challenge included social skills. My chances of winning would be practically zero if I couldn't speak.

"Alright," I said. I could beat him.

Air hockey reminded me of the game with women. The puck zigzagged, and while it bounced off the walls, you barely had any time to think. You just relied on your instinct, hoping your programming was quick enough to counter. The interaction constantly shifted. You had to be strong enough to defend against her tests, but sharp enough to respond elegantly. Breaking past her defenses and winning her heart.

I lost 6-7.

"I like guys like you," he said. "You put everything on the line, but you're not a gambler, you strategize."

I actually learned to risk from Alexander. The person who put his all on the line every interaction. Usually, he failed. In fact, he failed 99 percent of the time.

Hakan, the Buzz-cut, and the greaser from the room walked in with a guard. I'm assuming they were the other survivors of the first round.

We were escorted down to Gary's limo, stationed in front of St. Elmo's steakhouse where the guards microphoned us up.

"You guys will be creating names for yourselves, and you have mics on because we will be listening in on your conversations. If you share information, you will be terminated. You will only address each other based on the names you decide on right now."

Buzz-cut spoke up first and said he wanted to be called 'Carbon.'

Hakan changed two letters in his name and added one to become 'Hacker.'

The greaser said he will go as 'Z,' the letter.

These were all cool names.

"I'll be passionfruit," I told them.

Z and Carbon burst out into laughter. "You know what fruit means?" Z asked.

"What do you mean?" I asked, red-faced.

"It means gay!"

Fuck. I thought it sounded cool. Now I was going to be known as this forever.

"Since you guys are acting like kids, I'll name you," Gary said. "C, Z, H, and T; you will address each other by your letter."

I was the letter C, Hakan was H, Carbon was T, and the greaser was Z.

"Alright," Gary said, clapping his hands together. "There is a penthouse pool party starting at 9 o'clock tonight. You all have two hours to get a girl from the streets and bring her to the limo. Whoever fails to do so will be eliminated. See you at nine."

It was already 7:30, so we had way less than two hours.

I was the last to hop out of the limo when he stopped me.

"Remember our bet," he said. "Not a word." He put two fingers to his lips as if he was zipping his mouth shut.

Hakan went to Brothers, T went back into the mall, and Z went to Revel. I could only imagine walking up to a girl on the streets at night, not saying a word, and trying to get her back to the limo. She'd call the cops on me; I'd look like a total creep.

I only had one option. He said I couldn't talk but never said I couldn't use notes.

"Hey doll," I texted KT. "Want to go with me to a private pool party with celebrities?" Gary never said anything about celebrities, but I threw that in because who could resist that?

"Um, yeah!" she responded.

"I need you to meet me at Circle Center Mall at 8:30."

Fortunately, she could, and she wanted to. If she didn't then I'd lose. She wore denim shorts, cheetah print sandals, and an L.A. Dodgers cutoff T-shirt with her platinum hair wrapped in a messy bun.

I pulled her in, made out with her, and put my finger over her lips to say no talking.

She talked to me while I brought her to the limo, where we found Hakan in back with a glass of champagne in one hand and a tall Russian woman holding his other hand.

"You've outsmarted me," Gary said, recognizing KT. "Welcome, dear." He kissed her hand. "I treat all of my partners' guests in the highest regard."

He handed us a mimosa.

The next to step in was Z with a stunning girl who I later found out had a mix of Egyptian in her. She was tan-skinned, tall, and had spongy black hair.

At 8:59, there was still no sign of T until he popped around the corner of Georgia Street running with a blonde girl on his back. When 9 o'clock struck, even though T was right there, Gary shut the door and told the driver to leave.

"Part of being in business is being on time," Gary told us. "If I can't trust your word, I can't trust you as an ally."

I watched T run after us with his fist in the air as we drove away. Gary didn't even care that he left his microphone with him.

On the way to the pool party, I was in high spirits.

"So, we're the only ones to make it?" I asked Gary.

"Not necessarily," he said. "There were two others who proved themselves early on, and I already sent them out for work in Milwaukee and Kentucky."

"Will we ever meet them?" I asked.

"Probably not," he said. "But I also moved one more to the promotion team. He was the exception to the rules."

It was letter-X. I felt like we were the best, but I sunk into my seat when I realized three others were so talented that they didn't even have to do this round.

It was also after this night that we left our regular lives behind.

I was a student-athlete at the university by day but a world-class promoter by night. I had to keep these two worlds separate from everyone.

Revolution

Pack the clubs with people, and you'll make money.

This was the summary of the ten-page strategic guide we were given on how to actually do this.

To me, this was *the* dream. Our team was paid to talk to some of the most beautiful women and get them into the club. We got free VIP access in most of the clubs we hosted, free drinks, free food, and got to stay in some of the classiest hotel suites near the clubs.

All we had to do was supply. My strategy worked for me. KT was striking, and she had plenty of friends who were the same. It didn't matter where we were, the results were the same. Hot women equal stampedes of men.

All I had to do was walk KT and her friends, who included underwear models, down the street a couple of times. The men accumulated behind us like a herd of zombies. All I had to do was walk them into one location, give them VIP access and drinks, and men then flooded into that location.

Usually, H, Z, and I worked separate clubs, but the best nights were when H and me were put into the same club because they were paying bigger bucks for promotions.

The first team-gig was on Halloween.

It was cold as fuck downtown. I wanted to dress as Hugh Hefner, but I would've gotten frostbite in twenty seconds in a paper-thin robe. Instead, I put on a masquerade mask. KT and her friends dressed as playboy bunnies, and Hakan introduced me to the girl he brought, who were dressed in Pacers cheerleading uniforms.

I quickly got lost in the fun, growing an unhealthy mentality towards women.

KT wanted me, but I wanted her and others.

It was like that Bryson Tiller lyric: "Give me all of you in exchange for me." I remade that song into my own disqualifying line when KT said, "Date me and only me." I told her, indirectly, that I wanted all of her in exchange for, you know, *some* of me. I didn't say no, but it definitely wasn't a yes.

Hakan said he was interested in KT, and I told him that I was interested in one of the girls he brought.

There's this type of girl who has tan skin, black hair, and dark-brown eyes, and it just gets me every time. One of the girls who showed up with Hakan was from Honduras and fit that description perfectly.

Her body, a magnet to my eyes, was perfect. Her skin was darkened from the Central America sun but looked a light tan when compared to her jet-black wavy hair. She reminded me of a black widow: dark, mysterious, and beautiful in its own alluring way. She was a killer, but it wasn't her bite, it was her dark eyes. Black mascara painted her eyelids, and they sucked men in only to spit them back out with a broken heart.

Her name was as sexy as her complexion; Nadia.

I brought a thin piece of red plastic in the shape of a fish that fit in your palm: the fortuneteller fish. When it rested in your palm, it would move a certain way and – depending on how it moved – determined whether you were jealous, indifferent, in love, fickle, or passionate.

Hakan said that there was no way it was going to work, but within minutes there was a crowd around us wanting to try it.

This fish was my bait; I wanted Nadia to make her move on me.

"Do me!" she said.

"Easy, tiger," I told her, reciting a misdirection, "let's just start with the fish."

She gasped and slapped my arm. "I didn't mean it that way!"

Physical touch is my weakness.

I felt this electric sensation shoot through my body when I made contact with her and put the fish in her hand.

174

"It looks like its tail and head are moving!" she yelped. I looked at the back of the packet it came in. I looked back at her with a shocked look on my face.

"W-what does that mean?" she stuttered, leaning in to see the back of the packet.

It was 'fickle,' but I lied.

"It's saying that you are feeling in love," I said.

In the heat of the moment, I forgot to disqualify, but I did a few moments after that. "I would've thought that you wouldn't be in love, but jealous because I love somebody else," I said. "I'm sorry. We would never work out."

She put the fortunetelling fish in my palm. "Let's see what yours is then."

I happened to be 'passionate.' I told her she brought it out in me to pull her in.

"Join us and have a drink," she said.

"You are so demanding," I said, pushing, "but I love girls like you."

"I'm a Pacemate," she pridefully intoned, testing me. (Pacemates are the dance team for the Indiana Pacers.) She was wearing a sparkling yellow dress that said 'Pacers' on it.

It was obvious that she was.

"I would've never guessed," I responded sarcastically, looking her up and down. It was a line that Ace would call a reversal.

She slapped my arm and laughed.

I told her a story about my friends and the pool party to socially proof myself. Sometimes a girl tells a man she's a model or anything in that league to see his response.

If he crumbles like sand or drools all over her, he fails the test. At least, that's what I would've done a year ago. I never imagined I could ever flirt with a Pacemate, or models, or anyone of that sort.

I remember the first time I ever got with a girl, I was so nervous that my dick wouldn't get hard. In reality, this game is almost purely mental.

I wanted to try an experiment called 'breaking her into parts' where you capture her interest by reading into her different sides. She was very shy, I noticed.

"On the outside, you seem shy," I told her. "But I can tell from the look in your eyes that there's a side to you almost nobody gets to see. A wild side."

She started blushing. The sexual tension was rising, but nothing really came that night.

I told Hakan to take a picture of us so I could get her number. The idea was that after the picture was taken, if she was interested in me, she's going to ask me to send the pictures to her. It also gave her a way to contact me if she was attracted and built physical rapport by scooting in close together for the photo. I sent it to her with the caption, "We're so hot together."

I had to have her if it was the last thing I did.

Puppeteer

My strategy was unique for getting people into the clubs.

In fact, it was so good that I started to make between $500 and $800 every night. Even though I only had to do this around three times a week, I felt like I was the richest kid in the world.

When I worked in a warehouse making $13 an hour, it was the most miserable time of my life. But overnight, it felt like my obsession with seduction started bringing in more than enough revenue to live comfortably.

I really only saw one way to do this. Some people, like Z, aimed like a shotgun. He tried to influence as many people as possible to get them into a club, and it worked for him. I was the opposite. I tended to try to scope out the individuals with status – specifically, the women who were sparkling.

After I built an emotional connection with them, it was like killing two birds with one stone. She would fall for me, and I would bring her to the clubs. The women I dated loved to party. When I said the words "VIP and free alcohol," their eyes lit up like a slot machine in Vegas when the cherries lined up.

From there, my work was practically finished.

My strategy was that the girl I chose to date probably had five to ten other extremely attractive female friends. These girls surely had a funnel of even more attractive friends, and they all wanted into the club. Not only that, but these other girls had ten to twenty men who were lusting after each one of them. All I had to do was really solidify that relationship with my girl, and the rest followed.

I would singlehandedly bring 150 to 200 people into a club.

This didn't even include the best part.

I would wine and dine the friends, winning them all over. Usually, an hour or two before I was supposed to actually be in the club, I would take some of the girls I wanted in VIP down-town or wherever the action was nearby. I told them all to dress sexy, and it was insane. Men of all ages would follow us in herds down the sidewalks. They'd ask where we're going and then go there.

Guys go to clubs for usually one reason, and that's to score. When they see a dozen model-status women walk into a certain club, they'll get out of the lines of the other ones and immediately pack the house.

Even if they didn't have a chance, they still followed us in there.

Sometimes, I would walk the girls back and forth down the sidewalks in order to accumulate the men to follow us into the clubs.

I was still in university, but I told my professors that I would have to skip some classes because I was already heavily involved in business. Part of me said, *Why stay in school when I'm making more money than the people teaching me how to make money?* I stayed in school, however, because I promised my mother that I would finish college.

So, what does a kid do when he starts to make money? He spends it.

There are a few things that I love most in life, and hibachi grills happen to be one of them.

I started to go to hibachi restaurants once or even twice every other day, and every time I had a different girl with me. I met one of my favorite chefs, who was named Yo-Yo, and he called me 'player' in Japanese.

They named one of the koi in the pond after me – a golden one with long tentacles that looked like beards. Prior to my parents' divorce, they made a koi pond from scratch, and I spent a lot of my time outside in my backyard watching them or feeding them. After the divorce, we left all of them behind. I missed them.

Admiring the giant koi pond in the hibachi was my favorite part of my visits, probably because of that. It brought out the kid in me when I would stand on the bridge and watch them. Besides koi, birds are my favorite type of animal. If I was ever promoting a club with multiple floors, you could usually find me at the top of the place watching from the balcony, like a bird high up in a tree.

I also tended to do a lot of shopping. I found a Supreme pinstripe jacket online that I just had to have. H bought professional photo-shoot equipment. We would take our girls back to the suite and take pictures of us all together. The girls could use them for their modeling portfolio, and it was just downright a fun time. Plus, some clubs used them for promotional use.

H and I started bonding on a deep level, naming our girls with fruit nicknames.

"This is so cool," H whispered to me. "I love this. I love you."

In that moment, I loved him too. This *was* cool. There was nothing more bonding than pulling girls together.

Mystery Box

We sat down in Fogo De Chao, a Brazilian steakhouse in downtown Indianapolis, for a business meeting with Gary.

Z was the first to get scolded when he picked up the wrong fork for his salad. He picked up the inside one of the three, and that's when Gary said, "You eat from the outside in, top to bottom… Unlike the pigs who raised you back home."

That's when I realized one of my biggest pet peeves. Z, from smoking, tended to cough a lot.

While we were eating, he sat across from me and coughed without covering his mouth, so it was going directly at my plate. I absolutely hated that shit.

Gary got up and decided to use the restroom, and that's when Z chimed in.

"This man Letter-C makes women fall in *love* with him," he teased.

I started laughing.

"Seriously, you should've seen him," he told H. "He's a sniper, not a shot-gunner. He goes for one woman. Some guys go for all they can get, and then you have him. He goes for the highest-quality woman and slowly wins her heart, and by the time it's set in stone, he leaves before you realized it happened at all."

"But it works for me, Z," I responded. "I don't need a lot of girls. Plus, usually the girl I go for has the world's hottest friends. I show them around the city first, and it's like these girls had a gravitational pull. Guys followed them down the streets for miles. They whistled at them. They wanted to know where they were going. When they saw the girls walk into a specific club, the zombie-like men also walked in there. The moment they pass the bouncer and pay is the moment my pockets get bigger."

"My strategy shits on yours!" Z argued. "I use social media. The guys on my social media will see me partying in VIP with the girls, and they swarm my DMs in order to figure out where I'm at. I play tough and say I might tell. Once I finally get them to commit to coming, they bring all of their friends. I make like $450 per night on average. Gary knows that I'm the best pillar we have."

"Whether you like it or not," Gary said as he sat down, "C's strategy has brought in more income then you two combined."

Their jaws dropped. I was Gary's favorite pillar. That's what he called us, 'The Pillars.' I felt like Giovanni in Pokémon when he had that cat that sat on his lap. I was the cat.

After everyone was done eating, H and Z got up to use the restroom; Gary and I stayed at the table. I realized I should've gone because now I was one on one with Gary.

I had never talked to him one on one before, and talking to him was like opening the mystery box in *Black Ops*. You never knew what you were going to get from it.

I took a chance and talked first.

"What made you want to grow to this level of fame and massive success?" I asked him, exercising a cold read. "I can tell there's more behind your actions."

I was gaming the creator.

"I needed money," he said. "I was desperate." The words came short and raspy as he stared down at his empty plate.

I wondered if I had gotten the jackpot from the mystery box of Gary – the real him.

"My fiancée got pancreatic cancer when she was 27. If you know anything about that, basically it means 'you're dead.' We were too poor to have health insurance, and even though I was starting to take off in business, the treatments were evaporating all of my money. I worked night after night in the clubs because every penny counted to save her. I was so close, but she died in my arms one afternoon. When

I ran out of money, I had no other choice but to watch her slowly die every day."

His words were short but hit like a sniper. It was in that moment that I saw his heart and who he truly was. He told me that he felt like a failure because he couldn't save her.

There was a line that stuck with me from an anime, *Attack on Titan,* where one of the characters says, "Everyone is a slave to something." I believed it was because everyone has something from their past that is driving their present actions.

Once you see what someone else's prime motivator is, you begin to understand what is driving their entire existence. There's the day we are born, and then there's the day we truly experience our deepest pain. I wondered if that was the climactic moment in his life – if that was his 'Toska', the day he truly forgot how to smile. I wondered what the old him looked like before that, how warm his smile was.

Money changes people. Women change a man. Love shreds everything.

I couldn't resist the power of vulnerability, however.

I loved it when people shared their greatest pains with me. I started to realize that these stories were the 'dark arts' of a love story. When someone shares something as deep as this with you and shows you their true colors, there's almost nobody else out there who they can share it with. When you're able to bring this out of someone you become an escape for them. It separates you into a whole different category.

It was because of this interaction that I perfected my secret weapon of the love story. I was trying to figure it out for months, but it came out naturally when I finally seduced Nadia.

Part

Shattering

It was a night of multiple heartbreaks.

Ace, Adonis, me, Alexander, and Hakan found ourselves back at Stephanie's for round two. However, this time we brought along most of the party, including KT and her friends as well as Nadia and her dancing friends. Alexander was in heaven as he went around and tried to do some version of the game on the girls.

While I was catching up with Adonis, he said to me, "I have a curse!"

"What?"

"I can't lose my virginity. How come all the girls who are wildebeests want me, but the hot girls, the sexy babes, only want you and Ace?"

When we were about to talk, Lexi came over and interrupted us.

"Hey, Stephanie said that she doesn't want Alex. She wants either you," she said, looking at me, "or she wants you." Then she looked at Adonis. I didn't want her, plus I thought Stephanie was Alex's girl.

"That's all you." I looked at Adonis. "But I thought that she and Alex were a thing. He's brought her flowers and said they were basically together."

"Yeah, she told me that he's been trying really hard for her." She scratched her head. "But Stephanie just wants to be friends." I shook my head. This was not going to end well. I hopped off the countertop and went over by KT.

"Just kiss me," I told her. "I can't take this anymore." It was totally random.

"You're crazy," she said, giggling.

"Crazy for you." I winked. It was a good counter.

She told me I was a flirt and slapped my hand. Touch is a sign to escalate.

I asked her to measure her hand with mine.

Then we were holding hands.

Then I made her stand up with me. "If you wanted to dance, why didn't you just say so," I insisted.

She pouted as if she didn't want to. "For our wedding night, we need to slow dance just like this," I flirted, spinning her around.

"Everyone is looking at us," she said.

I whispered in her ear, "Would you rather be one of the jealous people over there watching us and wishing they could have this? Or would you rather be the girl who's actually doing it?"

The moment was ruined by none other than Alex.

"Fine!" he yelled in the kitchen. "I dare you to take him upstairs and fuck him!" KT and I stopped dancing together, and everyone's eyes turned to Alex. He slammed his drink on the counter. Red alcohol splashed out.

I raised an eyebrow, and KT grabbed my hand tight. He was yelling at Stephanie. She must have told him that she wanted Adonis instead and, out of anger, he said something he'd soon regret.

She said nothing. Shrugged her shoulders. Grabbed Adonis's hand, leading him down the hall and upstairs to a room.

Nobody said a word. We just looked around waiting for someone else to say something. I cleared my throat, looking at Alex. "What was that about?"

"She wanted Adonis, so I told her to have fun," he seethed.

Ace chimed in. "Well, I bet they are having fun alright."

Alex squeezed his hand into a fist. "Shut up!"

There were two things everyone was thinking right now, and I didn't want to be the guy to bring either one up. We wondered how Alex felt and what was truly going through his mind.

I knew he wanted Stephanie to be his girlfriend. He probably felt destroyed.

I was in mid-thought about Alex when Ace blurted, "Let's go

listen to them." This was the second thing everyone was really thinking.

"Okay!" I said after a short pause. I couldn't hold it in.

Ace and I led a mob of about fifteen people shuffling down the hallway to the base of the stairs where Adonis and Stephanie had disappeared. It became a concert of shushing.

We stood silent at the base of the stairs, anticipating hearing anything.

Part of me hoped for my sake I would hear them having sex, but for Alex's sake, I hope they weren't.

After a couple of seconds, I could have sworn I heard a faint moan.

I looked at Ace. "Did you hear that?" I whispered.

Right after I asked him, we heard what sounded like a cat stuck in a tree. Ace's eyes widened. Everyone looked up the stairs. Ace began to laugh. "No, but I heard that!" We all started laughing. Except for Alex, who ran out of the house and slammed the door. He reminded me of myself in a way. There was a time when I wanted a woman so bad, just like the way Alex wanted Stephanie. I became too attached, and it pushed her away. I didn't know what was happening; it's like we're blind to our own mistakes.

Part of me felt the urge to go outside and talk to him. He needed somebody. However, I had KT, Nadia, and all of my friends here. I didn't want to be like the others, and most would just laugh at him. A lot of the time I did the wrong thing, but occasionally – in a moment like this – the right thing came out. I needed to be the person for others that I always wanted to be but never had when I was struggling. My body moved on its own, and I walked outside.

He was sitting by the pond behind the house watching the fountain in the center. I sat next to him. When the breeze picked up the pace just enough, a slight mist from the fountain's recoil dampened my face.

He held a bottle of Bacardi with a few fingers. I'm not sure how much of it he'd drank when I got out there.

"Let's go for a drive," I told him.

He looked at me with tears in his eyes. "I loved that girl. Why am I never good enough?" Memories flooded into my head. I felt for him.

I helped him get up, and when he stood up, he took the glass bottle and threw it at the white brick that formed the side of the house. It shattered. He started screaming.

After he got done yelling, I remarked, "I'm assuming you're not going to finish that?" I pointed to the shards of glass on the ground and puddle of alcohol.

"I can't live without her." He began a drunken babble about suicide.

"Life is trying to tell you something." I put my arm around him. "You have so much love to give. Don't give up. Find a woman who is deserving of you and everything you can give."

My plan was to just take him home; he was obviously too drunk to drive. On the way there, he stared out the window.

"I didn't think Adonis would do that to me," he sniffled. "He knew how much I loved her." I felt for him, but at the same time, I questioned it.

If he was in Adonis's position, what would he have done?

I pulled up to his house. Before he got out, he said, "Thanks for being there; you're my best friend." I smiled and nodded back. On my way back to Stephanie's house, I didn't play any music. I sat in silence as my brain went to autopilot while driving on the lonely country roads. Alex's words cut deep. They brought back memories that I'd always tried to forget about certain people and events.

Sometimes, long drives by yourself, with your thoughts, are the most healing.

I drove through the gate and parked next to KT's car. My headlights caused the broken glass of the bottle that Alex shattered to sparkle back at me. I stepped out of my car and looked up at the sky again. Everything was quiet.

Finally, after a night of drama, I felt some peace. After a night like this, it was soothing to look at the stars and hear the crickets chirp. The frogs added their croaks near the pond, and I took a deep breath.

I stared into the universe.

Stars seem to glow brightest when they are all alone in the dark because it's the dark that makes them shine.

I dragged myself up the steps and put my hand on the brass knob.

It was cold for a summer night. Right before I turned the knob, I heard a coyote howl off in the distance. I had never heard one before this night. "I'm really in the backwoods," I said to myself.

For doing the right thing with Alex, life had decided to reward me.

When I walked in, Nadia was snuggled up in a beige fuzzy blanket on the couch in living room 'A' wearing a red hoodie. It was going to be one of the most artful seductions.

Instead of a battle, it was a dance.

Lonely Island

The S-Rank, in Japan, typically means so superlative that it cannot be described by any traditional ranking system. Lonely Island is a technique of the forbidden, the S-Rank of sparking uncontrollable desire.

Nadia was undoubtedly one of the most beautiful girls I had ever seen. The moon was directly over her in the living room. She was wrapped in moonlight while the rest of the room was pitch-black.

It was one of the most romantic scenes I'd ever star in.

She laid right next to a window that covered most of the whole wall, and the moon sparkled through it. It lit her face, her lips, and her dark-brown eyes. Everything about her sung to me like a song I played on repeat. Her dark-brown curly hair draped over her left shoulder.

I had to make a choice. KT was sleeping in another room, but Nadia was here.

In that moment, the choice was easy. "I don't want to leave you alone," I told Nadia. "I'll sit with you and tell you a bedtime story."

She laughed and scooted for me to fit with her on the couch. I lifted the blanket over myself as well so we were sharing it.

"I have to try something really cool on you," I told her. "It's called 'Lonely Island.'"

"Lonely Island?" she repeated. "What's that?"

"Imagine you got lost at sea and ended up on a tropical island. When you start walking on the beach, you notice how the island is either big or small. Which is it?"

"It's a small island." She emphasized 'small' by holding her thumb and pointer finger close together and then closed one eye to look through the gap.

"That's interesting," I said. "I could see that."

"What does that mean?"

"I'll tell you after," I said. "On the island, are there people or not?"

"There are quite a few people!" She paused. "I want to know what your answers are."

"Maybe after," I said. "Now this is where it gets interesting because on the island you notice what looks like a home. You decide to approach it and notice something about the door." I looked at her deeper as I leaned in. "The door is either a deep sapphire-blue or it's a burning crimson-red. Which color is the door?"

"Oh, it's definitely red."

"My door is red too," I told her. "But you decide to open the door to the house, and I need you to describe in three words the feelings you get from the vibe of this home. For example, what you see on the inside, and it can be anything you want."

"Hmm, so when I walk in, I get this complex feeling because I see a spiral staircase. It's overwhelming at first, but I realize as I walk around it's actually very simple and beautiful. It's strongly built and put together, but there's also a lot of fragile things on the inside."

I began to smile because this was going to be perfect. "Got it," I said. "So, it's overwhelming at first but simple, strong, and has fragile things on the inside."

She nodded.

"Last one," I said. "The weather on the island. Is there rain, sun, or maybe a mix of both?"

"It's raining heavily on and off," she said. "But sometimes the sun peeks through, and there are rays that come through the clouds around sunset that create a rainbow."

"Are you ready to find out what all of this means?" I asked.

"Yessss! I've been dying to know!"

She wanted something I had. I wasn't just going to give it to her as most would, but I'd make her work for it.

"Okay," I smirked. "I'll tell you in the morning after we wake up."

I stood up slowly and acted like I was going to go to bed.

189

She grabbed me with her legs and pulled me back onto the couch.

"Uh, no," she demanded. "I want to know now." She had one leg hanging on my leg after I sat back down.

"You love touching me, I see," I pointed out with some sarcasm.

"Shut it," she said, kicking me under the blanket. That reminded me of something.

"Okay," I smiled. "I will shut it and say nothing more."

"No! Not like that!" she whined. "Tell me what it means!"

"I've heard that women are very sensitive behind the knee," I told her, beginning to lightly graze the back of her knee. I moved my hand to the top of her knee, and then I looked at her.

"You seem like the ticklish kind," I said next, squeezing the quad muscle.

She jolted and spilled some water on herself. I laughed.

"I don't like you," she told me, wiping the water off. A test, but I didn't take her bait.

Too bad for her, my fortunetelling fish told us something different last time.

"That's true," I told her. "According to my fish, you're in love with me."

"Whoever said it was you?" she retorted. A good counter to my counter, I'll admit, but not good enough to knock me out.

"Well, uh," I said, looking at her leg on my lap, "if it's someone else, it's obviously not going too well, honey." I smirked.

"Oh," she chuckled. "You're so cocky."

It was so obvious she wanted me; it was all over her like a tattoo.

"Now please tell me," she added.

"Fine, fine," I said. "I'll tell you, geez… The first two are simple. The size of the island is your ideal life. You said the island was small, and what this means is that you don't necessarily desire fame or a huge lavish lifestyle. I feel like you are more of a simple person who may just want a family, a nice career, and you don't need a whole lot to make you feel happy and comfortable."

She began to nod.

"Then you said that there are a lot of people on this island," I continued. "This means that you like to be around others. Possibly living in a neighborhood when you get older with a lot of people and being close to family and your friends. It's like being around other people brings energy and life to you in a way."

"This is actually scary accurate," she said. "I love people, and I don't need a lot to make me happy."

"This is where it gets interesting based on the color of your door," I smirked. "The door color that you choose is basically the romance and love you secretly desire."

"Oh no." She held the covers over her face as if she was bracing herself.

"Red means passionate, exciting, and adventurous," I told her. "You want a man who doesn't hold back, and you want that crazy love story. A man who can make love to you all night long and make you feel like a woman. Someone who makes you feel beautiful and can handle your wild side. This color also means that you tend to fall in love quickly, if it's the right person, and you can't seem to help yourself."

She was nodding up until I said the last part, and then she gave me a skeptical look as if it could be wrong.

If it appears she might disagree, I say 'but,' and if her reactions are agreeable then I will say 'and,' adding to the story. In this case, she might have been skeptical of falling for someone quickly, so I added, "*But* maybe you haven't had that experience, or you have and it's been a bad thing because you've probably trusted guys or cared for guys who have only hurt you."

She rolled her eyes. "Yeah, I've dated some real assholes."

I looked into her eyes. "No wonder you like me," I said, moving her leg off of my lap. I scooted closer to her. "I'm just another asshole." I smirked.

"I don't think so," she giggled. "You're different than most guys."

We were looking into each other's eyes. I leaned in past the comfort zone. She leaned back slightly and darted her eyes at my lips.

Our faces were only inches apart. I felt her breath. It was the special moment right before a first kiss. My breathing slowed while my heart picked up its pace.

"They say that if you like somebody, your pupils will dilate, and then your heart rates begin to sync when you look into each other's eyes," I whispered, reciting one of the five kissing routines I'd memorized.

"R-really?" she stuttered.

I closed my eyes in sync with her. She leaned in, exhaling softly. Our lips met.

I've kissed a lot of girls, but this felt different. It felt like kissing a cloud. Our lips released with a slight smacking sound. Then she came back, gently biting my lower lip.

"You still haven't told me my last two," she whispered.

"I'd much rather do this."

She pushed me away, giggling. "C'mon, Connor."

"Alright, the inside of the house is a symbol for how you view yourself. The color of the door is kind of a metaphor for what a man will experience after you've opened up to him."

Her ears perked up like a deer and she bit her lower lip.

"You said 'overwhelming at first.' To me, this means that if I was the man dating you, at first, it may be hard to handle you. At first, your emotions, and your love is overwhelming. You're complex, but over time I would look past that and understand you. Your complexity is also your beauty, and it's only meant for the type of people who can figure you out. You also said strong but with fragile decorations on the inside. You see yourself as strong, but your heart is very delicate and fragile. You're careful about who you open up to because the wrong people will be careless and break what's valuable and fragile in you."

She was speechless. "I have to know yours," she said.

When we are talking about their answer regarding the weather, I usually ask them what they think their answer means. I let them open up about themselves because usually people associate rain with sadness. They will tell you about how they have had heartbreak or have dealt with insecurities. You let them take a few guesses and really let them invest. Sometimes, I never tell them what their answer means because they get so interested and involved with trying to figure it out.

At least that's what I did with Nadia at first.

The answer is that this is how one tends to see life.

Nadia said that sometimes it rained, but in between storms, the sun shined through the clouds. To her, sometimes life is difficult, sad, or hurtful, but this could mean she sees that those hard times create something beautiful afterward. For example, she said that there was a rainbow created by the mix of rain and sun. The rainbow is a sign that she will get through those times.

That's what I told her.

It would've been the perfect moment when we started kissing again, but while she was straddled on top of me, we heard someone walk into the kitchen.

It was KT. She made eye contact with me while Nadia was on top of me, walked back to her room, grabbed her car keys, and left.

Lost

"Love". I always wondered what love felt like.

These thoughts came to the surface after Ace got into a serious relationship. I felt numb to it, and I felt so cold like I was turning into something. That I was too late to turn back. There was a small voice inside of me begging me to just quit.

I already far exceeded what I came here for, but the other half of me loved every drop and every sense of validation. The money, the girls, and the power were so seductive that I came back for more. It was like a drug. Part of me felt like I just needed to duct-tape that voice in my head. Some people call it the 'inner bitch.'

There's a reason why seduction is a forbidden and dark art. Its secret requires a sacrifice, and I felt like my insides were slowly decomposing. After I got too far into this, I would only be a shell of my former self, unable to recognize myself.

Every time I got a woman, it was the same story. She was different every time, but it was the same story every time.

Part of me wanted something deeper. I wanted to explore the world with one person where that fire never burned out.

I also knew that only the coldest made it to the top, and that's why I started. I had to see this thing through until the end.

Every line I said made her desire me more, and in the moment, it felt so good. I was addicted to this game, but after they left to go home, I felt all alone once again.

Even in this community, surrounded by people, everything felt temporary.

People were dropping out of this community like flies. Gary had reported that he'd kicked two key people out in the past week, which meant he needed me and Hakan to fly out to Milwaukee to cover their spots.

I'd always wanted to have cool experiences. The first time I ever went on a cruise, I was sitting in a hot tub in the back of the ship with a few other people, and in the distance was a tropical storm that was following us. For about an hour, we watched waterspouts following our ship.

Gary flew us out to Wisconsin on a private jet, which was one of the best experiences. It was small but extremely fixed up on the inside with a bedroom, couches, and TVs. The best part was avoiding security because we were taken in a Cadillac Escalade directly to the plane, so all we had to do was walk up into it.

When my dad was at the peak of his Indianapolis 500 career, he told me about how their team would be flown in the sponsor's private jets. He said that when he had to race in Wisconsin, he sat in the cockpit with the pilots. On their way there, he saw the Northern Lights, describing it as a glowing blue, green, and purple curtain waving in the sky.

I decided to do the same, asking to join them in the cockpit where the pilots would tell me stories about the crazy things they had seen like potential UFOs. We didn't see the Northern Lights, but they were on my bucket list.

Also on that list were seeing a real dust devil in person and visiting a black-sand beach.

When the pilots asked what I did for a living, I replied, "Um, I'm not really sure."

I couldn't quit now when it felt like I was on the verge of massive success. I had made it to the final round. I needed to see this all the way through until I was either forced to quit or dead.

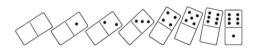

Chapter VII

Cavoli Riscaldati

Trying to Rescue What's Already Lost

*[Cavoli Riscaldati: An Italian term defined as "reheated cabbage."
It is used to describe an attempt to save or restart a relationship that
can't be revived.]*

Fourteen days of reoccurring memories.

Ace and I had been experiencing some weird form of déjà vu. We kept running into people who had significantly impacted our lives in the past. Ironically some of these people were the same. People we knew from high school who had faded away. But I never thought that I'd run into *her* again.

While in Milwaukee, we had a full load. I almost kept forgetting that I was a university student. I was thinking too much again.

But it stopped when déjà vu decided to strike a whole two states over from my home. The DJ on the stage of Site 1A was the girl who Caitlyn was with the first night I met her at Skateland. She had hired Gary to do marketing for her, and then he sent Haken and me to meet her in person.

She was cute; perhaps I would have her. I couldn't figure out if it would be easy or tricky because of Caitlyn. Maybe she would want me more because I was already socially proofed by getting Caitlyn, or maybe she would give me resistance because she was her friend. Or maybe they weren't friends anymore. Maybe Caitlyn was there.

Fuck. My mind just wouldn't stop.

In the VIP section, I sat with a drink in my hand. A guard came up to me and talked in my ear. "Someone is requesting you to come outside."

"Identify them for me."

"She told me not to say."

I smiled ear to ear and then started laughing. I knew who it was.

"Alright, alright," I sighed as I stood up. "I'll play your game."

I walked outside and down the street, following directions from the bouncer, to a trailer.

I figured I had the right one when I saw the logo of the DJ painted on the side. I opened the side door and stepped in. Red neon lights filled the room, but nobody was inside – at least I thought so. It was a long RV kind of thing. So, I walked to the back where a bed was.

Suddenly, someone with a gentle touch like an angel wrapped her arms around me.

"Long time no see," Caitlyn whispered.

"It has been, hasn't it, Caitlyn?"

I felt like part of the reason that I was so obsessed and addicted to women like her wasn't just because of her looks or her fame but because these women tended to distract me from my thoughts. My brain would constantly be running and thinking, and usually overthinking and over-analyzing.

She gave my mind a purpose. Instead of my mind resembling a Jackson Pollock painting, it became focused on finishing what I believed would happen the next time I saw her. I decided to skip over flirting and get to the point because I was tired.

"Let's play a game," I smirked. "If I win, you have to kiss me."

"Oh God, you are as lame as ever."

"But it seems to always work on you." I winked.

Over time, I began to perfect my misdirection. It was as simple as finding the weakness in her words and then forcing the attention on that. It's the perfect counter.

"You have guards," she asked. "What do you do?"

"Tell me," I responded, ignoring her question. "For you to make the effort for me to play hide-and-seek with you, there has to be a reason."

I turned around and looked into her eyes. The tube lights glowed her skin a burning red. It was like being in Christian Grey's Red Room but brighter.

"I felt like I needed to…probably to say that I'm sorry."

We paused for a moment and stared into each other's eyes. I pulled her in close.

"Then show me," I said, kissing her.

For a moment, passion exploded like a firework. She stuck her tongue down my throat and then pulled away.

"I shouldn't do this," she hesitated. "I have a man back home."

"But you want to," I whispered, reassuring and misdirecting her denial. "I can feel it in the way you kiss me. You don't kiss any other man like that."

"I do want you," she said as if she was fighting herself. Then she laid me on the bed.

She wore the same Calvin Klein black thong as last time.

"Is this the only underwear you have?" I teased.

"I get them for free, so probably."

I assumed through sponsorships because she had become a full-fledged underwear model by this point. Her career had skyrocketed.

She rode me condom-less.

It took everything I had to not cum in less than a couple of minutes. I had to take control or I would explode.

I was just grasping the concept of dominant and submissive. I could tell she was holding back. I put her on her back and stared into her eyes intensely.

"You're holding back with me," I said, reciting a line I had created for deeper feeling. I circled my hand around her throat. "Don't hold back. It feels good, so say that. Express that. Give me all of you." I wanted to witness her full open sexual side, and by saying that, it brought out a hardly recognizable woman from moments before.

I saw a different person in the bed, and she uttered three of my favorite words.

"Cum in me."

I obliged after thirty seconds.

I started to get dressed, and she laid in the bed under the silk covers.

"Your smile hasn't changed," she said. "But you're so distant, almost cold."

"I've heard that a couple times," I said nonchalantly, putting my shirt on.

"You used to be so warm… What happened to *that* Connor?"

"He was lied to and taken advantage of," I snapped, implying what she did to me before.

"I want to make it right," she argued.

I put my jacket on and began to walk towards the door.

"Why are you always so quiet?!" she yelled, wrapping the blanket around her naked body.

"Shhhh," I said, putting my finger over her lips.

I brought her in for a kiss, making out with her, and then I walked out with her yelling after me. I didn't like confrontation. When my parents used to yell at my brother and me all the time when we were kids, I just sat there. I stared blankly off into space and listened to my thoughts.

Now I couldn't stop my mind.

Part

Wronging My Rights

The third and final déjà vu happened back in Indianapolis at the Patron Saint.

Gary had informed me that some of the world's most well-known musicians and DJs, including one by the name of Nghtmre, were going to be performing on a Saturday. He offered to buy me a VIP pass to that event as a reward if I could work overtime on Thursday and Friday.

I walked Nadia and her friends around Indianapolis for about an hour both days. They were all high-class models or dancers.

I wined and dined them. I would take them to the club Gary had assigned, then lead them back out. Then I would do it a few more times because every time men saw these girls going into that club, they tended to form herds and follow us into the club – paying the cover every time.

Exhausted, on Saturday as promised, Nadia, her friends, and I sat in VIP at the Patron Saint for the show. I wanted to meet some of the world's best DJs and musicians.

The crowd in this place was a little strange for my taste.

I liked strange, but I saw why this club was underground. It was purely EDM music that was so loud, my ears rang for days. The people had multicolored hair. Men wore eye shadow and had rings in their ears that stretched the lobe so much you could put your finger through the hole. The club glowed a mysterious purple hue from the blacklights reflecting off of the smoke. That's when my third ironic moment appeared.

I ran into a girl I knew from years ago. She was one of the hottest cheerleaders at my university, and when I asked her out, she called me annoying and a loser. I wish I knew back then that she was just testing me. My life could've taken a completely different turn.

Her name was Patricia, and she had a skinnier, almost anorexic look with golden-blonde hair and striking blue eyes. She had just enough meat on her bones to have an ass – barely, but it passed.

Noah started talking to her. "Have you met my friend Connor?"

"No, I haven't."

I was almost angry. She knew exactly who I was but still acted like she didn't. She was a very stuck-up girl, kind of like Stephanie at first with Alex.

"Nice to meet you," I smiled, extending my hand.

"What's your last name?" she asked in a drunken babble.

I started laughing. "You know what my name is."

"I really don't."

I told her my last name.

"That's you? Aw, you've grown up so much!" she said in a degrading tone, baiting to see if she could get an emotional reaction.

"Likewise," I replied.

It had taken me a long time to get the one-word replies down because, sometimes, girls will pride themselves on acting like they are superior to a man due to a certain status they have. She happened to be a former Pacemate, so she thought she could walk all over most men. If you give into that frame, you lose. If you get emotional and say, "I'm not a little kid," then you also lose. It was a trap that sprung if you did anything at all, so all I had to do was sit idle.

She pinched my cheek. "You are adorable." But it wasn't flirty, it was to piss me off.

"I don't know what this game is," I said in the same high-pitched-talking-to-a-baby-voice she used with a fake grin. "But I'll play it." I was implying that she was acting really weird for talking to me like this.

She laughed. "Aw, are you mad?"

That was a loaded question. If I said no, she would push it further to get me there. If I didn't respond, she would assume I was mad, completely hijacking my mind and throwing me off my center. I had to go with misdirection.

"Oh my god. You are turning me on right now." I got up to walk away. "I have to get away from you. You make me want to kiss you."

I saw a sparkle in her eyes as soon as I walked away.

She giggled as I stepped behind the velvet ropes of the VIP section.

I heard that Nghtmre was sick so he couldn't perform, which I was kind of upset about, but one of his companions was there by the name of Company. I asked him, "If you were giving advice to a beginner about how to grow and become successful in music, what should they do?"

"I usually mix about four hours a day, and then watch YouTube videos about mixing."

"Awesome, thanks." I had no idea what DJing had to do with cooking, but I loved his performance. Multiple DJs came up on stage, but Patricia eyed me, not them. She came up to the velvet rope that divided us.

"I hardly recognized you," she said. "You used to be such a…"

"Such a what?"

"You've just changed a lot."

Seeing me in VIP changed her mind completely. I didn't even have to game them anymore. She was, in fact, a pure gold digger.

I figured, why not play the game anyway?

I push-pulled one of her tests.

She tested me again.

I misdirected it on the fact that she wouldn't be standing here if she really thought that. (I forgot what she said, but her actions said otherwise).

She laughed.

I told her that it looks like she hadn't been eating much, so I would buy her dinner.

She slapped my chest.

"Touching costs extra," I told her, pushing her away verbally.

I grabbed her hand and brought her into VIP (pulling her back in to balance the push), then I kicked her out after ten minutes for not obeying my role-play.

I told her that if I let her in, she had to be my mistress.

She agreed, so I let her in and then she asked me to get her a drink.

"Bad!" I responded. "Go out there in the crowd and think about what you said to me."

She laughed, begging me to stay. I told her to come back in five minutes with a drink for me.

I made out with Nadia.

Patricia came back with a Red Bull vodka. I got her alone and presented Lonely Island, my newfound power.

I told her that I couldn't see her until later, but she had to come see my room.

When she came to my suite that night, I asked her on the rooftop, "Would you like a kiss?"

She would. We did.

"You've changed so much," she cooed.

"I'll be your biggest mistake," I told her. She thought I was flirting hence the slap of my arm. I was serious. I spoiled her for one night. Showed her everything I had. Her brain was frying just as I saw Jay do to the girl at IU in fifteen minutes.

Then I simply let go.

After giving her everything, she wanted monogamy. I never talked to her again after that night.

It's the game. For someone to win, another has to lose. She lost.

Signs

The challenge of taking girls from the clubs back to my place no longer existed for me.

At first, when I told her that I had a suite, she wanted to come home with me almost immediately, but I didn't want to use material things to get her back. After Patricia, I wanted it to be because the girl desired me and not what I had.

One of the best ways to isolate a girl is to get her to commit early on. Plant the seed early. For example, "You seem like you have this side to you that's very spontaneous or adventurous."

Then later you can pull that card back out by telling her you two should go explore, grabbing her by the hand and leading her around to random places. If she were to decline then she would be going against her word that she was adventurous. People want to stay consistent with what they say, so I used that against the brain.

I would also tell her about something cool where I stayed that she had to see, but when I would ask her to come back, I would tell her, "I have to be up early for some business, so you can't stay long." She would end up spending the night.

One afternoon in Broad Ripple, I had to host an event on the strip with some of the major clubs. It ended at around 5 o'clock, and after I got paid, I decided to take Nadia on an interesting date, or I guess an adventure.

Spirituality had always been a serious part of my life growing up.

My mom tended to believe in spirits and ghosts. My dad tended to not believe in any of that "stupid stuff," as he put it, until he had his own experience. In our old house, he said that he once walked out of his room, stopped, turned around, and saw an image of an old man appear right before his eyes.

He said that ever since that night, it spooked him enough to believe.

Then there were my mom's stories.

After my grandmother passed away, my grandfather was admitted to the hospital a short time later. He began to experience cardiac arrest, and they had to perform surgery immediately. My dad was freaking out, but my mom paused. She said that while the doctors hovered around my grandfather, a woman appeared. It was my grandmother in a pink Hawaiian shirt that she always used to wear, and she went in between the doctors, peering over their shoulders. She couldn't believe her eyes. It was either that day my grandfather passed away or a few days later, but my mom said that it was my grandmother's way of guiding him to the heavens.

I tend to be a believer, and women always enjoyed those types of stories when I told them. Guys tended to say, "Oh that's a bunch of bullshit." But spirituality and the divine were able to open some women up because it's a unique topic.

On our adventure, I found myself standing in front of a fortunetelling place. I took her inside, and we sat down for a tarot card reading.

I kept getting a sword card in my reading, which meant battle and masculinity, but also misfortune. My last draw was my future card, and I drew the King of Swords.

"I can feel conflict in you," she said. "This is your six to twelve months reading, which means in six to twelve months, you are going to be faced with a choice. The King is a very cold card, and it's calling to you. It's a haunting feeling. Can you feel it?"

"Um, yeah."

"This choice it may be trying to tell you about is one that turns you cold or one that reverses this and creates a new version of you."

Perhaps she was doing her own version of cold reading on me, and I was a sucker for my own medicine. I played it off as if it was bullshit, but she did guess my life exactly right.

I drew the 10 of Wands, which meant I was carrying a heavy load on my mind due to past experiences with family, relationships, and life in general. She claimed that's why I felt so cold and closed.

I did feel cold because it was all an act.

Every time a girl opened up to me by telling me her hopes, her dreams, her fears, and her story, I only listened to use it for material later. I revolved my technique around what she wanted, making myself seem like the perfect man for her – 'the one' destined to walk into her life. She had a puzzle piece that fit hers, and I molded myself over the course of twenty minutes to match hers.

I was heartless, and deep down it bothered me that I viewed such a pure heart so poorly. I was only dehumanizing and then manipulating people to get what I wanted. Almost like she was nothing more than a pawn for me, knowing I would sacrifice her later on for a piece that I wanted more, breaking her heart in the process.

It takes a broken heart to break another's so easily.

Part

Roaring Applause of No Audience

Everyone has an experimental and adventurous side to them; luckily, I could experience Nadia's wild side down to its core.

In the off-season, she spent her time doing competitive cheer, and she invited me to watch her team compete against multiple other teams at a stadium in the city. The only downside to this was that her team won, and the winner was going to Florida for thirty days to train for some elite competition.

She was dressed in a green-and-black skintight cheerleading uniform. She hugged me, and her perfume tickled my nose. In the stadium, beautiful cheerleaders flooded the east side, so I took Nadia's hand and walked her to the other half of the stadium where nobody was.

It was like a ghost town. No security, no people, and it was just us. The lights weren't on, and the entrances to the seating were blocked off with a curtain.

This moment unfolded itself and felt like it was just happening.

She grabbed my hand. I pulled her into me and kissed her.

While we were making out, I pulled her behind a curtain and into a blocked-off section. I slid the curtain shut so nobody could see us.

"Wow," Nadia whispered. I turned around thunderstruck to see the entire stadium of empty seats. It was quite the view.

We couldn't see anybody, and that meant nobody would see us.

Confucius said, "He who believes he can and he who believes he can't are both usually right." I believed that we could make this a lifetime memory.

She pushed me into the wall. We began to make out.

Then I spun around, pushing her into the wall aggressively. Our emotions were heightened on a level I'd never felt before. It felt like I was high, feeling the nerves of first-time intimacy plus the excitement of potentially getting caught by security at any moment.

I kissed down her neck. I tasted the perfume. Even though I didn't like the taste, I didn't stop. I didn't care.

"Are we really doing this?" she asked.

"I can't believe you're making me do this," I told her.

"We need to hurry," she said as I felt her entire body. I went under her dress and felt her over her 'spankies' (cheerleader tights). This would undoubtedly be one of the kinkiest experiences of my entire life. I slowly unzipped the back of her uniform.

She was wearing a bright-red Nike sports bra that matched her bright-red lipstick.

We undressed each other. She took off my shirt. Then she kissed my neck, to my sternum, my chest, and licked down my abs to the line of my jeans. She put my shirt under her knees because the floor was cement and unfastened my belt. Part of me felt scared. *What if we get caught… Should we even be doing this?* I questioned myself.

In my head, I pictured myself asking Jay, Ace, and Adonis if they would do this. They all nodded as if it was a stupid question.

It was.

There's no guy in the world who wouldn't do this, so, we did.

She wrapped her mouth around me, and while she was blowing me, I looked at the empty seats around the stadium. It's like I had a crowd of ghosts. I could almost hear the cheering for me.

"I want you to cum in my mouth," she said.

I did.

A few days after Nadia left, I found myself back in Revel where it had all started. I wanted to rebuild my connections while she was gone.

I had noticed a group of three girls sitting at the bar with guys huddled around them.

I opened them by asking them about their opinions on the club. I teased the cutest but shortest of the three girls about her aggressive personality. Her face reddened, and she slapped my arm playfully. I pulled her back in with the eye-color cold read (saying that her eyes told me a lot about her). Whether they were hazel, blue, green, or any eye color, I'd say that I'd heard that people with X-colored eyes are usually more difficult to open up, but once they are open, they have a very interesting and wild personality.

I asked her two friends if that was true about her. They said it was. Now I had won them over. "Let's have a drink together," they said.

Right before I could start transitioning into Lonely Island, a British accent came from a man a few seats over. "So, are you going to fuck him or what?"

Ouch.

I have five pet peeves that piss me off:

1. Walking into a spiderweb face-first. It takes something like fifteen minutes to get off.
2. The kinds of people who come up behind you and look at your phone as you're texting someone.
3. People who don't cover their mouths when they cough or sneeze.
4. When you are going 60 in a 30, and the driver behind you is still riding your ass.
5. The types of guys who act like this.

This guy was messing up my sequence. This guy was what Jay called a 'cock block.'

The British man continued, "He's saying this stuff to get you into bed." He pulled out a cigarette and lit it. "I remember when I used to say stupid little stories like this to girls. That is such a little kid thing."

The girls looked at me. He needed to be removed. 'Power in numbers' was his motto. 'Eagles fly alone' was mine.

I tried to be a ninja, keeping my presence in the shadows, but people started to take notice of me. I had to learn not only how to influence a woman but manipulate a man. Misdirection can work in this situation just as well. In people's words lies weakness. They tell us unknowingly their inner intentions, thoughts, and insecurities.

"Well, I'm glad we know what your secret intentions are for these girls," I said. "Nobody will say or do anything that isn't a reflection of their thoughts in a specific moment."

The girls looked back at him.

He smiled and took a puff from his death stick. "You're American, aren't you?" he asked.

"Yes."

"I could tell… Americans have no brain."

"You're British, aren't you?" I asked.

"How could you tell?"

"Your breath smells like shit." The girls laughed and walked away. I ordered a shot and looked at him. "I'd stay," I told him, "but I'm tired of talking to you."

He flipped me off. I knew the DJ from other clubs, so he invited me into VIP. While we talked, the shortest girl of the three tapped me on the shoulder.

I turned around, and she handed me a drink.

"I'm sorry about that guy," she said. "We have been in an on-and-off relationship, and he tries to control everything I do."

She was around five feet tall with blonde highlights mixed in with dirty-blonde hair. Her hazel eyes sparkled, and a smile that was so warm. She was the very opposite of Nadia with hardly tanned skin and wore bright clothing, notably her sparkling pink dress. She was eye candy, and I realized I wanted her more when I found out she was a cheerleader for the semipro hockey team in Indianapolis. Her name was Melanie.

The moment I won her was when I told her, "I feel like you don't want a nice guy, but you don't want a guy who's a total asshole either." I held my hand to my chest as if I was talking about myself. "You want a guy who doesn't tolerate your shit, but at the same time he'll be there for you more than anyone." She listened as I continued. "There are too many guys who are pushovers," I said, pointing away. "And also, too many guys that won't give you the clarity and certainty that you truly need." I moved my hand back in, pointing to myself. "But then there's the kind of guy who you can't have your way with, and you say you don't like it, but deep down it turns you on," I whispered.

She laughed. "The kind of man who will fuck you the way that you need but is in it for deeper reasons other than sex... He's in it to truly love you."

"And you're one of those guys?" she said sarcastically. A test. I wanted this because tests come out when you've made progress.

I turned my head and smirked. "I never said that... But at least we both now know how you truly feel about me." I winked.

She laughed, hitting my arm.

I wrote my number on a napkin. "When you're ready for something real, I'm only a phone call away."

Part

Red Wine

Melanie and I bonded deeply.

She called me not even twenty-four hours after I gave her my number and told me she broke up with Oliver.

"Is that your way of inviting me over?" I asked.

"Only if you want it to be."

She told me that she wanted to make dinner for me, and I figured it would be a nice change of pace. The story usually went: She comes to my room, I tell her we can't be together, and then we wind up together. But perhaps this story would go: I go to her place, and she tries to seduce me.

When I showed up at 8 o'clock, she was dressed in casual light-blue jeans and a black hoodie. Her highlighted hair was wrapped up in a bun with bangs hanging over her eyes. Her mascara was what made me hot, but it was her effort that made me feel something different.

Her one-story house was cleaned spotless, there were candles lit, and she truly spent a lot of time preparing a dinner for me.

I think that effort is one of the sexiest things a woman can give a man.

She made spaghetti and poured me a glass from a new bottle of red wine. She complemented my personality like salt on a margarita glass.

When we sat down at the table sparks began to fly instantly.

Typically, women would ask me, "Do you say this to every girl?"

I reversed that line and used it.

"Do you do this for every guy?" I asked Melanie.

She laughed and said, "Only the guys who deserve it."

She told me about her life. How her father left her when she was little and how it left her struggling in relationships.

I found it strikingly appealing.

"Guys chase me," she said. "But I feel like they don't want me for me, but for my body, so I usually never go out."

"So, basically, guys try to talk to you, and you can tell that it's not because they truly desire you but desire you sexually, and it makes you feel unappreciated. Then you may find a man but slowly start to lose interest, and you don't know why. You're looking for something that's real, something that will last."

It was a perfect pace and lead.

I'd recited what she told me but added a little cold read at the end to help her feel like I truly understood her.

It deepened our connection.

"Yes," she purred. "Are you like that?"

"I've never really met a girl who made me want to be exclusive," I told her. "She'd have to truly be special to change my opinion."

We talked for hours and went through a couple more bottles of wine. I was slightly flush and tipsy.

I noticed in her backyard she had a hot tub.

"Let's get in," I said.

I started taking off my clothes. Luckily, I was wearing my burgundy half-tights from the track team. She stripped down to neon-orange Nike spandex shorts and the orange sports bra to match.

"Can you get two towels out of the hall closet?" she asked.

I did, and I acted like I was going to hand the towel to her. She reached her hands out, then I took it away.

She rolled her eyes. "Give it to me."

"I like you," I said, "but let's take it slow." I couldn't help it. I started laughing.

"I wasn't talking about sex!"

She tried to steal the towel from my hand. I tossed it at her, hitting her gently in the face, and I laughed as I ran off. She chased me outside into the backyard.

"Alright…alright," I said, catching my breath. "Let's get in." I lifted the hood of the hot tub. Steam hit us right in the face. Then she felt the water and splashed it in my face.

"Gotcha," she said. I picked her up. She yelped like a small dog, and then I tossed her in.

"Don't think anything is going to happen between us," I told her, sipping the wine. "I could never hurt Oliver like that."

I was putting up the idea of a barrier – like in *Romeo and Juliet* where their families said they could never fall in love but that made them deeply desire each other even more. Putting some sort of barrier between you and her as to why you can't be together is like attraction on steroids.

She swam over and started playing with my gold chain, asking me something about it that I've forgotten.

I answered her on autopilot.

"If we stare into each other's left eye for thirty seconds, our hearts will beat at the same pace and our breathing will become in sync," I told her.

After four seconds of staring, she began to chuckle, and then she laughed, spitting water all over my face.

"Well, I learned a lot about you," I mocked her, wiping my face. "That you can't control yourself."

"I can!" she whined. "Let's try again."

We stared into each other's eyes again. I looked at her lips and then her eyes.

I pulled her in for the kiss and then pushed her away.

"Your bad news," I said. "But I can't help it."

She giggled, and we started to make out. I bit her lower lip, pulled it back, and then let it go. It snapped back into place. Then she bit mine, and I pulled loose.

"Hey, not so fast," I told her.

I leaned in again. She closed her eyes.

I did the almost kiss. Our lips barely touched. But I pulled back again.

"You're such a tease," she whispered. After a few moments, she added, "When I first met you, I thought you were the hottest guy I had ever seen."

I brushed a damp strand of her hair out of her face and placed it behind her ear. "Go on," I whispered, telling her to compliment me more.

She laughed and hit my chest. "You're full of yourself."

I made it seem like it wasn't a big deal, but in reality, this was the first time a girl ever told me this. I was touched.

As I was staring into her eyes, I noticed in the distance something big moving in the yard.

She turned around. "What is that?" she gasped, backing into me.

It was huge, walking towards us on four legs.

My heart began to pound.

I was almost certain that it was a coyote, and it was going to attack us.

It was dark and probably as big as me. I pictured us getting clawed and chewed.

What do I do? I thought.

It's so close that if we make a run for the door, it would easily catch us and eat us for dinner. When it was about ten meters away, I stood up.

"I'm so scared," Melanie squeaked.

"If it's a coyote, I'm going to distract it, and you have to run to the house okay?"

She nodded.

I took my phone and shined my flashlight at it, hoping to blind it.

When my light illuminated its face, the dog squinted and started wagging its tail. Our fear evaporated when we saw what it was.

"Aw!" Melanie purred, jumping out of the hot tub.

It was a beautiful black-and-white Siberian Husky with different-colored eyes. He was whining and wagging his tail as if he wanted to play. When Melanie tried to pet him, he started running around and barking, expecting us to play.

We didn't know who or where the owner was, but we had to catch the dog because maybe that information was on the collar.

That would be almost an impossible task. We chased him around the yard for what seemed like an hour.

He dodged us, he weaved, and he ran around.

Out of breath, I looked at Melanie. "Wait here," I said, "and keep him occupied."

I went inside, dug around in the fridge, and found some microwave bacon.

I set it by where we were sitting, and I brought out a rope that I could tie around him. He began to eat the bacon, and that's when I snuck up behind him, grabbing his collar.

After we caught him, he sat there with his tongue flopping out of his mouth and licked Melanie on the face.

"I want him," she cried.

It was late, so we'd call the owner in the morning. I thought he could sleep outside, but after we went inside to lay down, a slight rain started.

We heard him crying. Guilt started to fill my head as I envisioned him lying in the rain.

Melanie was upset, and I was feeling bad, so I got out of bed and opened the door.

He wagged his tail and came to the door as I dried him off with a towel.

I led him to the bedroom, where he hopped in bed with Melanie and laid down next to her. She laughed. That night, he shared the bed with us and slept in between us. Exhausted from constant travel, networking, and the wine I ended up passing out shortly after giving her a simple kiss goodnight.

Overnight, we fell in love with that dog. The next morning, we made breakfast together but ended up feeding the dog most of our bacon.

"This is why you and I can't have children," I said, "because we would spoil them like this." She laughed but disagreed.

"We should just keep him," she gushed. "I love him."

"We can't do that to those people," I said. "He wants to go home."

The owner came by to pick him up.

His name was Wolfgang. Melanie and I watched as they drove away. Wolfgang stared at us from the window, and Melanie stared back, curling her bottom lip and pouting like a child.

The Ultimate Obsession

For some reason, I couldn't part from Melanie.

She wasn't someone I wanted to get rid of, and as the weeks went on, we bonded deeper. Effort was extremely sexy, and she gave it to me in every moment.

Hakan also noticed that I was spending a lot of my time with Melanie, more than I did with any other girl. Melanie had beautiful friends who were cheerleaders, so business remained constant in the clubs for me because they all loved to party.

The first time we had sex, I came in about eleven seconds. It reminded me of that line in *The Wolf of Wall Street* where Belfort said, "I fucked her brains out for eleven seconds."

"Did we just have sex?" she asked.

"Somebody did," I replied.

I just couldn't get enough of her for some reason. We were hanging out all the time. Right after I would get paid for the weekend, I would usually take her out.

One Saturday night after a promotion in Indianapolis, Hakan, me, Melanie, and a girl he brought went to the Indianapolis Canal at around midnight. We found a paddleboat off of its ropes and decided to get in. We paddled down the canal together, isolating Hakan and his girl alone so they could share some bonding time before we took them back to the suite.

Melanie sat on my lap, and I started to get hard. She felt it. Gasping first, then rubbing it second. She gave me a blow job, but it wasn't technically 'road head.' I guess it was 'boat head.' I really wanted to join the mile-high club, but that wouldn't be possible because Gary said no girls were allowed on his jets.

One of my favorite lines from *The Walking Dead* was when Negan said, "I love it when a woman buys me dinner and doesn't expect me to put out." I used it when we attended our last penthouse pool party with the newbies to the community, and Melanie brought me a plate of food from the outdoor buffet. She still got me to put out that night, however.

What changed my life happened during a contest in the pool called 'chicken.' The girls had to sit on the guys' shoulders, and the point of the game was to knock the other duets down. The last one standing won a grand prize of $500. I certainly wasn't the most muscular, but together we were the strongest team.

We made it to the final, with two teams left standing. The other team was Hakan and one of Melanie's friends. I was a little concerned that he was much stronger than me.

For about ten minutes we kept pushing, but neither H nor I would fall. Out of breath, I slipped but held us up. They were exhausted too.

"We aren't losing this," Melanie said. She inspired me. I came up with a plan.

The fifty-plus people there all cheered the two teams on.

If I couldn't outmuscle him, then we would outsmart him. Usually, in every pool, there's a shallow flat half and near the center, it angles down into the deep end. I lured him towards the middle where the pool floor began to angle. Melanie saw my plan, and when we were right on the edge, we pushed him onto the angled part. He lost his balance, and they went down.

Melanie celebrated, and then we hugged each other. Our connection felt like none other.

"We're the best team!" she screamed, kissing me.

Then three words slipped out.

"I love you!"

I was speechless. We stared at each other.

When I was young while my mom was dating my stepdad, he broke up with her for someone else after telling my mom, "I love you." She told me to never tell that to a woman without actually feeling it or it would hurt someone. Even if I wanted to feel desired, love was a word I tended to avoid. Even though love is the ultimate obsession.

I had to make a choice. I always felt that love should be for one woman.

"Do you feel the same?" she asked.

"I think so," I told her.

"Then tell me."

"I love you," I said, kissing her. I think I truly felt it for the first time.

Choices

"I'm sorry, Nadia, but I really like Melanie."

I was practicing, in front of the mirror, what I would tell Nadia that night, but that's not exactly how it went.

I felt that I needed to tell Nadia in person what had happened while she was away because she returned that night asking to see me. I stepped out with Hakan and Alex

When I thought about it, I never apologized to Hakan for kissing his girlfriend at Stephanie's house.

"Hey, man," I said to him in the car when it went silent. "I really didn't mean to kiss Holly that night. I just wanted to let you know that I'm sorry."

"Thanks for that," he replied. "But we broke up long ago."

"What happened?"

"Well…" He smiled at Alex. "She thought I was cheating on her and tried to run me over with a car one day."

We stepped off the elevator into a penthouse, and the girl who answered the door was the same girl I danced with in the club on top of the booths with Jay before I was even in this industry. Now she was a Division 1 volleyball player.

When we walked in, we saw other volleyball players from her university. Some of the girls played softball or soccer for other big universities. These girls were hotter than hell, and if I died and went to heaven, I knew in my heart it would look something like this.

Then there was Nadia. She had a glass in her hand and was talking to two other girls. She looked my way when we walked in. She ran over to me and gave me the biggest hug. She missed me and said that I was on her mind every day that she was gone.

How could I do this?

She really did care about me, but telling her that I wanted to be with Melanie instead would break her heart. We talked about how her past four weeks had been and what she did.

She looked stunning that night. She wore a skintight black dress, and in the light, the sparkles woven into the dress glistened. Her dress matched her wavy black hair, and her perfect white teeth shined when she smiled. The straps of her dress wrapped around her Florida-tanned shoulders, which blended with the black dress perfectly.

Could I do this? Could I even tell her?

In this moment of watching her talk and watching her pupils dilate, I felt how much she wanted me. I felt how much she missed me. In this moment, I couldn't deny that I desired her.

We sat on the couch, and that's when she started to make her move on me.

She scooted closer and put her hand on my lap.

"Watch out, Nadia," Hakan teased. "He's taken."

In this moment, I hated him, but I shouldn't have. He was looking out for me.

He walked away, and I expected the saddest look from her when I turned my head.

She was smirking at me. This wasn't right, I thought.

"You have a girlfriend?" she asked, laughing.

"Slow down," I said, smirking. "I think we should just take it slow before we start talking boyfriend and girlfriend."

She laughed and hit my arm.

I put my hand over my mouth. *Stop talking,* I thought. I was gaming unconsciously at this point. Everything that came out of my mouth was playful, flirty, and made her want me more. I continued to scold myself in my head. *If I don't talk, she won't fall for me anymore.*

When I was in mid-thought, she scooted in close.

"We didn't take it slow in the stadium," she whispered in my ear.

My heart picked up the pace. Her lips grazed my earlobe as she whispered. I could feel her breath – so warm.

Chills went up my spine and then to my right arm as goosebumps formed. I took a deep breath and closed my eyes in an attempt to contain myself.

I looked back at her. "You were rushing me? Otherwise, we would have been there for hours," I said.

I put my hand over my mouth again. *Don't say another word,* my inner voice demanded. I had a girlfriend, but now Nadia wanted me even more because of it. Whenever I moved, she got up and followed me. When I sat down, she sat down next to me.

I looked straight ahead and gave her no attention.

"What are you doing tonight?" Nadia asked me.

I bit my tongue.

If this was yesterday when I was 'single,' I would've said, "You. If you're lucky." Then laugh and say, "Just kidding."

I couldn't say anymore. I looked away from her.

"H, what are you up to?" I asked. He was talking to three beautiful women.

She pestered me. "Hey," she said. Then she took her leg and spread it like a pancake across my lap. "Feel my legs. I shaved today; aren't they smooth?" she asked.

The last time she had her legs on my lap was the night Adonis slept with Stephanie and Alex had a meltdown. She was wearing sweatpants that night, but now it was a dress, and I could see her legs.

She took my wrist, moving my arm, and then positioned my hand on her inner thigh. She was hitting me in my weakness. I love nice, thick legs.

My eyes slid up her legs with my hands as I felt them. I looked at her red toenail polish all the way up to where her dress covered her thighs.

Thoughts were going through my head when I realized we still hadn't had sex. *What would it feel like…the rest of her body…inside her body…* I rubbed my hand up and down her thigh. In my head, I was seeing her all over me. I think I moaned a little bit.

"What was that?" she asked.

"Uh," I said as if I was caught, "just clearing my throat."

I took my right hand and grabbed my left wrist, pulling it away as if I was fighting myself.

Just like a *Tom and Jerry* cartoon, I had the devil on one shoulder and an angel on the other. I had the devil on my shoulder telling me, "There's the three-second rule when you drop food on the ground, so isn't there maybe a three-day rule to sleep with anyone after a commitment? Shouldn't you text Melanie and break up with her? C'mon, just take her to bed this once; nobody has to know."

The angel was telling me that it was wrong and reminded me that I'd waited so long for this with Melanie. I'd given Melanie my word.

Then the devil interrupted. "Imagine what it would be like…what it would feel like when you aren't rushed this time. Imagine everything you could do to Nadia…imagine the sounds she would make." He was right. I wanted to do everything to her, but the angel had a point too.

I needed advice, so I unglued her legs from my lap.

"I'll be right back," I said. I pulled off my hoodie, throwing it over the back of the couch.

I walked up to Alex in the kitchen. "Dude, Nadia wants to sleep with me," I said.

"Then what are you doing in here?" he asked as if I was stupid. "Go do it."

"But what about Melanie?"

"I mean," he smirked, "she doesn't have to know. I won't say anything."

I went up to Hakan and asked the same thing.

"Listen, man," he sighed, "I've made that mistake. It was fun, but I don't think it was worth it." He shook his head. "If that's what you want to do, then that's your decision."

I came back to Nadia wearing my hoodie. She pulled it up to her nose.

"This smells just like you," she told me. Obviously, it would. It was my sweatshirt. I didn't say that to her though.

Instead, I asked, "You like my scent?"

"Yes," she swooned. "It smells so nice."

"May I have it back?"

"If you take it off of me." She was implying if I undressed her.

"Sure." I reached my hand over to her and tried to take it off.

She grabbed my hands and then leaned in right by my ear. "No…" she whispered. "Let's go to a room."

She grabbed my hand and started to lead me to the room.

As I walked, I saw Alex give me the thumbs-up, and I saw the other girls covering their mouths saying, "Ooooh."

My heart started to beat faster and faster.

I was sweating.

I knew when I went to that room what was going to happen, but could I live with myself?

She was going to pounce on me like a leopard as soon as that door shut. Why wasn't I saying anything?

Say you can't, I thought. But no words were coming out of my mouth.

Why couldn't I speak? Did I want this?

Am I really going to be branded with a 'cheater' label forever?

Was this going to be worth everything I built with Melanie?

The thirty minutes or, depending on how long it took, thirty seconds would be beyond great.

I had a girl in my life now who was in it for more than a couple of minutes. She was in it truly for me. Those few minutes, from a different perspective, wouldn't compare to the many months or possibly forever that I'd spend with Melanie.

Most people would say, "Just tell her no," but that is such a shallow thing to say. I had one of the hottest girls in the world, to me, asking and begging me to do anything I wanted to her. Put yourself in that same position with the girl you fantasize about when you're alone – the girl who turns you on just thinking about her name – and I dare you to 'Just say no.'

She opened the bedroom door.

My mind went a million miles per hour.

H came out of nowhere. "We have to go right now," he panicked.

Nadia and I stopped at the doorway. It was apparently an emergency.

Nadia whined, asking me to stay.

"I have to go with him," I told her.

We started jogging down the street to his car. We hopped in and he hit the gas so hard that the tires of his blue Corvette skidded on the asphalt.

Part

Sirens

(WARNING: The content in this section may be disturbing to some individuals. Reader discretion advised.)

"Where's Alex?" I asked Hakan.

"There was no time," he said. "We needed to go now."

"Can you tell me what the hell is going on?" I leaned the seat back.

"I just got a call from my best friend's fiancée. She told me that he just got into a terrible car accident."

The route to the scene was a straight shot.

We saw all of the ambulance and police lights long before we arrived. We rode in silence anticipating what we were going to see.

Blue and red flickered stronger as we got closer.

Then we arrived at the scene.

We couldn't get close, so we parked on the other side of the street, farther back. We got out of the car, and I stood up on the seat so I could see.

I saw his car; it was sideways and had hit a telephone pole on the driver's side. It looked like someone took a piece of paper, crumbled it into a ball, then stretched it back out again.

The car was wrapped around the pole. It was devastating.

They were trying to get him out through the passenger side or the roof.

His left arm and leg must've been crushed.

I saw the fiancée, and I realized that I knew her. I also knew her boyfriend, who was in the crash, whose name was Blake. I had met him long ago, and he wouldn't hurt a fly. The guy was nice to everyone and always had a smile on his face. There was also something else I knew about him. He truly, deeply loved her. They had set a date for their wedding months before.

She was there. She was crying and fighting to get through the first responders.

She didn't know if it would be their last goodbye. Hakan ran over to the scene, but the paramedics and police held him back as well.

I watched from the car. After ten minutes, they had cut through to him and began to pull him out. Multiple paramedics held a stretcher right by the door.

I didn't want to look. I should have looked away, but my body froze. All I could do was watch. Something bigger than me was telling me that I needed to see this. My eyes didn't blink, and I don't even think I breathed.

The sight I was going to see would scar my mind.

When he was loaded onto the stretcher, his left arm bent in four different directions. There was blood everywhere, and his leg…there was no leg.

She put her hands over her face and screamed his name.

She was crying uncontrollably. His family members did the same.

I froze, and as I watched, I didn't cry. I felt paralyzed. Writing this right now, I'm crying as I type on my keyboard. It was so fucking sad. This was one of the saddest moments I've ever known. What was she feeling and experiencing? What was she going through?

She loved him so much, but he was gone.

This bone-chilling feeling that I experienced as I watched and listened to the cries and screams carved into my pupils and brain. I could never 'un-see' this… I could never 'un-hear' this… This was permanent.

This feeling was what we call death.

What was it like to know that every time you kiss the person you love, one of those kisses might be the last one? What was it like to know that a couple of hours ago, that kiss would be their last?

If she would have known this, would she have kissed him differently? Would she have held him differently?

For those who are reading this with a wife, husband, boyfriend, or girlfriend, what if today was the last day of their life or yours? How would you treat them? How would you kiss them? How would you talk to them?

If you have children, every time you see them, one day it will be your last time.

Every time you see the love of your life, eventually it will be your last time.,

One of these days coming will be your last one.

Is that scary? Does it make you reconsider how you've been treating people all this time? Even if you argue with them and get mad, why take away your love? If they went out and died in a car wreck, would you want those words to be your last exchange?

And it's only after they are gone that we realize we should have treated them differently. We should have spent our time differently. Why not do your best to make each moment special for her, for you, and for everyone in your life?

For men, would you argue, or would you want to spend every last second loving her more than she's ever been loved before? Would you hold her like you never have before? In this moment and in this state, you wouldn't argue with her. You'd cherish her. Time is our most valuable asset. If we all knew when our time was coming for us to die, then we wouldn't waste it on bullshit that doesn't matter.

But we will never know.

Lucid Dreams

The way to love anything is to realize that it might be lost.

After seeing Blake in the car accident, it made me reconsider who I was and what I was about. After hearing his girlfriend cry, I asked myself what I needed to do from this point forward. I wouldn't go unpunished for this though…because that's when the nightmares started to come. Night after night, I was being tortured. After hearing her scream, it haunted me. I couldn't sleep because every time I slept, I heard her crying. Every time I fell asleep, I saw him being removed from the car.

Occasionally, I dreamt that I was in Blake's body. That I was trapped in a car, bleeding, and in immense pain. I tried to get my phone out to call my girlfriend because I knew I was going to die. I woke up every time I realized that I was missing my leg.

I had nightmares about it every night for ten days, and it was driving me insane. Every night, I woke up in a cold sweat and in tears.

I began to go days without sleep, showering, or shaving.

I splashed cold water on my face to keep me up, and then I looked at myself in the mirror. My bright-blue eyes turned dark and bloodshot with bags underneath. I was exhausted, but if I fell asleep, I'd relive that night. Seventy-two hours later is when I began to 'lucid dream' – awake but dreaming at the same time from exhaustion. Reality began to blend with the dream world. One moment, I would be lying in my bed reading or watching a video, and the next I would jolt up in a panic because my bed turned into my car. I saw myself heading straight for a telephone pole.

I wondered what that feeling was like looking death right in the face. Waking up to yourself in that condition. When I was young, my father told me, "Every time you count to six, someone has been born, but every time you count to eight, someone has died somewhere in the world."

Eventually, one of these sets of eight seconds will be for me, you, or our loved ones.

After seeing this firsthand, death in the movies was no comparison to seeing a person die like this. It hit me hard because the feeling of watching someone die, especially a kid that young and especially in this way, was something I can't put into words.

I went to Blake's funeral with Ace, who I hadn't seen for weeks.

I didn't want to talk to anybody. I only texted Melanie, so he didn't hear from me for a while.

"Are you okay?" he asked, concerned.

I explained to him everything that was going on. My nightmares, visions, and dreams. As the service started, the same cries that I heard from that night rang in my ear. Blake's fiancée was there and began to cry. I began to breathe heavily as the same feelings from the nightmares returned.

I walked out. I went to the bathroom and gripped the sink tight.

I will never take Melanie for granted again," I said, but I was talking to nobody. "I'll never take love for granted, and I'll live every day giving it everything I have. Just please get out of my head. Please make these nightmares stop...

That night, I went to sleep and had the greatest slumber of my life.

Finally, I was at peace. I slept soundly through the night as the ten-day cycle finally broke.

Life really is for keeps. This isn't a game. We only have one chance.

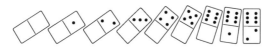

Chapter VIII

Onsra

A Love That Will Never Last

[Onsra: A term from a language in India defined as "that heart-wrenching moment you realize that a love won't last."]

I really had two major regrets in my life up until that point, and life helped me see them.

Life tends to speak to us in ways only we can understand.

After that night, I realized that I needed to realign myself. I needed to focus on the things that truly mattered in my life. Chasing women was a shallow pursuit, and sacrificing those who I cared about was beginning to put me into a bad mental spot.

I wanted to reunite with my family and focus on rebuilding those relationships.

My first regret was my real blood brother. He was the polar opposite of me: jet-black hair, dark hazel eyes, and extremely awkward and shy. Ever since our parents' divorce, we rarely talked to each other. When we were young kids, we used to play together all the time and bond.

We had a bunk bed with a slide on it when I was around three years old. One of us got the idea that it would make a great water slide, so we dumped soapy water down it and the water splashed directly into the carpet. We got in big trouble with our mom, but my dad thought we were prodigies.

After their divorce, my brother and I went from bonding to fighting with each other every other day. I took my misery out on him because some people are easy targets, and he was one.

He was probably more fucked up from it than I was. I had an obsession with chasing women, and I went out every night, but he tended to lock himself in his room and play video games until dawn.

The only time I heard him try with a girl was when he gave her a card on Valentine's Day, and she never replied. After that, it seemed like he just kind of gave up.

I attempted to reconnect with him when I came home.

"High school was one of the shittiest times of my life," he told me.

I remember one time when I was walking down a hallway in high school, and my brother came up to me and put his hand on my shoulder. I gave him a disgusted look, and then he walked ahead of me without a word. One of my biggest regrets was letting him walk away.

"I felt like you didn't want to be seen walking with someone uncool like me," he said.

I was on the football team and tried to be involved in track and he thought that I was Mr. Popular because of it. At least I had Adonis, Ace, and another friend, but he truly had nobody.

"I had no friends," he told me. "So, at lunch, I sat with the special-needs kids because I didn't want to be seen alone."

It was the very opposite. He thought he wasn't cool enough to walk with me, but I realized I wasn't strong enough to walk with him.

For the first time since we were kids, I gave him a real hug.

When I came home, I saw my second-biggest regret. It was simple, but it hurt.

It was my dog, Reggie. My mom bought Reggie as a present for me right after she went through bankruptcy with the only spare cash she had.

When he was a puppy, I walked him all the time, but when life hit harder and harder, I tended to neglect my dog. I stopped walking him. I stopped giving him attention and treats.

Eventually, Reggie just moped around. It appeared he had become depressed over the years. He would just lay there staring out the window, wishing he could be out there. Even though he is now thirteen years old, I promised myself that I would make his remaining years the best of his life and walk him every day.

I knew that nothing I could have done would make it up to either of them except to give my very best effort like Melanie did for me.

Change

Life tended to balance. As I rebuilt, I also tended to lose.

"I'm sorry, but you will be flying solo from now on," Hakan told me. He was leaving his letter and the club scene in the past, starting a new chapter of his life. Like Jay, he had fallen in love, and that night of the accident had also impacted him deep into his core.

"I feel like life has been telling me to start transitioning out of this and focus more on the true meaning of life," he told me.

"And that is?"

"I'm not really sure, but clubbing isn't as fulfilling to me as it used to be. I want a family, and I want to be happy with my new girlfriend Faith."

Experiencing death in person was life-changing for us.

"I understand."

"What will you do?" he asked.

"I'm going to stick with it for a little while longer," I told him. "I'm not sure what I really want to do yet."

"Well, if you ever need anything, just know that I'm only a call away."

He hung up, and we have never spoken to each other since. I found it fascinating how two people can be best friends in one moment and then never talk again in the next.

Over the next few days, I wanted to start bonding with my parents again because, after the divorce, we didn't bond that often. I started with my mother.

She told me stories about how she wanted to name me 'Rowdy' when I was a baby and another story about how I was supposed to be a twin but my twin sister died in childbirth. I couldn't ever imagine myself as a girl. She would've been either the most beautiful girl in the world or the ugliest – nothing in between.

My mother, like me, communicated her love through physical touch. The times when I saw her light up were when I tickled her when she was in a grumpy mood or when my stepfather kissed her in the morning.

My father was who I needed to set things right with the most though. I always found it difficult to look him in the eye. One of the things that inspired me to start working out was when I was around ten years old and walked into his bathroom in the 'house of pain,' and I saw him doing pushups against the rim of the bathtub. Ever since that day, I've done pushups every day.

Slowly over time, and after another divorce, he started to lose hope in life. He tended to watch TV late into the night by himself while eating pizza. I felt that he was dying for some sort of connection because, like me, he seemed very alone.

I usually texted him that I loved him, but I never said it to him in person when I truly felt it.

I remember I told him that I loved him and thanked him for everything he had done in my life, and for a moment his eyes lit up like a sparkler. It was uncomfortable, but I did it.

He answered nonchalantly as usual, as if it wasn't a big deal, but deep down we both knew it was.

When I introduced Melanie to my family, they loved her and treated her like she was a queen. I started to realize that as one's life tends to grow, the quantity of people in our lives shrinks significantly, but the quality and depth of the relationships grow beyond anything we've experienced before.

Part

Letter-N

Hakan's replacement was none other than Noah, Letter-N.

He had a new look every time I saw him. I remember when Nadia once told me, "Noah is going to be very attractive one day." She was right. He had finally molded himself into a solid womanizer.

He went through tryouts one and two with ease – more ease than me seducing multiple cheerleaders, actresses, and models.

Prior to test two, I challenged him to air hockey in the Circle Center Mall.

"What are you willing to sacrifice for this game?" I asked him just as I once was.

"Everything," he responded.

I beat him 7-4.

However, Letter-N hit the boards like a tornado, completely revolutionizing the industry. Gary had a new favorite.

He started to give a lot more of the nights out to N, and even though I was on a mission to rebuild, things kept leaving my life, time after time.

When I showed up at Hirosaki, first I discovered that Player, the fish named after me, had died. After I sat down at the grill for some food, Yo-Yo came out and said, "Oh! Where are your usual friends at?"

"I decided to come alone to have a little 'me' time."

"Well, I'm sorry to inform you on such short notice, but I'm going to be leaving this restaurant to transfer back to Tokyo because I want to start a career out there."

"So, this will be the last time we see each other?"

"Probably," he told me. "But it's been a privilege to serve you."

He gave me the best show ever with constant flames, extra food, and magic tricks. He even let me try to do some tricks on the grill.

Over time, I realized that the hibachi grill was one of the places where I began to lose my anxiety when I talked to women.

When they flipped food into your mouth, everyone watched, and it made you feel pressured to catch it. The next time I went, I was the only one in my family who wanted to attempt to catch the food. If you can risk rejection and embarrassment in front of others, you start to realize that it's not as bad as we make it out to be in our heads.

Echoes

"I'm going to divorce him. I've fallen out of love."

Those were the words of my mother while we talked on the phone about my stepdad.

It was like an echo or a loophole that kept coming back. No matter what, I could never escape divorce. I felt like this was an inescapable part of me. No matter where I went or what I did, divorce happened like some nightmare that kept reoccurring.

While I was home, I discovered what I believed to be my true passion. It was relationships and the healing of them. Over time, my stepdad stopped dating her. He stopped loving her. He just kind of sat there in front of the TV and never talked to her. He never asked her how her day was, or looked her in the eyes, or made her feel cherished.

They argued constantly, even in front of me.

Mom: "I'm kind of just over men."

Me: "You're going lesbian?"

Stepdad: "I must really love you for putting up with this shit."

Mom: "Oh yeah? I put up with you calling me a bitch."

Stepdad: "She does so much work, and she eats this popcorn all the time."

Me talking to my mom: "What did he do in the past to make you fall in love with him?"

Mom: "He used to wine me, dine me, and buy me things all the time. I just want a man who is nice to me all the time."

Me: "Would you really respect a man like that though?"

Her: "Probably not."

Me: "Why did you fall in love with my actual dad?"

Her: "He was very romantic. We moved to Colorado together after we got married. We would ski together and lived in the mountains where we would watch it snow while we sat by the fireplace."

Internally, I knew that I actually got a lot of my style with women from my father. He knew how to tease them perfectly, but also knew how to listen to her and make her feel cherished.

Me: (I waited my whole life to ask this question) "Why did you guys get divorced?"

Her: "Well..." Her phone rang, and I never got that question answered.

Stepdad: "She just blows up out of nowhere."

Me: (For the first time I lost it) "Dude, you're pointing your finger, blaming her for everything, but you aren't loving her. You aren't looking into her eyes, treating her like your lover. You never ask how she's feeling, and when you're out to dinner with her, you sit on your phone the entire time. You never hold her, but it's when I see you kiss her in the morning that she lights up. She's filled with affection, and it's overflowing in that moment because that's the only love she feels from you during the day."

Stepdad: "You know how I grew up. My parents never did that, so that's just not me."

Me: "And you know mine. I didn't know how to either, but I'm figuring it out."

Sadly, they still got divorced. I could date and make anyone fall in love with me, and I even taught it to my closest friends bringing them similar results with women, but this was the third or fourth divorce I saw my parents go through. I went to counseling with them and tried my best to help save it, but I always felt like I never had the power to revive a dying marriage. I blamed myself even if it wasn't my fault. Getting girls was a game to me, but I knew that relationships and love wasn't a game because it needed a person's entire heart.

240

Joker

The king had made contact.

Jay had called me, but it was due to grief.

"I found out that my girl was cheating on me," he said on the phone. His voice sounded faint and unlike the unshakable version of himself when I had first met him.

"I'm really sorry to hear that. What are you going to do now?"

"I'm not going back to clubbing, but I want to go start my own business out in California. Perhaps I can start a new life out there."

"Remember what you told me long ago? This is a game, and in order for someone to win, another will lose."

Life came back into his voice for a moment.

He chuckled. "Someone's grown."

Jay was one of the few people I stayed in contact with.

Little did I know that Jay and I had a bond deeper than the clubs. I was about to be in his exact position.

After I got off the phone, I showed up at Ace's spot because it was his birthday.

I bought him a burgundy leather jacket and a designer watch because he always commented that my leather jacket was really an eye-catcher. Even if it was August and hot as hell outside, he could save it for the next couple of months.

The popular thing to do at his house was play pool. One of his friends from the Marines bet all the money in his wallet that he could beat me. When I was visiting for his birthday, the Marine put $70 down on the table, and I pulled out $360.

He lost on his very first hit by scratching on the break. He demanded I play him again.

Luckily, I had already learned that as soon as you go for more, you tend to lose it all.

I pulled out the old Adonis line. "Sorry," I told him, scooping up all the cash. "I'm retired."

The reason I say 'old' Adonis was because, over the past few months, Ace and I noticed that he'd started to change after he lost his virginity and tasted the forbidden fruits of this lifestyle. He lost that charismatic voice that he always talked in, and wasn't the unselfish and funny Adonis we used to know.

He started doing a lot of drugs and alcohol, but when we would tell him that he was starting to get a little carried away, he would say, "Mind your own business. I know what's good for me and what's not."

He was like a shell of his former self, caring only about what he called 'busting a nut.'

Apparently, he had a girlfriend now, but it sounded like he was only with her for the sex – and when he talked about sex, it wasn't interesting anymore.

"She kept sucking after I came. I was practically twitching! Like those memes you see where the comment is, 'When you nut, and she keeps sucking.' That was me."

"Nice," I told him. I didn't know what else to say.

That night, I bonded with Ace on a deeper level.

I was always semi-jealous of Ace. I thought he had everything growing up that I didn't. But I was surprised when he said that he was always envious of me.

"You were the athlete," he said. "I felt like you and Adonis could always talk about that stuff, and I was left out."

"Your parents were always together," I replied. "You always had a girl, you had money, and I was always jealous of you."

Since my parents' divorce, they tended to be not strict at all, but his parents were strict about everything he did. I guess I was jealous because I believed that strict parents really cared while parents who weren't strict couldn't care less. He said that he was jealous that mine didn't give me a curfew or any rules to follow, and I was jealous for

242

the opposite reason.

It was an interesting perspective change. We were both able to feel grateful for what we had.

That is until Alexander pulled me to the side.

"I've been trying to find the way to tell you," he said, hesitating. "Melanie is cheating on you."

Part

Hemorrhage

"Hemorrhage" is a song by Fuel that my father and I bonded over.

After his divorce, I heard him listen to it constantly. The lyrics went, "Don't fall away and leave me to myself. Don't fall away and leave love bleeding in my hands."

I never knew what those words truly meant until I witnessed it myself.

Alex's words about Melanie's infidelity hit me like a dagger, but it wasn't the words that ripped it back out of my heart – it was the proof.

He showed me pictures of their messages. He showed me videos of Noah taking her back to his suite from downtown. He showed me pictures of them making out in the window of the hotel. He showed me screenshots of her sending him nude pictures.

I couldn't believe it.

This feeling that conjured in my chest when I saw those pictures and videos was indescribable. It was a mix of anger, sadness, and my heart sunk into my stomach all at once.

I left Ace's without a word, speeding down the road at midnight.

That's when I almost hit those geese I talked about earlier. Where I knelt in the shit. The orange glow illuminated my face and showed me for what I was. I went over to sit at the outdoor basketball court and called my father.

"She cheated on me," I whispered.

"Oh, man," he sighed. "I'm so sorry."

"What do I even do now?" I asked.

"You don't have a lot of options. You can't ever trust her again. Just know that I'm here for you, and I know you'll make the right choices," he told me.

From this point, would I?

Even with the proof, I didn't want to admit that it could be true.

I had to see for myself.

I didn't know how I would approach her about it. I didn't know what I would say, but I knew that I had to.

Frozen

The next night, Melanie came over.

Even with all of the evidence held up to my face, I didn't want to accept it to be true. I had to check her phone to see if the evidence was real.

In bed at around midnight, the blue clock reflected off her phone screen. It was calling me to look. She was fast asleep, laying on me.

I had to move slowly, very slowly, so I didn't wake her up.

My hand was almost there.

I grabbed the phone, pulling out the charger.

She moved a little bit and let out a big breath.

I didn't move a muscle. I was frozen. I hope she wouldn't see me going through her phone. I sat there absolutely still for a second to make sure she was asleep.

Luckily, the way she sleeping, her palm was face up, so I took the phone and gently put it on her finger to unlock it. It was a thumb passcode. If her thumb touched the home button, it would let me into the phone. It unlocked.

I turned down the brightness on the screen and began to search. I began to scroll through the people who she was messaging.

I couldn't believe what I saw…

Nothing. I saw absolutely no evidence of what Alex had shown me and told me about.

Not in the messages with her friends. Not any messages of her texting other guys. Not in her call history. Not in her photos. Not in her social media accounts. Nothing.

I felt like an asshole. I was supposed to love this girl, but here I was going through her phone behind her back. I didn't know who was lying. What if it was just a girl who looked exactly like Melanie? But I knew in my heart that couldn't be true.

I didn't know what was going on.

While I was on her phone, I shared her location with my phone and then deleted the evidence. I could now see where she was at all times without her knowing. I felt so wrong doing this, but I had to see it with my own eyes if it was true.

Sadly, I knew her. When she was falling in love with me, she wanted to be with me 24/7, and I had noticed that over time, she gradually stopped wanting to be with me as often. That Saturday night, I noticed that she was driving to Indianapolis. She told me that she was just hanging out with some friends, but I knew this would be the final step in seeing whether her infidelity was true or not.

I went to Stephanie's mansion in the hills because she was one of the only people I could trust.

I had her disguise me once again with makeup.

"Just one more time," I told her, "and don't you dare tell anyone."

"What's wrong?" she asked, lining my eyes with mascara. "I can tell something is on your mind."

"I don't know what you're talking about."

"Alright, live in denial."

"I'm being cheated on," I admitted. "I need evidence."

"Oh my gosh!" she gasped, staring at me in the mirror. "What is she thinking?"

"Have you ever been cheated on?" I asked her.

"Twice," she said. "I tend to fall for the guys who aren't good for me."

Before I could tease her, she spun me around and said, "All done!"

The Jack Sparrow/ Ghost Rider look had returned. I finished the outfit by putting on my dreadlock wig. Before I walked out of the door, she offered parting advice. "Remember that if a girl doesn't appreciate you that there's always another girl who will." She winked.

"No thanks," I said, winking back. I shut the door right when she gasped.

As I drove the forty-five minutes back to the city, I had plenty of time to think. She left a guy for me, and history tends to repeat itself.

I was only next in line. I stole her away from someone, and now someone had apparently stolen her from me.

I parked near her location, The Sky Bar, and I waited. At 1 a.m., she was still inside, so I decided to make an entrance. As I was walking towards the doors, an entire group came out including Melanie, but she was only with one friend and four other people.

I couldn't believe who was walking out with her. Hakan, his girlfriend, Alexander, one of Melanie's friends, and Noah. Hakan made eye contact with me, and I made a sharp turn down an alley behind the clubs.

They walked to the Westin. The hotel was a long walk, and they were drunk and laughing the entire way. They didn't notice me.

I stood outside, staring through the glass and watching them step inside the elevator. Then I walked inside the building. The lights above the elevator door told me they were going to the third floor.

I waited, taking off my wig, and rubbed the makeup off my face.

That late at night, the halls were quiet for about fifteen minutes before Alexander burst out of his room laughing and yelling. He tended to have a loud personality. I hid inside the ice-machine closet.

He walked in holding the bucket to fill it with ice, and I jumped out, pinning him against the wall by the collar of his shirt.

"Holy shit!" he screamed, dropping the bucket.

"You two-timing, lying fuck," I growled. "Tell me what room she's in."

"It's 423, bro," he rasped. "Just let me go."

Without a word, I ran upstairs frantically looking at the room numbers until I stood in front of the door.

I pounded on it, covering the peephole, until it opened.

Melanie answered the door wrapped in a bedsheet. Her nipples poked through the silk, and her hair was messed up.

"Connor…" she whispered.

Last Breath

Sometimes what we are holding onto so tight is what we need to let go of most.

She burst into tears.

"I'm so sorry," she said.

I said nothing and started to walk away. I hurt, but right after the hurt came nothing. I didn't feel anything in this moment. No pain, no hurt. Like a heart monitor flatlining.

I was numb.

She begged and grabbed onto my feet as I started to walk away. I opened the doors to the elevator, walking in. She cried at my feet on her knees, holding the door open.

"No," I whispered.

She cried in the elevator on the ride down.

"Why was Alexander and Hakan with you?" I asked.

"They promised they wouldn't tell you about my situation if we helped him sleep with one of my friends."

"How you're fucking my friend behind my back?"

"Connor, I'm so sorry."

I was walking out when she started screaming. "If you don't stay with me, I'll kill myself!"

I stopped. She stood up and wrapped her arms around me. She dug her face in my chest. I looked down at her.

Part of me still wanted to save our relationship; part of me still cared. She looked up at me, and our eyes met one last time – hers bloodshot from crying, mine ice-cold.

Her face was wet from the tears. Little balls of water remained on my waterproof windbreaker where her face was. The tears didn't soak in like they would in normal fabric. Instead, her tears rolled down then fell off the jacket, splatting onto the tile. For a moment, she stopped crying. I was going to say something, but then I saw images in my head.

If she needed me as badly as she showed right now, then why did she do this? What was going through her head when she began to kiss him? When she was getting felt on and her clothes were coming off?

I said nothing.

I unwrapped her hands, beginning to walk away.

She cried that she'd take a handful of pills, saying she'd take her life.

She was the love of my life, but for someone I claimed to love, I didn't care what she did. If she took her own life for me, it was only the destiny that she chose. I was so cold that I didn't care what happened to her; I wouldn't have shed a tear. It disturbed me that when I thought about her taking her own life for me, I asked myself, *Would you feel anything, Connor? Would you even cry?*

I used to feel people's pains. I used to embrace the world, but now my heart closed. I armored it, locked it, and threw the key into the ocean. I couldn't let anyone in again.

Her tears, when she cried, used to soak into my heart, and I'd hold her. Now, her tears rolled right off – just like they did on my jacket – and would be forgotten without the slightest clue they were trying to ever reach me.

This is human. I am human. Therefore, I am cold. I am selfish.

I was going to take from the world what it took from me.

I thought I was warm. That I was nice. I thought I did what was right, but I got everything taken from me when I was.

Was right wrong?

Was wrong right?

No matter which path I chose, either way, I always lost.

It was what Masashi Kishimoto's Itachi had said: "So tell me where should I go? To the left where nothing is right or to the right where nothing is left..."

An Eye for an Eye

Sometimes sacrifice is a part of life.

Revenge was something I wanted against Noah, and I had my perfect opportunity, but it would take my greatest sacrifice.

Ace had always been my best friend but also my greatest rival since middle school. We had a weird relationship where we would argue but our arguments were fake and full of love. It's how we bonded. He was the piece in my life that I valued the most. The one person who I didn't want to throw away.

I was once told that *life will sometimes give us what we want but with a distraction to test us on how badly we truly want what it is we asked for.*

I was dying for something real in my life, but I sacrificed that which I loved for revenge.

I had to make a choice: my best friend or Noah's girlfriend.

Noah had been cheating on his girlfriend – who he had met through this community – with Melanie. By fate, life put her right in the palm of my hand.

Two weeks after that night, Ace returned from a getaway in the Philippines. He wanted to spend some time with Adonis and me. Quality conversations and time were the things that I observed meant the most to Ace.

All three of us met at the bar for a drink and, about an hour in, I realized that sitting a few seats down at the bar was Noah's girlfriend, Alysa, and her friend. Alysa was a blonde who wore tight clothing to show off her body. She wore jeans with more holes in it than actual denim, and when she smiled, it was kind of crooked. Like the shape of a raindrop, but it was cute for her. Her friend was Karsen, a short and skinny brunette who wasn't a hair past 100 pounds.

I shut Ace out and focused entirely on Alysa at the bar.

"Hi, I'm Connor."

"Oh," she insinuated, reaching out her hand, "I know." She was already implying the situation with her boyfriend and Melanie.

Adonis won her friend over. Over time, he had gotten better with women, but that changed after he slept with Stephanie. Especially when Stephanie told him that it was only a one-night stand and didn't want anything long-term with him. I think deep down it affected him, but he covered it with marijuana and cheap vodka.

After twenty-five minutes, Alysa and Karsen asked if we wanted to go back to her house.

Ace hesitantly said, "Okay" but didn't look me in the eyes. He looked down and away. I knew something bothered him, but I acted like I didn't notice it.

He had just gotten into a relationship with a woman and loved her deeply, so he didn't want to do anything like hang out with one-time flings behind her back.

"I'll follow you guys in my car," he told us.

Adonis and I went in their car, but midway through the drive, Ace took a hard right in a different direction.

"This isn't you," he texted me. "The Connor that I know is above getting revenge. You've changed after Melanie. What happened to the times when it could just be fun with just us? Why do we need to have girls for fun? What happened to the times when we would sit in my basement and watch shows? What happened to the times when we could stay up all night just talking about life or play basketball until two in the morning?"

I knew, in that moment, that I'd hurt him. But I felt that eventually everyone close to me would stab me in the back at some point. Therefore, I should be close to nobody, I thought. I should accomplish what I wanted no matter the price – no matter who I had to cut off – because soon enough, they would do the same to me.

When we arrived at Alysa's condo in Indianapolis, they put on the movie *Halloween*. I always loved horror films but hated them at the same time.

"Do you have any water?" I asked.

"Sure," she said, hopping up. I watched her walk away. She was cute. She changed into short grey shorts with a yellow T-shirt and had brown glasses that brought out her brown eyes.

She brought back a glass bottle with the letters 'V-O-S-S' printed on it.

"Someone's boujee," I smirked.

"I just like having the best," she countered without missing a beat.

When the movie was over, Adonis and Karsen went to a bedroom. Now it was awkwardly Alysa and me alone on the couch. She threw off her blanket and hopped up.

"I'm going to go take a shower and get ready for bed." She stretched and moaned.

I stared at her. "Are you inviting me to join or something?"

"Noah wouldn't like that very much."

I smirked. "Neither would Melanie."

She laughed and rolled her eyes. "We're not talking about that." I could tell she really wanted to say something about it.

"You and Adonis are more than welcome to spend the night." She paused. "Well, I guess Adonis has already made himself comfortable with Karsen, but there's a guest room here."

"Fine, I'll stay as long as you tell me a bedtime story," I flirted.

She rolled her eyes. "Whatever, I'll show you where it is."

I was trying everything, but she was ice-cold.

I thought that something would happen. When the door shut, I believed she would instantly hop on top of me or make her move, but it was the opposite.

"Let me know if you need anything," she said and then walked out.

I could vaguely hear her walk back to her room and run the shower.

I shut the door, turned off the lights, and laid down in the bed.

I guess nothing is happening tonight, I thought as my head hit the pillow.

A girl's room is always clean, it seems. It smelled like a candle had been burning. It was comfortable. Everything seemed soft. I played around on my phone for about twenty minutes, then I started to drift to sleep. I put down my phone and rolled over, facing the window. The buildings outside were so tall that the moonlight couldn't reach the window.

I thought that either Adonis or Karsen was walking outside my door because I heard footsteps, but then I heard my door handle jiggle.

I froze.

The door opened, and a warm body crawled in bed with me.

"Adonis?" I asked.

"Are you awake?" the soft voice of a woman asked. It was Alysa.

I felt her body pressed against my back, and I realized she had no clothes on.

"Are you…" I began, but I couldn't finish my sentence.

"Shh," she whispered into my ear. I felt her nibble my earlobe.

"Don't you have a boyfriend?" I asked.

"Yes, but he cheated on me with Melanie," she said, "and she cheated on you with him."

I rolled over so now we were face to face. She lifted her head off the pillow and combed her fingers through her hair. It was still damp from her shower, and the scent of fruit hit my nose when a wet strand landed on my face.

She ran her fingers through my hair. "I've found you to be one of the hottest men I've ever seen since I first saw you in middle school," Alysa expressed to me.

Do two wrongs make a right? Maybe it wasn't right. She had a boyfriend, but that boyfriend took everything from me. He slept with Melanie. Melanie wanted him just like Alysa wanted me now. Maybe it wasn't right, but she was in my bed, she was beautiful, and she was warm. Her damp hair draped over her face with the scent of citrus shampoo. I didn't need much convincing.

254

I wanted this from the start. I wanted to take everything from him that he took from me. I pulled her into me. "Convince me," I whispered. My nails ran up her spine to her neck, to her scalp. Her skin was pocked with goosebumps.

A breath, sounding of relief, came out in a moan. It wasn't about the harmony of a man and a woman coming together anymore. This was personal.

I was aroused by the feeling of revenge, not necessarily her. She leaned in close. Our lips touched. "I'll let you do anything you want to me," she whispered.

When my hand reached her scalp, I grabbed a chunk of her wet hair by the roots. I pulled it back firmly, and her head went back like a Pez dispenser.

I breathed in her ear as if I was fogging up a window, and then I sucked on her earlobe.

"Oh…" she exhaled, "my God." Testosterone fueled me; every vein in my body showed.

She put the condom on me and bent over. I shoved her face into the pillows and smacked her ass. It felt very alpha. I flipped her on her back, wrapping my hand around her throat.

"Tell me this is mine," I whispered in her ear.

"It's yours," she breathed. "Take off the condom."

I threw the lubed rubber on the floor, and she wrapped her mouth around my shaft.

"Cum in my mouth," she said, jacking me off.

I did.

After, as we laid there, that feeling of satisfaction turned into confliction. The very people I hated I'd become. I'd sacrificed everything, even my closest relationships, to win. In my head, I saw a picture of Ace and my friendship being ripped apart.

Just how far would I go? I won, but at what cost? I had to leave; I needed air. I got dressed and told her that I was leaving.

"I'll call you," I promised her, but I knew that was a lie. I'd never call.

The next day, she messaged me. "Noah heard that we were together last night and is asking me about it." She sent me screenshots.

"What do I tell him?" she asked.

I wasn't sure how he found out because I didn't tell a soul.

"Be honest," I said. "Tell him every detail."

She did.

It was ironic how the roles were reversed. He was waiting in anticipation to see if Alysa cheated on him with me. Four weeks ago, I was waiting in anticipation to see if Melanie cheated on me with Noah. He was feeling, at that moment, everything I felt before. She sent me screenshots of what he was saying.

He was cussing her out.

Alysa needed to be honest with him just as Melanie was with me and just as I needed to be with myself.

I felt like a scum.

Chapter IX

Jinxed

The Right One, the Wrong Time

[Jinxed: An English term meaning "misfortune."]

We attract who we are on the inside.

This is one of the universal laws, and ironically, Letter-X made his first appearance into my life.

When I walked into his penthouse in downtown Chicago, he was about as unnatural as they came, both physically and in the clubs. He wore glasses, an aggressive baggy dress shirt, and khaki pants. He walked around with a laptop almost all of the time. His skin was pale white as if he never went out during the day, and he was skinnier than I was when I started.

The old me would've judged and thought, *There's no way this guy is as good as his reputation.* But over time, I realized that this community is full of surprising people. I just hoped he wouldn't be another flop like Alexander.

Here's his story as he told it to me:

"I was a computer person who never even kissed a girl until I was 24. I was socially useless. When I talked to a girl who I found hot, my voice was able to barely squeak out a word or two. I was so nervous, my voice was cracking at 24 years old, and then the girls would ask, 'Are you still going through puberty?' When I finally got a girlfriend, I went on a trip to California, bringing her back a $250 necklace, but she dumped me on the plane ride back, so I never gave it to her. It was embarrassing – so embarrassing that I purchased every single pickup, dating, mind control, and seduction course I could find."

He told me he invested more than $16,000 on courses, and they helped him to evolve into the man I saw. Apparently, underneath his exterior was a dangerous man, and I couldn't wait to see.

When I offered him $1,500 cash for copies of the CDs and courses, he said he would give them all to me for $2,800. We settled on $2,250.

I realized that everyone I had met had some form of a 'La Douleur Exquise' – basically, the girl they could never have or who got away – and it inspired most to take some sort of action.

I had three days with him, so we had plenty of time to bond together. I wanted to sap all of his game from his head. We analyzed each other's style, and I learned that we were strikingly similar.

"Tell me your stuff," he said. "Show me your technology."

"My technology?"

"I've heard a lot from others on how you operate," he told me. "I've actually modeled some of my style from you."

I specialized in emotional connections while he used that and a form of hypnosis known as Neuro-Linguistic Programming (NLP) to solidify the connection.

He was like a more advanced form of Hakan.

After Letter-X would secure her heart, he would then make her think about him all the time by giving her a small gift: a necklace, a swizzle stick from a drink, or one of his shirts or jackets. Whenever she took the presents out, she would start thinking about the great connection she had with him. When she thought about him, the attraction would simultaneously grow. It was an advanced technique, one I needed to apply.

"My routine is simple," he said. "I'll do it to you."

Fuck yes. I was waiting for this.

"I call it 'purple potion,'" he told me. He really was a geek. "I open with a cold read: 'You take your time with love, don't you?'"

"Yes," I responded.

"But did you know it's been scientifically proven that people can fall in love in two-tenths of a second because of the way the brain chemicals work?"

"Really?"

"Yes," he told me. "Actually, I took a test to determine if I was the type of person who falls in love quickly. I have to try it on you."

He sat next to me on the couch, invading my space slightly.

"So, imagine – I say the word 'imagine' because it's a trigger word to stimulate the mind's eye – that you met the love of your life. (I hold my hand over my heart to indicate that I could be talking about me.) You find out that he – well for you it would be she – lives in the same town as you. Does she live close? Like right next door, or is she across the town?"

"She lives on the opposite side of the city; we met by fate," I told him.

"Okay," he said. "When you met, did she wear a plaid or pinstripe dress?"

"Plaid sounds nice," I responded. I am a pinstripe guy, but I switched it up.

"Describe in three words what she's like – her personality, shit like that."

"She puts in effort; she wants what's best for us, not just herself; and she expresses her love without holding back."

"Alright," he said. "Let's find out what this all means... It doesn't mean shit. I was just messing with you."

He started laughing. "Just kidding. That's what I normally do."

It was similar to how I performed Lonely Island – which is what I gave him for this.

Depending on whether he/she lived close or far determined the amount of time it took for one to fall in love. If they were far apart, then the answer was: "You tend to take your time with love and fall in love slowly over time. Maybe because you've been hurt before or you're wanting to give a man a challenge." If the answer was close, then he would say: "When you meet someone, you're really into, you can't help yourself but feel those feelings quickly. It's riskier, and it's probably hurt you, but eventually, you'll meet a person who's the same."

The outfit is the type of love story that you tend to experience. Plaid stands for obstacles, hence the boxes. You may run into walls and challenges, but it also helps you both fall deep into love, or it can tear you both apart. The pinstripes represent a straight-line journey, one with passion and fire, and the only downside is that it could either be the love of your life or something that runs out of fire early.

The three-word description includes the words that someone tends to bring to a relationship. When you fall in love, this is the experience that the other person will receive. These qualities are very important to you.

"The best part about this," Letter-X said, "is that when she's telling you the things that she needs for her to fall in love, she's already talking to you like you're her lover."

I told him about my technology. Lonely Island and the hand routine to escalate physically.

I'd say, "Wow you have man hands." She'd argue this, creating that tension.

Holding her hand, I would interlock our fingers, describing to her how interlocked couples means they have a very close connection with each other. Then I switched our hands to the palm hold, which symbolized that they know each other very well.

"Here's the interesting part, though," I told him. "The person with their palm facing backward has a stronger personality, so I need to always have my hand in front."

She would either argue it or laugh.

If she laughed, I continued, you spin her around or take her to go dance, but if she argues it then you remove the touch, matching her test with a tease.

"Clearly, I'd be the one dating down in our relationship, so we couldn't hold hands in public."

Random but fun, free-flowing, and effortless.

In any case, I'd remove touch first because it's two steps forward, one step back to keep her guessing. She probably holds hands with people who she views as special, so her brain internalizes you as that.

We reviewed some of the CDs I bought from him, and then he showed me around the town. The next night, he told me the plan:

"We need to get people to Oak Beach," he said. "Have you ever been to a beach party?"

"No."

"It'll be a wild time, especially because it's Mardi Gras-themed."

Mardi Gras Sunrise

It was on this trip that my abilities peaked.

Letter-X took me to multiple clubs in Chicago including Prysm and Lite. Part of me wished that I lived in Chicago so I could promote a club as red-hot as those. They had fog machines and lasers, and the light effects in the ceilings were insane.

The beach party started at 10 o'clock and went until sunrise, so it was going to be a late night for us. We wanted to get people there.

The way he won over a crowd wasn't my biggest surprise. It was his transformation. He switched personalities as soon as he stepped in the club. He was a computer geek by day but then transformed into a world-class player as soon as the sun set. Shedding his glasses, he wore all denim like he was from the Eighties, slicked his black hair all the way back, and stuck a toothpick in his mouth. Then he simply went to work and performed as flawlessly as a robot.

I perfected the eye read that came directly after a slight push.

For example, a girl tested me by saying, "Oh you're a promoter? Are you going to do some sort of trick on my mind?"

"My tricks only work on the weak-minded," I told her. "So, yeah, I could." I smiled as I said that, and she gasped, playfully hitting my arm.

Implications were one of the most lethal ways to push and pull a girl. I heard Letter-X do another indirect and then direct version where he would tell her, "I was going to a party tonight, and I wanted to invite my favorite girl."

Then he would pause while she says, "Aw."

"But she wasn't available, so I decided to call you." It was all playful and wrapped in a vibe that was fun and kept everyone on their toes not knowing what would happen next. The best movies are those that trigger the parts of the brain that anticipate what's going to be said or happen next.

As soon as she loses interest because you've pulled or pushed too much, she's probably going to find what does interest her. After some form of a tease, I would then move right into something to capture the interest and pull her back in. Usually, it was something I noticed about her that had some sort of meaning because of what I learned in Carnegie's *How to Make Friends and Influence People* – that people's favorite topic is themselves. The most common one I pulled out was the eyes.

"[X, Y, or Z] colored eyes are said to have trouble opening up to people," I would tell her. "I get this feeling that you're closed off slightly like you're skeptical because possibly you've opened up to someone only for them to hurt you before."

If it clicked, which it almost always did, she would open up about what hurt her in the past, and I would simultaneously reassure her indirectly that I was the man she's been looking for.

"I feel like you need a man who is able to make love to you passionately but won't leave you after sex. But also, the man who doesn't put up with your bullshit and a man you can't walk over. The one who turns you on so deeply that you can't even describe it but also makes you feel special, cherished, and loved."

I would imply that I was that type of man and then solidify that I was.

"Look at all these guys in the club," I told her, turning her to face the crowd. "Most of these guys look desperate. They'd take anything they could get their hands on. How is that something that would make a girl feel special?"

It basically applied the role-play that it's the two of us together. The 'us' frame is a powerful tool if used correctly. However, if she had friends, then I would win them over as well, telling the others, "I feel like you have struggled financially." Then I would connect with them, telling them how I did as well growing up. The truth was, I liked connecting with people, but the shame was that I used it only for my gain.

Letter-X had a limo take us, his friend, and all of the girls we collected over to the beach.

"If you're going to be partying, you need these," Letter-X told me.

He pulled out multiple bead necklaces to wear.

"It's Mardi Gras-themed, so just know that it's going to be wild."

I stripped down to my neon-green swim trunks, and we all went to the beach for the fun. I had never been to a beach party, but it was everything I had dreamed of.

Some girls didn't wear tops, just beads over their breasts, and they wore masquerade masks covered by glitter.

There was drunken volleyball where losers had to take shots of tequila.

Over time, I had overcome the shyness about my body because I had been lifting weights consistently for a year.

But there was one fear that I'd never faced.

The crowd formed a circle, and my chest began to thump fast. I'd almost forgotten about one of my greatest fears: dancing solo in front of others. Even though I was slightly intoxicated, my heart pounded through my chest. When I tried to walk away, Letter-X grabbed my hand and pushed me into the center. I tried to copy some of the moves from Michael Jackson and other dancers I'd studied.

Let's just say that it didn't work.

I made a mental note to take one of the dancing courses I saw advertised for $27.

Letter-X did body shots off of multiple girls at a time. He was becoming so drunk that he left his phone everywhere he went. Luckily, I picked it up for him each time, but it would come at a price. I decided to pull a prank on him and set multiple alarms on his phone for the morning. After we got back and he fell asleep, the alarms would start going off. I gave it back to him while he was doing another body shot.

"Join C!" he yelled.

I did.

264

"You do this *every* weekend?" I asked him, slurping tequila off the body of a tanned brunette.

He beamed a smile. "Every Saturday," he said. The 23-year-old Milwaukee actress, who he took a body shot off of, held a slice of lime in her mouth. After the shot, he glided his tongue up her chest, between her breasts, and took the lime from her mouth with his.

At 3 a.m., the DJ started to play EDM music. After that one time at Patron Saint, I became addicted to this type of music. I had a blonde in a red bikini wrapped around me. I didn't know her name. Letter-X had a beautiful Latina in a neon-green two-piece bikini dancing with him. We danced for hours to the music, and it was one of the most sensational experiences of my entire life. Fists in the air, she stared into my eyes with the biggest smile on her face as people with squirt guns sprayed the entire crowd.

At around 5 a.m., the four of us walked down the beach away from the loudness in order to lay in the sand to watch the sunrise. I cuddled with the blonde in the sand as the horizon began to glow. The me from years ago would've probably moved here, but the current me just wanted to enjoy it once. Sometimes, once is all someone needs for a lifetime because, at 6 a.m., Letter-X showed me his true colors.

Every robot eventually breaks down.

"Dude," he told me. "I'm tired as fuck. Let's go back."

"Five more minutes," I responded.

"No, asshole," he said in a serious tone. "We're going back now or I'm leaving you behind. I don't give a fuck."

I couldn't tell if it was the alcohol or the sun rising, or if this was just another side to him, but that was enough for me to never want to go back again. That attitude was toxic to be around. I knew he was hiding something behind that smile. At least I had insurance to pay him back for cussing at me. At 7:30 a.m., about forty-five minutes after we drifted to sleep, his alarm went off.

He turned it off. Then another came on at 8:30.

"What the fuck?!" he yelled.

Part

Options

There was this idea floating around the community known as 'state transfer' where if you're around someone else then their feelings, mental state, and attitude rubs off on you.

Letter-X had done some sort of state transfer on me because I went haywire.

I met a skinny cute blonde named Kelsi at a museum. "I'm a teacher," she said. "I'm used to having people listen to me."

"I'm a writer," I responded. "I'm used to leaving women always wanting more." She wanted to see me that night. I saw her that night, and then I left her wanting more.

Jessica was a short mixed-race girl who had a master's in business and sold alarm systems. It was my game versus her degree. When she showed up at Stephanie's mansion to sell her an alarm, I answered the door. I told her that she only had fifteen minutes to sell me on one. One hour later, we were in bed making out, and then she gave me a blow job. I never purchased the alarm system.

They called it 'Jersey Night' at my university. Her name was Ally, a tall volleyball player with blonde hair and a skinny body. After we went back to her dorm, she had to take several pills including an anti-depressant, birth control (I removed those pills because I told her sex wasn't happening), an antipsychotic for bipolar disorder, and one for anxiety relief. I felt a little bad, but only a little. She ended up needing the birth-control pill, and when she fell asleep in my arms, I slipped out because I didn't want to wake up next to her in the morning. The problem was that when I realized I'd forgotten to put my shoes on, I was locked out of the room and snow covered the ground. I ran to my car at 6:15 a.m., a quarter-mile in socks in the snow.

It sucked.

I saw Melanie eight months after I had last seen her. I gave her a hug then pointed to my cheek for her to kiss it. She leaned in, and right before she reached my cheek, I turned my head and she pecked my lips. She screamed and smacked my chest. I found out she was engaged. She had told her fiancé that she just needed to pick up clothes at my place that she left when we broke up. She came by to pick up the clothes a few times a week.

Kate was a 19-year-old blonde who unleashed her inner country by wearing a NASCAR denim jacket that I teased her about one or five times. I met her in a parking lot one night. It was her dream to be a singer, and I had her sing to me while we drove to the closest university's football field. I had a blanket in my car. "C'mon, let's go," I said. I jumped out of the car. She asked where we were going, but I said it was a surprise. I grabbed the blanket and walked to the field. It was a huge campus, and this was probably trespassing, but we hopped the gate. We went to the 50-yard-line, and I laid the blanket down on the logo. I pulled her into me, and we made out on the field for a while.

Turf stuck to our hair and skin.

I was finding it for days afterward.

When I was on a business trip in Milwaukee, I met Hillary, a single mother who liked doing hot yoga. She was also exactly double my age. "Join me for dinner?" I asked. She obliged. Thirty minutes into our conversation at dinner, she said, "You're a bad boy...a player." I asked her what she meant. She said that I talked with such confidence and passion. Then she said that if she was twenty years younger, she would have been chasing after me. "Listening to you right now, I can't tell the difference," I said. I winked at her and leaned in smiling. She offered me $2,000 to sleep with her. I rejected the invitation.

Jasmine had a boyfriend when I met her, and she told him about me. He made her block me on everything. Four weeks later, they broke up. He was probably insecure and pushed her away. She unblocked me on all of my social media and, when she followed me, I sent the words 'welcome back' to her. She told me it wasn't her with an eye-roll emoji. I took her out that weekend. When I dropped her back off at her apartment, I told her to kiss me goodnight. We made out. Then she asked if I would like to meet Bosco and Dash. I asked who they were. She showed me a video of her smoking a marijuana bong and then snorting a line of cocaine. She asked me if I agreed that high sex is the best sex. I left immediately and blocked her on everything that night.

Sydney was a cute redhead who worked at H&M. When I walked up to the register to check out, she said, "I can't check you out because the register is broken." I playfully interpreted her words and told her to stop checking me out. We exchanged social media after a few minutes of talking. "If you follow me on Instagram, make sure you like everything. If you don't then I'll block you," I joked. That night, she liked my pictures and sent me a message that said, "I liked a pic of yours and now I'm waiting for my like back." She sent a wink.

"How about I show my appreciation over dinner?" I replied.

"When and where?"

We went out a night later.

Gary hosted a private party on a beach in Wisconsin a few blocks from where I was promoting. I went out twelve hours before to explore the city. I found myself on the beach right outside of Milwaukee. On one of the piers, a gorgeous blonde wore super-tight black spandex pants to show off her body and a tight white Nike tank top. She laid her yoga mat down and began to do all these different stretches. I had to have her. My opening line was, "Teach me how to do yoga." From there, it was game-set-match. That night, we sat on some of the rocks lining the side of the pier. The waves crashed against the rocks, and the mist painted our face.

"This is the most romantic thing I've ever done with a man," she told me after we kissed.

It was a special moment, but I still felt the same way. Even after all of this, I felt this loneliness in my heart. I tried to ignore it, but every time I swept it under the rug, it grew more and more. I couldn't take it anymore.

No number of women could ease the pain I had because of what I had done. I pushed everyone away and even my best friends in this life, and now I was paying the price.

I was reverting to the way I was at the very beginning of my life.

All I wanted was a connection.

Part

Letter-V

Two people helped me bring the light back into my life.

The first was the final person I met in the industry. He went by the codename 'Letter-V.'

He was fit and stylish in a grey suit and brown hair gelled up into a messy part. He was one of the two individuals I noticed in the first meeting with Gary besides Letter-Z who had been recently kicked off the team for trading secrets about the business to other promoters for profit.

Recently, Letter-N had also been banned from the industry for trying to start his own business on the side, using Gary as a pivot to attempt to take over the Midwest himself. It didn't work, and when Gary found out, he was extremely disappointed.

I had to accompany Gary when he approached Noah, and it wasn't pretty.

We walked to his suite, and Gary pounded the door until Noah answered with some girl.

"In business, man has to be ruthless," he told Noah. "If you think that I give a fuck about your feelings, I don't. I was soft back in the day, and I lost everything. I won't make that same mistake again. Pack your shit and get out."

Without a word, Noah packed, and I smiled when we made eye contact. I was one of the veterans.

Gary had Letter-V come from Kentucky to assist me in Indiana.

On the Friday he came, he didn't talk to a single girl. He just talked to managers and other promoters. He wore the same grey well-fitted suit and a silver Rolex. When you would put him in an awkward position by either complimenting him or trying to joke about how cool he looked like he was trying to be, he laughed it off. Then he would respond with the same five words that I said to him: "Have to impress the ladies." I liked him because nothing got to him.

Rarely did you ever see him get worked up. He was the definition of stoic and indifferent, making me wonder if he even had anything he liked or disliked.

He was just always in the moment with his feelings. I tended to talk to the hottest girls, but Letter-V talked to everyone.

That night in the club, he didn't care what status you had, how you looked, or what you did because he seemed to just want to connect with anybody.

When I asked him about it, he said, "Might as well take your time and hear people's stories."

He wasn't flashy. He never had a crowd around him. Instead, it was usually a group of three or four people maximum, but the few people who surrounded him really enjoyed his company. I'm not sure if he was a sniper or a shotgunner, or if he was anything at all.

At the end of the night, two girls wanted to come back to our suite, but he insisted that we had a one-on-one talk.

"No girls," he said. "I hope you don't mind, but I want to talk to you alone."

"Um, sure."

We walked a mile back to The Westin; the same building where I found Melanie cheating on me. We shared a bottle of wine while admiring the city on the patio.

He opened up to me about his story. He got married when he was twenty-four, and his family begged him not to, but he didn't listen to them. He moved halfway across the country to be with this girl in New York, but after he dropped everything to be with her, they divorced not even a year later. He said that it crushed him. From there, he found his way back to the Midwest and was introduced to Gary the same time I did.

"But I've had my fun," he said. "I'm thirty-two now, and I got engaged to another woman last year. I thought I'd find 'the one' in the clubs, and I searched but I never found her."

"If not in the clubs, then where?"

"I found her by doing the things I enjoyed. I realized that I loved my family and friends. After I returned, I rebuilt those relationships, and she appeared through them. We fell in love."

It sounded romantic, like one of those fairytales that children read when they're little.

"You and I seem to be a lot alike," he told me. "You're different from X, N, Z, H, and D [another guy who was partners with V in Kentucky]."

"What do you mean?"

"You have a heart, but it's buried under all this stuff you want to call 'seduction,'" he told me. "I shared with you who I was, so you tell me who you truly are. No tactics, no lies, just raw."

He was the opposite of Letter-X. He cared when I opened up to him about Melanie, why I got into this to begin with, how I let go of Ace, and all of my other wrongdoings. He just listened to me. He was a lot like the warm side of me, the type of person you could just open up to.

I told him about my past and how I got into this industry. I told him about Melanie and how I thought we were soulmates until she ended up cheating on me.

"We dated for over a year," I told him.

"Who cares?" he asked. "A successful relationship is not determined by the amount of time you've been together but the depth of the love both of you share."

He was like the Buddha – full of wisdom.

"Why are you even here?" he asked. "Why are you doing this?"

I searched deep down for an answer but came up empty-handed.

"If you're looking for love, you won't find it in there," he said, pointing to the strip.

"Then where must I look?"

He pointed to his heart. "In here."

I chuckled, looking off into the distance. "So cliché," I told him.

"Then you tell me," he said. "When is enough, enough? You've given up your best friend, you've sacrificed so many things to get here; you don't even know who you are anymore."

I just stared off into the distance.

"You have a gift," he told me. "I'll admit that, but how about you use it for good? Men like you are the ones you describe in your routine. You tell a woman that a man has broken her heart and built up her walls, but it's because of men like you that those women exist. The ones that hurt, the ones that can't trust men. You can fool them, but I can't help but see that you're the only one who's hurting."

His words hit deep. A single tear slid down my cheek. "I've been hurting my entire life," I whispered. "I got in this because I was alone; I couldn't take not being wanted. I had no friends. I have no life or love. I needed something. Everyone told me that I was worthless, that I'd be alone forever, that I wasn't special..."

He wiped his eyes.

He saw a side to me that I never showed anyone. I never even showed myself. He stood up and put his hand on my shoulder.

"Love requires openness and vulnerability," he said, beginning to walk away. "You're a good man; don't be like N or X."

"Where are you going?" I asked.

"I'm leaving," he said.

"But we still have work."

"I believe that people come into your life for a reason," he said. "I taught you something just as you taught me."

"I taught you what?"

"Well, I guess I feel like life has been telling me to make a change," he told me. "You were the person who persuaded me to finally go through with it."

"With what?"

"I'm retiring," he said. "I'll give *him* a call tomorrow morning."

Just like that, he shut the door and I was left on the rooftop, but I didn't feel alone at that moment.

His presence lingered; he was the definition of warm.

Part

Restart

The next person I made a genuine connection with since Ace, Melanie, and Letter-V was a man named Kyle.

He seemed simple but had a charm about him. The first time we ever went to a party together, he was making out with some random girl within fifteen seconds of walking in. It was in a basement, and when we walked down the stairs, someone said hi to me. I turned back to see him sucking faces with a girl we had never met.

We were good friends after that night.

His charisma went beyond his complexion. He had black hair gelled to a point occasionally, but it was his eyes that women loved. That was one of his most lethal cards because they were turquoise, and it just hooked them.

It was his story that hooked me, however. I think we became really good friends because we shared similar pasts. Commonalities are one of the things that can connect a man and a woman, but great friendships are also made from them. It was the way he opened up and described his past to me that did it:

"I was around ten or eleven when my parents yelled at each other a lot. I was always scared growing up, but it was on one particular weekend that I experienced the most painful moment of my life. I still remember the day like it was yesterday."

He said that him, his sister, and his mom went to a cottage without his dad to go boating, but then decided to come home early because it was raining, and they couldn't really do anything.

"When we pulled up to our house," he told me, "my dad was packing his belongings in the truck. My mom hopped out of the car, and they started to argue on the front lawn. Then she started to cry.

Her crying always hurt the most; it's like it stains your brain. I didn't know what was happening, but my sister and I went inside. I sat watching out the windows, and that's when he shut the doors to his truck and left forever."

"Have you ever seen him since?" I asked.

"After I started getting really good at track, he wanted to come back into my life." That's how Kyle and I first met. We were on the track team together, and he always kicked my ass.

"I would expect you to hate him," I told him.

"I did at first, and my sister still does," he said. "I know it sounds crazy, and most people won't understand, but I don't hate him. I know that people have their own reasons for doing something, and he has a lot of hate and pain inside of him. I don't want to live my life with those same feelings, so I've chosen to forgive him."

I guess Letter-V was right – we can learn something from everyone. I used to view my family as the source of the life I was placed into, but without learning to forgive them, I would hold onto the pain forever.

Women often complimented my smile and Kyle's. It wasn't a coincidence that the brightest smiles are usually created from the world's deepest pain.

Synchronizing

I found it easy to get the girl, but staying interested was my struggle.

Instead of clubbing, I found myself doing the things I was interested in exploring; that's when I met *her.*

Haley was a surgeon who sat in front of me at a wine and canvas; a place where you do art, such as paintings, and drink wine.

She had dirty blonde hair with highlights in it, kind of like a golden zebra. She had hazel eyes and dressed casually in light-blue jeans with a long-sleeve red T-shirt. To me, her body was a perfect ten with an ass that had some gravitational pull effect on my eyes.

Her canvas looked like shit, so I teased her on it and smiled.

"Wow, you are quite the artist," I told her.

She blushed and told me to shut up.

During the two hours, she pointed to a guy sitting on the opposite side of the room.

Apparently, he wouldn't leave her alone. She pulled out her phone and showed me a message from him on Instagram that read, "The last time we were here I forgot to ask for your number, but you are cute as fuck." She opened it and didn't reply to him.

"I don't like when guys message me on Instagram," she said.

"So, you're more of an in-person kind of girl?" I asked.

"You could say that."

"Okay, how about you come back here and sit by me?"

"No, I'm shy," she whispered. "Everyone will see me stand up and move everything to come sit by you."

I chuckled a little bit and raised my eyebrows. "Oh," I said. "I must've heard you wrong."

"What do you mean?"

"I thought you said that you would rather have someone ask you in person." I paused. "Next time I ask, I'll just shoot you a message on Instagram instead," I smirked, turning my attention back towards my painting.

"Shut up," she giggled.

Before we left, she continued to keep the conversation alive – the sign of a girl in the orange part of the chart.

I didn't want to game anymore to get a girl physically, but I wanted to use these techniques and lines for the right reason – to search for someone I could connect with.

I discovered a way to imply value without directly saying it: complaining about girls that won't leave you alone. "Sometimes it does get annoying because there are some girls who just don't get the hint and won't leave me alone."

"Oh my gosh, I know!" she said, pulling out her phone.

Her DMs were like a waterfall of men wanting to sleep with her, get her on a date, or do anything with her.

While I was on her phone, I went to my social media. I commented 'heart eyes' from her account in response to one of my pictures so it looked like she did it. Then I gave her the phone back as if nothing happened.

My plan after we both left was to get her to message me.

I would comment back to her 'heart eyes' comment from my account and say something like, "Can you please control yourself?"

She would see this and most likely send me a message about it, saying how that wasn't her. It's an underrated technique to get her to message you first and start it off with her chasing the man. If she didn't message me, I would then know she wasn't interested so I'd move on, possibly to another girl in the wine and canvas.

To solidify the connection, I used some NLP that I learned from Hakan and Letter-X.

I asked her about the necklace she was wearing. It was special to her. I took my chain off and looped it around her neck. Then I asked her to take her necklace and put it around my neck. I told her that next week when we came back for our next wine and canvas, we would give each other our necklaces back.

"Deal," she said. "But please don't lose it."

Now that she was wearing my chain, every time she looked at herself in a reflection, she would think of me. I would be running through her mind constantly.

That night, she found my social media and messaged me a picture of her wearing my necklace. She told me that she didn't like messaging over social media at the wine and canvas, which was funny because she was messaging me over social media. When she found my social media, she went through every picture. I knew that when a girl likes a guy, she will go through all of his pictures, probably with her friends.

It didn't take her long to find the 'heart eyes' I put there earlier from her account. When she made a comment about it, I told her, "I know you like me, but please try to control yourself."

When I saw her in person the next night, we opened up to each other. It felt right.

I laid her on her stomach, took off her shirt, and began to massage her back.

"I'm a masseuse," I told her.

"Really?"

"No," I said. "But my love language is physical touch."

My thumbs slid down her back and into her muscle. I noticed a tattoo on her ribs right behind her breasts that were pressed against the mattress. I thought a tattoo on a girl's ribs was one of the sexiest things I had ever seen. But it needed to be simple: a quote or a word.

"If a rose can bloom after a hard winter, so can you," it read in cursive. I traced the whole thing with my nails. It gave her goosebumps.

When I asked her about it, she slowly opened up about her struggles with her past. Her father passed away when she was young, and she told me about a park that's close by that he used to take her to. He would push her on a swing at the park and play tag with her.

278

Then he died in a tragic car accident when she was eight years old. I felt for her.

I realized that a part of connecting with someone is removing all judgment. Judging before understanding is the world's epidemic. I wanted to perceive the world through her eyes, her pains, her views, and her challenges.

"I only just met you. I don't know why I'm telling you all of this," she said.

"Because you feel that I'm different than most men," I responded.

She rolled over, and we began to kiss.

Then we stopped, and she looked in my eyes. "You are different," she whispered, moving a piece of my hair.

I wanted to see her again.

Lowering the Heart's Wall

It wasn't long before Kyle was scooped up.

A blonde cheerleader danced all over him at the clubs, and I invited Haley along.

We all danced together. Kyle and I had our backs to a wall while the rest of the room watched us dance with the hottest girls there. We looked each other in the eye while it was happening, smiled, and nodded our heads.

This was what bonding was.

He always used to ask me why I stayed single, and I tended to avoid the question. I wanted just one special girl, but then again, I didn't because it was a disaster last time. When Haley danced with me, I felt those feelings again when she turned around and wrapped her arms around me.

"I like the way you hold me," she said.

I liked holding her.

When we all got back that night, Haley invited me over, and this was the first time that we had sex. I learned that if you do it the first time with someone and you're doing it for the sake of doing it without a reason, usually the other will be misled and become attached. Which means they will get hurt in the end. I didn't want to hurt someone anymore; I wanted intimacy.

Over time, I also mastered being the dominant leader in the bed. I made her work for me. After I licked, sucked, and kissed every inch of her body, I grazed my hand up and down her inner thigh. It was radiating heat. I rubbed all around it, over it, on her underwear lines, and beside it.

"Please," she begged. "Just touch it already. I can't stand this."

I stuck my hand down her pants, and she was the wettest I've ever experienced. I slid inside of her, condom-less.

"I just got a Brazilian wax," she moaned.

"What?"

"Where they wax the hair off the vagina so much that it doesn't grow back anymore. It's so smooth. I did it for you."

While I was fucking her, I felt up her arm. I stopped when my fingers touched a metal rod the size of a matchstick. It was a birth-control implant. After thirty minutes, I flipped her over, smashing her breasts into the mattress, and took her from behind. I grabbed her hair by the roots and pulled. Lions tend to bite the manes of each other during sex; this was my way of doing that.

She loved it.

"Cum in me," she said. "I'm on birth control."

I did just that.

After we were done, she acted strangely. She laid on her side and away from me. I could read her like a book. I knew something was wrong.

"What's wrong?"

"Nothing," she whispered.

I didn't say anything, so I laid next to her but away from her. A few minutes later, I heard her sniffling. "Are you crying?" I asked her.

"No," she sobbed, rubbing her nose and wiping her eyes.

I grabbed her shoulder, rolled her on her back, and laid above her staring into her eyes. I wiped a tear away. "Babe, what is it? I'm here; please talk to me."

"You're not acting like it," she cried.

"Like what?"

"Like you're here," she snapped. "Like you care."

I didn't know if this was a part of the whole connecting and bonding process, but she clearly wanted to feel some sort of certainty from me.

I understand that words don't really have meaning unless there's action that backs them. Anyone can say anything, but the gesture, the heart, the thoughtful gifts, and the little details you act on seem so much more real and authentic to her.

I just stared at her as she talked. "I'm complicated, I'm sorry."

"You're not complicated at all to me, Haley," I said, moving a strand of hair behind her ear. "You just want to be loved."

"That's the first time someone has ever said that to me," she said.

"I don't know much about the people or the guys in your past, but I have a feeling that you've been hurt before," I said. "People left you, they hurt you, and they broke your heart. That's them, and that's not me. I'm asking you to trust me and leave them behind."

It was beautiful, and this was from my heart. For her to open, I had to be open.

"Even when you're crying, I can't help but find you so beautiful."

"I'm so ugly when I cry, don't look at me," she whined.

"You're not ugly," I whispered, holding her.

The next morning, I took Haley to a coffee shop downtown where I did a lot of my writing.

"Do you come here often?" she asked.

"A lot," I said. "Usually every Sunday." We spent the day together and that night she asked me to stay once again.

She had to be at the hospital at 5 a.m., and when I woke up, I saw that she had left me a note.

"When I'm away from you I can't stop thinking about you. XO"

I couldn't stop thinking about her either.

London Bridge

Sometimes simple is better.

Kyle and his girlfriend's friends tended to be simple. They liked to drink, dance, make out with random guys at parties, scream when their favorite songs came on, and mostly loved sports.

Kyle had tickets to a suite at an Indiana Pacers game and invited me to fill the last seat. I was usually into the wild and crazy scene at night, but part of me liked the more laid-back idea of watching a basketball game.

While I was in line to get in, I noticed this striking woman. She stuck out like a single red rose in a meadow of grass. There was a difference between the girls from the club and the girls who were truly classy.

She wore black high heels with burgundy-painted toenails that matched her fingernails. Her legs went all the way up to her skintight leather dress. Moving up from there was a tucked-in grey shirt with a black choker around her neck. Her brown hair draped over the front of her shoulders like a silk curtain, and when she flipped her head, a wave of brown followed. She had her arms folded not with aggression but with sass, slightly putting one leg ahead of the other. She looked identical to Gal Gadot, the actress who played *Wonder Woman*.

I really wanted to talk to her, but for the first time in a long time, I chickened out.

When I got into the suite that night, Megan, a girl who had beaver-like teeth and a touch of masculinity, and Kennedy, a shorter blonde soccer player, were already on their fifth beer and screaming when random songs came on. They would talk randomly and out of the blue because they were drunk.

"When's Londyn getting here?" they asked each other.

When I asked Kyle who she was, he said he'd never met her before. I realized that Londyn was the girl I saw standing in line; fate gave me a second chance. When she walked in, Megan and Kennedy hopped up. "Londyn!" they screamed.

"Oh my," Londyn said. She knew they were drunk. Then she added, "You guys look cute tonight."

"Thanks," I interrupted. "You too."

Londyn looked me up and down. "Right," she mocked, rolling her eyes.

"Meet our friends," Megan interrupted our connection. "This is Kyle, and this is Connor."

"I'm Londyn," she said, grabbing my hand.

"I'm...madly in love with you," I joked, acting like I was going to kiss her hand.

She pulled it away but blushed. "Slow down, Romeo."

"Oh my gosh," I gasped. "We already have nicknames for each other. That's so romantic."

Usually by this point, I would have her in the palm of my hand. She would chase me, flirt with me, and couldn't get enough of me. But Londyn simply rolled her eyes and walked off, which left me scratching my head. I was thinking, *What's wrong with this girl... Why isn't she wanting me yet?*

When she had a beer with her friends, I overheard her say, "The opposite of love isn't hate, it's indifference." I guess this was what I was getting from her – indifference. When she walked into the suite to get a plate of food, I decided to wander in and try to ignite this fire that she was clearly denying.

"So, if I'm your Romeo," I told her. "You're saying that you're my Juliet?"

She laughed and rolled her eyes.

"Why don't we discuss this tomorrow," I said, beginning to smirk. "Like over dinner or something?"

"Not a *chance*," she replied, emphasizing the last word.

284

I wasn't about to go out so easily. I had no choice – I had to pull out my old self.

"You probably say that to every guy, don't you?" Usually, this line worked.

"No," she countered. "Just the dangerous and charming type like you."

It's almost as if she had automatic responses to shut down a man like me. Everything I said missed, but everything she said was delivered with such grace and elegance. Before I could respond, my phone started to vibrate in my pocket, and my jeans were tight against my legs so it took me a second to pull it out.

"If you'll excuse me," I looked at her. "Someone is trying to talk to me." When I finally got it out, it was a missed call from Haley.

Why was she calling me?

I walked away from Londyn to call her back because if she heard me over the phone talking to Haley then I would clearly prove her point that I had other girls and was, in fact, a charmer.

I went outside on a patio where it was quieter. I put my hood up because it was cold, and the fur tickled my cheek. It was almost Valentine's Day, around twenty degrees at that point in the year. When I called her back, I sat in front of a fire tower listening to it ring. I breathed slow and deeply so I could relax but also so I could see my breath. I still acted like a child no matter the age.

When Haley answered, I could hear that she had been crying.

"Is everything okay?" I asked, concerned.

"No, it's been a rough night," she said sniffling. "I've cried twice." It sounded like she was about to start again.

"I'm out with Kyle and some other people. Can we talk in a few?"

"Or," she said, "you can just come over."

"I'll be there in twenty," I told her. "I'm leaving now."

I stood up and remembered Londyn. Part of me didn't want to leave. I was having so much fun with her, and Kyle and my friends, but I also needed to be there for her when she needed me. When I got back to the suite, Kyle was one of the only ones in it.

"Where did everyone go?" I asked him.

"To the bathroom," he chuckled. Some people's wonders of the world include aliens, the pyramids, and do ghosts exist? Mine was why women travel together to the bathroom.

"So, I don't have much time," I told Kyle. "Haley called crying, and I think I'm going to head over there."

"Yeah man, you should go," he said. "I'll hold it down here."

"Alright," I said. "But if Londyn asks where I am, ask her if she misses me or something. Then when she says 'No,' look at her skeptically and say, 'Uh-huh, sure.'"

He looked at me skeptically instead.

I pointed at him. "Yes, look at her just like that."

"I think Londyn is into you too, but you have Haley to worry about," he said. "But I'll get some intel for you."

"Let me know what she says." I quickly started to walk out.

When I stepped into the elevator, the doors began to close. Londyn came around the corner with her friends.

Maybe she didn't want me to leave. Maybe she really was interested in me. Maybe she was 'the one,' and my leaving tonight would mess up a great opportunity with a girl like her. Maybe I was overthinking it.

Our eyes met and remained locked.

The doors closed.

Crossroads

Blaming everything sexual on her, telling her to slow down or that sex isn't happening, and challenging a girl are intoxicating for her.

For example:
"Why do you make me think these thoughts?"
While kissing her, you whisper in between, "You're so bad, you know how to get me every time."
"Stop trying to seduce me. I told you that sex is off the table."

It's forming the role-play that everything she's doing is trying to turn you on. I told Haley that sex wasn't happening, and when I challenged her, she wanted it more.

I could tell because when I got there, we didn't make it to her room. Instead, we pushed everything off the kitchen table and began to undress each other. We fucked against the fridge, on the counter, on the table, and finally laid together on the floor next to everything we pushed off earlier. When the tile got uncomfortable, I carried her to her bedroom, and we laid in each other's arms.

It was one of the most passionate times I've ever shared with a woman. I didn't know if it was Haley or the fact that I was riled up from Londyn. Londyn made me feel so alive, but in the next few moments, Haley made me feel like a wilting flower that hadn't been watered for a week.

"When you said that you were having a rough night, I wasn't thinking that you meant this kind of rough," I flirted.

"Shut up," she said, pushing me. "I was having a rough night." I didn't say anything. I just held her and ran my fingers through her hair.

A few moments passed when she shifted her tone from tranquil to depressed. "I'm just confused."

"Confused about what?"

"A couple hours ago I wasn't sure about us, but laying here now in your arms feels so right," she whispered. "I don't want to lose this."

"Why would you lose this?"

"Well, tonight before I saw you, I was out with my roommate, and I ran into my ex-boyfriend." She moved out of my arms and sat up, putting her hair in a bun.

"What does he have to do with us?" I asked.

"Well, we broke up six months ago, and I thought I was over him, but tonight we talked about things."

Londyn's word 'indifference' was the key to this situation. I remembered when Nadia knew a lot of DJs and had a lot of guys talking to her, but I didn't get jealous. "I think it's so hot that you don't get jealous or insecure that I have guy friends," she told me. This situation was tricky because if I got mad then it would show neediness, insecurity, and clinginess, pushing her away into his arms. All a man can really do in this position is just be the best option.

"Okay," I said, giving her permission to continue.

"I like you a lot, but I'm also not over Jeremy. I thought I was, but part of me still misses him," she explained. "He told me tonight that he's been struggling without me. He's been hurting, and it hit me harder than I thought it would."

I realized Jeremy was her ex.

I couldn't deny that listening to her say this was difficult. No man wants to hear something like that. I knew that if I didn't stay centered, I'd lose her.

"I want you to be happy," I said. "If that's with him, then so be it. I just hope that you will make the right decision for yourself because if you do want him and choose that, just know that you will lose me in the process." I had to be honest.

"Even if I did get back with him, I'd still want to talk to you because you're a great guy."

I shook my head. "I'm sorry, but I won't do that."

"W-why," she stuttered.

"I'm not going to be second place or a friend. If I'm going to be with you, I'm really going to be with you. I'm going to love you and be that man," I insisted. "If it does come down to that, just know that I'll cherish these moments forever, and if you don't choose to have more of those moments with me, I know another woman will love, respect, and cherish what I'm giving you."

She laid back down in my arms and rested her head on my chest, "You are one of a kind," she whispered. "I know I'm difficult, but just be patient with me. I'm getting over him, but it just takes time."

"Take your time," I whispered back. "I'll be here for you." She kissed me.

This situation reminded me of the one years ago with Caitlyn and Mitch. I wondered if it would end the same way or if she would do for me what Caitlyn couldn't.

This was the true meaning behind Jay's ideology of being high-value. If I tried to argue for myself as to why I was the better option or be logical then it would push her away. Why would I try to prove that I'm better? I needed to prove nothing. If I kept giving reason after reason as to why I was better, it would just show more and more that I didn't believe in myself. If she didn't see how valuable I was, I wouldn't prove to her that I was or tell her I was. I'd walk away because that's what a strong man does. He doesn't chase what does not want him or respect him.

If people learn that they can disrespect you, then it will continue to happen. *What we allow to happen to ourselves is what will continue to happen.*

We continued to lay together. "What are our Valentine's Day plans?" she asked. "It's next week."

"I have everything arranged already," I told her. "Just be ready by 5:30 on Friday."

I had nothing arranged yet.

Redirection

I sat looking out the window of a coffee shop trying to figure out Valentine's Day plans.

The front door opened, and the bell chimed in sync. With my back facing the entrance, I turned around and side-eyed the door when I heard the bell. Londyn and Kennedy walked in. My heart skipped a beat, but I didn't say anything. I turned back around quickly. I acted like I was intensely reading something on my laptop so I'd look cool when she saw me.

They got their coffees, and Londyn casually strolled up next to me.

"So, you're just going to sit here and act like you didn't see me walk in?" she asked.

"Well, hello." I looked her up and down. "Wow, you are one hell of a sight to see." I was flirting with her because I smirked right after I said that.

She did her typical eye roll. "You keep trying to charm me, but it's not working."

"Oh yeah?" I countered. "I feel like when someone says that, it's only because it's actually working, and they are denying it." She smirked and shook her head. We held eye contact for a few seconds.

Kennedy yelled to Londyn, "I'll be in the car waiting!"

Londyn turned to me. "Whatcha working on?" she asked.

"I'm just reading something," I casually said.

"There's nothing on the screen though." Her eyebrows raised as if she'd caught me.

I looked at my screen and saw that there was nothing there.

Dammit, I thought. *Smart women are tough.*

I had to come up with something quick. "Oh," I said, waving my hand as if it was no big deal. "I was just working on our Valentine's Day plans, so of course I exited out."

I hoped she would buy it.

"Our Valentine's Day plans?" she cringed.

I'd saved myself; she bought it. Then I realized I might have put myself into a situation. If she said yes, then who would I blow off, Haley or Londyn?

I looked out the window. "I'm thinking dinner, some wine..." I paused, beginning to smile. "Some kissing."

She gave me a look that I read as *you've got to be kidding me.*

"I thought you already had a date because that's who you left us for the other night." Kyle told me that after I left the bar, Londyn pestered him about where I was going and who I was going to see, but he didn't tell her. "I know you went to go see a girl," she added.

"I promise I'll cut her off for you," I said, trying to create the dramatic role-play of a love triangle between us with another woman involved.

She laughed and rolled her eyes. "Whatever, I need to get back to Kennedy."

"Wait," I said. "Before you go, what's the most romantic thing a guy has done or could do for you?" I asked. I was trying to make these plans for Haley.

"Why?" she asked as if it was a stupid question.

I smirked. "Because I need to know for our date."

She turned around and started to walk away. "I'm leaving, Romeo," she called back to me. I was checking her out as she left. She was just sexy to me for some reason.

The guy at the table next to me saw me staring. "Get it over with and ask her out before some other guy does," he said.

I continued to stare at her, and when she walked out of the shop, I said, "What?" Then I turned my head to look at him. This guy was maybe sixty-five years old.

"I heard the way you guys were talking to each other..."

I interrupted. "It's just friendly banter," I tried to argue.

"Explain why you were staring at her like that then," he countered.

"I don't know what you're talking about."

He turned back to his book. "Well, her friend in the car knows because she was watching you stare at her the entire time she walked out."

My eyes widened. "What? Did she really see that?"

"No," he laughed. "But at least we both know the truth now."

"Damn, you got me," I laughed, rolling my eyes. This guy was cool, but I never got his name. If you're the man in the coffee shop reading this now, thanks for a good laugh.

Within two hours, I made the best Valentine's Day plans for Haley and I. Out of nowhere, creativity hit me.

This was the plan:

I called Hirosaki and scheduled a hibachi grill for six o'clock. I told her to be ready at 5:30, and we would drive there together. We would have dinner, and I asked for the best hibachi chef in the place. From there, I would take her back to the park where she told me her father used to bring her. When the day came, I would have to go to the park around five o'clock and hide flowers in the playground. If someone did show up, hopefully they wouldn't find them. While we were at the park, she would stumble upon them.

There was one last thing though. I paid the owner of her twenty-story condo building $80 to leave the rooftop unlocked for us. Where I left two blankets, one to lay on and one to bundle up in since it was the middle of February. I also had a bucket of ice with a bottle of champagne and two glasses up there. Under the bucket was a card that she would open that said 'Happy Valentine's Day.'

I knew she was going through a lot these past few days. Sex is great, but seeing her light up with a smile made me feel beyond great. Women may think men live for sex, and we kind of do, but men live to make their women happy. Sex isn't good if she isn't happy. If a guy plays her a great song or shows her a really cool video and the next time he's with her she plays that video that song, he says, "Well, I did that. I showed her that, and she liked it." That makes a man feel good, like he accomplished something.

She did mean a lot to me. I wanted to give her a night she would remember for the rest of her life, something that would mean more than material things like gifts. A memory.

Valentine's Day ended with a woman, but it wasn't Haley.

It was Londyn.

Let me explain...

Chapter X

Koi No Yokan

Knowing They Are the One

[Koi No Yokan: A Japanese phrase meaning, "The feeling upon first meeting someone that you will inevitably fall in love."]

"Not here?" I asked. "What do you mean she's *not* here?"

Haley's roommate answered the door to their condo with her boyfriend.

"I was supposed to take her out at 5:30," I told her. "We had a date."

Haley's roommate looked at her boyfriend and then back at me but didn't say anything. It finally hit me.

"She's with Jeremy," I said, looking away. "Isn't she?"

She looked down at her feet. "I'm really sorry she didn't tell you."

I nodded my head and began to walk away, but then I stopped because I remembered something.

"Oh, I almost forgot one thing," I told her. She was about to shut the door but stopped and poked her head out. "Don't tell anyone this, but I paid the manager here to leave the rooftop unlocked. There's champagne and a lot of cool things up there. If you guys aren't busy, feel free to check it out."

Then I turned around and left.

I wasn't going to be needing it, and I knew now they were curious. They'd go check it out.

My dad once told me when I was learning how to drive, "Expect the unexpected. Expect people to do the stupidest thing they could possibly do so you're prepared for it."

This was the stupidest thing she could possibly do.

Kyle texted me earlier around five and asked, "What are you doing tonight?"

"Nothing, why?"

He called me, and when I picked up the phone, he said, "I'm here at a party with Megan, but I'm going to leave soon to hang out with my girlfriend. But Londyn is here too."

I heard Londyn's voice in the background. "Who's that?" she asked Kyle.

"It's Connor."

"Is he coming here?"

"She wants to know if you're coming here," Kyle monotoned through the phone.

"Send me the address and tell her, 'Only if she's my Valentine.'"

I heard him get Londyn's attention. "He said, 'Only if you're my Valentine.'"

"Whatever," she uttered back to him. I assumed she threw in an eye roll.

"She said she wants you here really bad," Kyle said back to me, loud enough so that Londyn heard.

"I didn't say that!" Londyn gasped.

I was fifteen minutes away. On my way over, I got a text from a random number. "Are you almost here?" it read.

It was Londyn. She must have gotten my number from Kyle. At a red light, I texted her back. "Be there soon, babe, don't worry."

Eyes of Desire

Her eyes were the color of my favorite drink - sweet tea.

It was a simple house when I arrived. Drunk people sprawled on the lawn outside, and music rattled the windows. When I walked in, I saw her immediately. I began to weave through the crowd of people to get to her. A hand came out of the crowd and stopped me like a toll bridge. It was a very hot blonde girl I actually knew.

"A-Alysa?" I stuttered. The girl I was with right after I broke up with Melanie. Because Melanie had cheated on me with Alysa's boyfriend way back, and then Alysa cheated on Noah with me, I was surprised to see her.

"I never thought I'd see you again," she said. "I've been waiting on that call."

I bit my lip. I'd promised I would call her, but that was over a year ago, and she was still stuck on me?

"Sounds like you've been missing me," I said, smirking.

"No," she argued. "Well, I did, but you lost your chance."

"How did I lose my chance?" I asked, pretending to care. I looked over at Londyn and saw her watching me.

"You promised me you'd call."

"Have you seen Noah lately?" I asked.

"No," she said. "We haven't talked since you came to my house." She shook her head. "What does he have to do with you not calling me?"

"I'll show you," I said. "Let me see your phone."

"Um, okay?" She reached into the back pocket of her tight blue jeans.

"Unlock it and give it to me." She did.

I went to her messages and sent myself a message so I had her number. She tried to look at what I was doing, but I tilted the phone away. "No peeking," I smiled. "Gosh." Then I handed her phone back.

"What did you do?" she asked.

"Wait for it," I told her as I casually tapped my phone.

One moment later, she was getting a call from me. She looked at her phone ringing to see who it was, and when she realized it was me, she looked at me with a look that said, *Really?*

Then she hit decline. She still had my name in her phone from two years ago. I kind of felt bad in that moment.

"See?" I asked. "I didn't call because you would do that."

"Shut up!" she blushed, looking away. "You are as stupid as ever."

"And you like it," I responded with a smile. She started laughing and slapped my chest flirtatiously. Midway through her laugh, I said, "Now if you'll excuse me, I'm leaving to find someone who would actually answer my phone call."

I started to walk away towards Londyn. Finally, I could go talk to her, I thought, until Alysa grabbed the sleeve of my arm and pulled me back in.

So close, I thought.

"We're about to head out," she continued, "but we're going to Steak 'n Shake if you would like to join us for a milkshake."

"I'm going to go grab my friend, and then I'll meet you there a little later."

"You'd better," she told me, walking out.

I didn't plan on going.

At first glance, if most men saw Alysa next to Londyn, they would ask why I didn't date Alysa. They would call me nuts. Not because Londyn wasn't attractive but because Alysa was probably the hottest girl not only in that house but within a ten-mile radius. Depending on your perspective, that's a big area. Sure, it was only a small dot on the globe, but it's all about how you view it.

Londyn didn't have what Alysa had...nor did I want her to. To me, she had beauty.

Hot girls don't normally have beauty, but I've found beautiful girls to be beyond hot. Hot girls are just an illusion. They are skin deep, and usually boring.

She had something that a hot girl never has.

There's a difference between hot and beautiful, and I wasn't sure what it was, but I knew that Londyn had it.

Conflicts

All I wanted was just one kiss.

There was a marble island right across from the counter where she was sitting. I sat there, right across from Londyn, while Kyle talked to Megan.

I patted the marble countertop right next to me. "Come sit by your husband."

"Husband?" she cringed right before she drank some wine. Then she hopped off the countertop. I thought she was going to sit next to me, but instead, she snagged the hat off my head, shook it as if I was a dog that would chase her, and started backing away. I looked at her for a second, contemplating whether I should play her game. I decided to play and hopped off the island. She put her wineglass on the countertop as I put my hands up as if I was going to tickle her and slowly crept towards her. She backed into the counter with nowhere to run.

She held out my hat. "Here! Take it!" she yelped.

I snatched it from her hands. Then I stared at her, deciding whether to tickle her. We stared into each other's eyes. She giggled. I could tell she was flush – a little tipsy from the wine. I leaned in close as if I was going to kiss her. She turned her head, but instead, I just grabbed her wineglass.

"You've had too much, babe," I said, walking away towards the marble island.

She took the bait and chased me.

"Give that back!" she said, reaching for it.

"Tell me how much you love me first," I smiled.

Instead, she tried to grab the hat off my head again.

"Easy, tiger," I said reciting the frame that she was coming on too strong. I gently backed her away. "When you're sober, you say 'no-no,' but it seems when you've been drinking, you can't keep your hands off me."

She crossed her arms like the first time I ever saw her in line, staring at me with a slight smirk. It was like she was playing a game with me as much as I was trying to with her.

"Drunk words are sober thoughts," I said. "Do you have something to tell me?"

As I pushed her away, it made her want me more or, at least, it seemed that way when she took my hand. "Let's go talk somewhere a little quieter," she said, pulling me away.

It's so on, I thought. But it wasn't.

As she pulled me down a hallway, Megan said, "I knew Londyn wanted him."

"It's not like that!" Londyn snapped. "We're just talking."

I looked at Megan and Kyle as Londyn was pulling me. "It's totally like that," I called out to them. Kyle mouthed the words, "Oh yeah," nodding his head, and raising his drink for a toast. Londyn took my hat and threw it to Megan. She put it on, and then Londyn aggressively pulled me into a laundry room.

"When I think of a laundry room, I imagine clean, but you'd be the one to make it dirty," I said as she sat on the washing machine. She stared at me. I was expecting her to respond, but she didn't, so I added, "But too bad for you I'm not that easy. I need more wine for that."

She couldn't help herself but respond this time. That's all I needed was just one reaction for her to take the bait, and then I'd escalate with comments like that.

"Whatever," she sneered. "I could have you right now if I wanted to."

I sat on the dryer right next to her, positioning my face six inches from hers. We stared into each other's eyes.

"Make your move then," I whispered.

I looked at her eyes and then at her lips, escalating the triangular

300

gaze. My heart was pounding, my body was hot, and I felt butterflies. This moment felt like an eternity. I wanted to kiss her, but I wanted her to come to me. I couldn't tell if she actually liked me or if she was one of those girls who – after a man admits his love – runs off because that's all she needed. I was not going to go down that way.

She backed away. "You say that I'm your 'wife' and whatever, but you don't even know who I am. You are just kidding around. I know women want you, but you're a womanizer," she told me. "Weren't you supposed to be on a date tonight?"

My heart locked up and then released. She'd called me out. I'd almost forgotten about Haley ditching me earlier that night.

"I didn't go," I told her.

When I said this, she showed me a different side to herself. She repositioned herself and went from spicy to sweet and gentle.

"Why?" she gently intoned.

"I told you in the coffee shop that I wanted to spend Valentine's with you."

"Oh, whatever, you're such a liar!" Her tone had returned to normal. "It's never going to happen between us."

"You're still playing that card, huh?" I asked. "You want me, but you hold yourself back from it."

"No," she protested. "You're hot, and you know you're hot. Women want you, and a lot of guys want me…"

"I know," I said, interrupting her, "including me." She rolled her eyes. She'd admitted I was hot, that I was attractive.

"But I lead a lot of guys on," she continued, "and I know you do the same with girls."

"We're so similar," I told her. "We might as well go get married now."

She brushed that line off with ease. "What I'm saying is that I'm not one of your other girls who you can charm with your eyes, your perfect smile, and your words."

"What do other girls have to do with us?"

"There is no *us*." She emphasized the word 'us' by making air quotes with her fingers. "I'm saying that I'm not just another girl who you can lead on or who falls for you."

Before I could respond, the owner of the place walked in and told us that the cops had come. Apparently, the party got out of control, and they had to shut it down. We walked out together with mobs of people but no sign of Kyle, Megan, or – most importantly – my hat.

"Walk me home like a gentleman," she said. "I live only a couple minutes away." My car was right down the street, but if I walked with her, I'd get more time with her.

"Hop on," I said, squatting down in front of her. She obliged, and she piggybacked on me all the way back. She took a selfie of us on my phone, and we both looked so happy. When we were almost to her house, she laid her head on the back of mine.

"You're so comfortable," she whispered. "I could fall asleep on you." Right when she said that, she took it back. "Ignore what I just said; I didn't mean it."

I had one last opportunity to get a kiss.

Red Lights

She was *so* problematic.

She questioned *everything*. If I told a joke, she would say it was dumb. My smile, which most girls loved, had no effect. She said that it was 'cheeky' or too flirty. I loved it, but I hated it. We got to her house, and she let me in. Just how I was thinking it would go. It quickly changed when she said, "Wait here."

She went upstairs and disappeared. I sat on the couch and looked at all the stuff she had laying around: medical books, a Wii gaming system with Mario Kart, and stuffed animals. I thought she was going to give me a tour, but she hopped back down the stairs jingling her keys.

"Okay, let's go," she said.

I acted like she meant we were going to bed. "Okay," I responded, walking upstairs towards the bedroom.

"Not up there," she said, beginning to smile. "To crystal," she added.

"Crystal?"

"My car," she said, "I named her that."

"Okay, where is Crystal taking us?"

"To your car," she explained as if I was in grade school. "And then you're going home."

"Oh yeah, totally," I said. "What was I thinking?"

What the fuck. I'd never had this much push-pull from a girl. It was like she wanted me earlier and now told me to go home.

I had met my match.

Adaptation was key. I still had a few more tricks up my sleeve to use while she drove me back to my car. As she started to drive, I only had a minute before we got to my car to spark something fast and hook her in a conversation.

"You talk about how you had this 4.0 GPA in college, and you think you're really smart," I told her, conjuring up a last-resort attempt to steal a kiss. "But I bet that before I leave, I can guess three things right about you before you can guess three facts about me."

"Alright," she said, accepting the challenge. "Let's see what you got."

I stared at her for a couple of seconds. "I bet," I said, pausing for effect, "that you're the type of girl who – when the waiter or waitress says, 'Enjoy your food' – you have said, 'Thanks, you too' back to them."

She laughed. "I have done that before."

"Oh gosh, I'm never going out to eat with you," I teased. "But your turn. It's one-to-nothing."

"I feel like you are the type of guy who has slept with a lot of girls," she stated. I figured that she would say something like that.

"What's a lot to you?" I asked.

"Like 10 girls."

I gasped. "I'm offended. Do you take me as a player?"

"Yes, I do."

"Um, no." I changed the topic. "It's still one-to-zero, but let's see…" I looked at her. I was going to pull out a cold read that I used only for times like this to secure a victory.

Just before my guess, we stopped behind a car at a stoplight. I looked at her while the red of the brake lights and stoplight painted her face. Her lips, her skin, and everything else glowed crimson. When she looked at me, I saw the beauty, and my heart thumped hard just one time before settling back down.

"You've had your heart broken once," I told her. "You thought he was or could be 'the one,' and you really opened up, but it caused you to get hurt in the process, so now you've become more aware. It's harder for you to open up to guys because of it."

She nodded as if she was surprised. "That's actually pretty true.

I hadn't thought about it like that before." We pulled up next to my car. "You're interesting," she added.

"Damn," I said, smiling. "You got me on one."

She tilted her head in confusion. "What?"

"You said that I'm interesting," I told her. "That's true about me, so I guess now it's two-to-one." I smirked at her. "You're good at this game."

She giggled. "Oh my gosh, you're so stupid."

Now it was time for my final guess. I was going to go big or go home with my final trump card, one of my most special moves for a kiss. This technique was almost forbidden, only to be brought out for a girl like her. The crème de la crème, as they say. It was set up from the beginning to end with a kiss. To make her open up to me with my first two guesses, and my third would be to get her to kiss me.

My heart picked up pace as I stared into her eyes. My hands went cold; my breath went shallow. I looked at her. "I bet that you…" I paused, "are a really bad kisser." My plan was that she would obviously challenge this.

"That's so wrong," she argued. "My lips are perfect for kissing."

It was falling into place according to plan. Now it was time to finish this with two words.

"Prove it," I said, leaning in a little bit because how could we know without trying it out? If she took up the challenge and we finally kissed, I'd pull back first and say, "I guess I was right," implying that she was a bad kisser. She would then laugh and probably tell me to shut up, all according to plan, and we would continue to kiss and go from there.

She smirked. Rolled her eyes and leaned in. My heart skipped a beat. I had never worked *this* hard for just one touch of lips.

I closed my eyes. *Finally*, I thought.

I felt the warmth of her lips but not on my lips.

I opened my eyes.

She was kissing my forehead then pulled back and giggled, "You never said where I was supposed to kiss you."

In that moment, I thought I heard a record screech like in the cartoons when something unexpected happens. I was shocked. I never thought she could find a way around this.

I shook my head. "My fourth guess is that you're a child," I said, opening the door to leave. "Three-to-one, I win." I shut the door as she continued to laugh.

She rolled down her window. "I never got my third guess!"

"I already won," I said, opening my door.

"I bet you are a great kisser," she purred. Hope came back to life in me.

"Want to find out?" I smirked.

"Maybe next time, Romeo," she called back to me, stepping on Crystal's accelerator and speeding off. I was left in the dust and saw her brown hair flowing out the window as she turned the corner. I was played by her, but it wasn't over.

Strange Tides

"So, Haley was with her ex," Kyle said. "Then Londyn took you to the laundry room but didn't kiss you?"

"Yes," I said, adjusting my seat all the way back.

I asked him to meet up that night so I could explain the trouble I was having.

"Well," he said, "I had a good night with my girl."

"At least one of us did." Right when I said that, my phone started to ring in my pocket. I pulled it out and saw that Londyn was calling me.

I looked at Kyle. "Maybe you're about to have a good night after all," he said.

I answered, putting it on speaker so we could both hear.

"Did you change your mind about that kiss?" I said into the phone.

"Nice try," she chuckled. "I have your hat actually." We flirted back and forth for a while.

"How about you give me the hat over dinner?"

She wasn't giving in. She was cold. "So, it's just going to be one of those love stories where the guy chases forever and ever. Then I eventually give up and find a different girl who's not as cute but force myself to believe I love her when deep down I still think about you."

"Connor," she laughed, "you're sweet and you're charming, but I just don't have the time right now to date. I'm so busy with trying to be a PA (Physician Assistant) that I couldn't be in a relationship if I wanted one."

"Okay," I said. "So, I'm thinking we go to dinner on Thursday."

Kyle laughed in the background. He tried to cover his mouth so she couldn't hear.

"I'm hanging up, Romeo." I could tell she was smiling and rolling her eyes.

She hung up. Still no dice.

"She is something," I said, smiling at my phone.

"I feel like she wants you by the way she flirts with you but is conflicted about it," he remarked. I agreed with a nod.

"I never got my Valentine's Day dinner," I said, putting my phone down. "Want to go somewhere?"

"Sure," he replied.

I pinkie-promised Alysa earlier that I'd go to Steak 'n Shake, and I guess this was my karma for telling her I'd be there when I planned on not going. She and her friends were still there waiting for me when I said, "I promised I'd come for you."

I played the part on the outside and flirted but thought about my time with Londyn instead. I watched Alysa's mouth move as I began to go into deep thought about Londyn. When she would talk to me, I answered on autopilot.

Part

Hot Shot

"I know you're asleep, but I had to tell you this."

The voice on the other end of the phone was a man. It was Kyle, and when I looked at the clock, it read 1:30 a.m.

It was a week past Valentine's Day.

He was invited over to Megan's house with Londyn and a few other friends.

They played Truth or Dare, and on her turn, she said "truth." Kyle spoke up and asked, "How do you truthfully feel about Connor?"

Apparently, everyone in the room had a reaction to this, and Londyn blushed. "Oh my gosh," she said.

Kyle continued. "Then she said, 'I feel like he's a flirt, but he's interesting,' but that's not all. We had a few drinks, and when everyone was hanging out, she sat next to me."

I couldn't help but want to hear more but tried to act nonchalant about it.

"Then what?" I asked.

"She asked me why I had brought you up during Truth or Dare, and I told her it was because I feel like there's a spark between you two," he said. "But right after I said this, she told me that it would never work because you talk to too many girls."

I chuckled. That sounded like something she would say.

Kyle elaborated on their conversation. "There are other girls who want him. I'll give you that," he told her. "But after he met you, he only talks about you. You'd be so surprised at the things he says about you."

Of course, when you say something like this to someone, they want to know more.

His only response to her persistence was, "You'll just have to ask him yourself if you ever decide to go out with him." While Kyle was telling me all of this, I heard Londyn in the background.

"Who is that?" she asked.

"Connor," he responded to her. "How about you talk to him?" She was hesitant, and then he said loudly into the phone, "Never mind, she's too nervous to talk to you."

She snatched the phone from him. "Kyle and your friends are here. Why aren't you?"

Even though I was really tired, I couldn't help but smile and wake up a little. I couldn't resist a chance to flirt. "You miss me?"

"And what if I do?" she snapped back.

I heard Megan in the background say, "You're so into him, just date him already."

"Shut up!" she snapped. "I'm not."

She turned her attention back to our call. "So, are you coming over tonight?" She slurred this sentence together.

"How much have you had to drink?" I asked her.

"Why?"

"You get affectionate towards me when you're drunk," I said. "Last week you were telling me no, and now you say you miss me."

"I didn't say I miss you, Romeo," she giggled. "But Kyle said that you talk about me, so what do you say?"

"Listen, I can't come over tonight," I said changing the subject. "I want to, but I need to be up early for a flight." I was leaving for Kentucky to assist Gary with some promotion in the country clubs. "I'll be back next Thursday, so can I take you out for dinner on Friday?"

I was asking her on a date. I had tried every other way. Flirty, indirect, and now it was time to just be upfront and direct.

"If you're too busy for one dinner, I understand, but I'd like to treat you to a real date. I want to see you again."

She didn't say anything for a few moments.

"One dinner," she said.

Tangled Souls

I pressed the silicone contact lenses against my eyes and rubbed the gel into my hair for the messy look. I put on my burgundy leather jacket (retiring my pinstripes), which got a compliment every time I wore it, with a white hoodie underneath, dark-blue tight jeans, and my tan suede boots.

Of course, I put on the colorful chakra bracelet Ace gave me that also drew a lot of compliments. However, whenever I wore it, I was reminded of how I'd killed our friendship. Even if he wanted nothing to do with me, the bracelet inspired me to cherish my new relationships. We hadn't talked for years.

Besides the bracelet, I wore my black Movado watch.

I had a plan for Londyn. First, I'd take her to the hibachi grill, and then around nine o'clock, I was going to take her to a club that I had to promote in Broad Ripple. I figured that if she could see my secret VIP lifestyle then it would be enough to break through and win her heart.

Around 6:30, I texted Londyn and told her that I was on my way to pick her up.

"I'm going out with Megan instead around eight, so tonight isn't good for me," she replied. That was it. No trying to make another date. No trying to hang out later that night. No nothing.

"Uh, we have a date?" I texted.

A few moments passed before she responded. "I'm already going out with Megan. You're not mad, are you?"

"Honestly, just forget about it." I expressed my aggravation in that text.

"Now I feel bad," she replied.

I didn't reply; I wasn't going to be her pen pal. I wanted action, not back-and-forth babble. My dad once told me, "I have no ears, only eyes, so show me." Basically, it's saying that you need to look at what someone does, not says. Do they put in the effort for you? Or when something comes up, do they put other things over you? Do they show you they want to be with you? Do they make the time for you and prove that you mean a lot to them, or do they make excuses?

I was tired of getting blown off. First Haley, and now Londyn. I'd planned out something again only for it to go straight into the trashcan.

Is it me? I asked myself.

That night, I got to Broad Ripple at nine, and two blonde soccer players I knew, who I always thought were cute, danced on a table. A mob of guys below them eyed the girls creepily and fake-danced. I walked through the guys and reached my hands up to the girls; they helped me up.

"Connor!" they screamed.

"My favorite girls," I said, hugging them both. I had them both kiss my cheeks.

I put my hands on their hips. "Let's dance," I suggested.

We started to dance, and they started to go down on me, and on their way back up, the girl on my right slid her hand up my leg and grabbed my dick, but slick. I wasn't sure if she meant to or not. They felt down my chest, down my abs, and it was no mistake – they both put their hands on my crotch. I forgot everyone on the floor was around when I started to kiss the girl on my right.

Then I kissed the girl on my left.

I felt my phone buzzing in my pocket, but I wasn't going to let anything ruin this moment.

I told them to kiss me at the same time, and we tried to share a three-way kiss, then they started to kiss each other instead.

I guess it isn't me after all. I told myself as I grinned.

I slipped away to go to the bar, but the girls hopped off the table and started to follow me through the club.

As I weaved through the sea of guys, one of them stopped me.

"Are you a pimp or something?" he asked.

"A what?" I asked.

"Y-you literally just walked up there and started making out with those girls," he stuttered as if he couldn't believe it.

I wasn't a pimp, or a pickup artist, or a belly dancer, or whatever anyone thought I was.

I was just tired.

I sat down at the bar, and the girls came up beside me.

Even during all of this, I thought about Londyn. I didn't know why I was stuck on Londyn out of all the girls I could have. I pulled out my phone for a picture in order to get both of the girl's phone numbers because that's how I'd send the pictures to them. "Take our picture," I told one of them as I got close to the other. I handed her my phone.

"Who's Londyn?" she cooed, looking at my phone. "She called you twice."

I began to get butterflies, and I wanted to grab my phone, but I also knew Londyn a little too well. She could just be calling me again to make sure I knew that she was rejecting me.

I held my composure. She took the picture, and I let the feeling of excitement pass.

I talked about how cute we were. Then I had her put her number in. That's when I saw what Londyn had texted me.

"Hi babe," she messaged with a kiss emoticon. She had to be drunk. She was only affectionate when she's drunk, otherwise it was games.

"You drunk?" I asked.

"I'm on my way back home."

"Why?"

"I felt bad, and I realized that I kind of missed you." I smiled when I read that.

I didn't reply for a couple of minutes, and I'm guessing patience was not her strong suit.

She sent another text. "I want to see you, what are you doing?"

I looked at the two girls I'd danced with as they talked to each-other. I could take them both home tonight if I wanted to. Then I looked back at my phone. I didn't have to think about the decision.

"I'll be right back," I told the girls.

I texted Kyle: "I'm going to Londyn's house."

Then I walked out of the club.

I knew I wouldn't be back.

Strange Tides

I took an Uber back to campus because I had been drinking.

I picked up some extra clothes and ran a quarter-mile down the sidewalk at midnight in my Timberland boots. Kyle always gets mad at me for wearing them because he said I was already too tall.

When I got to her house, I waited five minutes outside to catch my breath so it didn't seem like I'd run all the way. I texted her that I was outside, and she opened the door within seconds. I casually strolled up the walkway as if I was just getting there.

"Were you waiting by the door for me?" I asked to start this off flirty.

"No, I saw you standing outside for a few minutes, so I came and waited by the door," she said. Then she glared at me. "Why were you standing around?"

I let out an awkward laugh. "I was, uh, making sure this was the right house."

"Right," she said sarcastically. "I'm pretty sure you saw Crystal, so you had to know this was mine."

"I did see her outside, yes," I said. I had to change the subject. "So, what kind of snacks do you have?"

She took me into the kitchen and pulled out Raisin Bran or something like that.

"Ew," I teased. "What are you, a grandma?"

We were right next to each other. She said something but I forget what it was. It was mindless babble. The kind of talk before a kiss. I looked into her eyes. The pupils were dilating. Her eyes lit up a bright amber color. *Kiss her,* I thought. *Just kiss her.*

"Do you know that feeling right before two people kiss for the first time?" I asked, reciting a line I had heard Jason Capital say.

"Yeah," she whispered. "Why?" She wanted me to kiss her; she didn't back away. I was frozen. Six inches separated our lips. I just had to basically fall into her.

"I like that feeling," I said, pulling away. I was too nervous.

I walked upstairs and found her bedroom. She followed. Then I took everything off except for my boxers and jumped into her bed trying to look relaxed.

"You don't get the bed," she said, taking her jewelry off. "I do."

"I am the guest," I gasped as if I was offended.

She unwrapped her hair out of a bun and shook her head. "We're sharing it."

"Okay," I said, misdirecting it to make it look like I was onto her plot. "But no funny business."

"You're so stupid," she said. She was bulletproof.

She turned off the lights and climbed into bed.

Eventually, I just had to ask. "Why did you come back for me?"

"Well," she said, "when I canceled, I felt like you were actually upset, and I realized this meant you must be into me." I just listened to her talk. I couldn't see her because the lights were out. "Kyle said you do have other girls," she continued, "but he also said that you talk about me a lot... I was starting to like you, and that scares me."

I rolled on my side to face her. "Why does that scare you?"

"I missed you tonight," she told me. "At the bar, every guy was buying me drinks, but I couldn't help but think about you." She paused, but I didn't say anything. "But I'm afraid that if I open up to you that you'll break my heart." Under all of her tough exterior was just a woman who was closed off.

"Sometimes, you have to risk being open with someone to have something special," I said. "What if I really do care about you and desire you but you don't give me a chance because you're too busy living in the past and judging me based on guys who broke your heart?"

"Why do you say these things?" she whispered.

"What do you mean?"

"I feel like you understand me, but you could just be saying all of this and not truly mean it."

"You could be right. I could be lying to you right now. I could have several other girls and just use you. I could have you open up to me and tear your heart apart. But I can promise you it's not that at all. I don't know how to prove it to you, and I probably can't, but I just know one thing, and that's that I'm here right now with you. I could be with any other girl, but I ran down the sidewalk to see you... I was so excited."

"You ran down the sidewalk?" she said in awe.

"Well, yeah."

She laid her head on my chest. "Your heart is beating fast," she whispered.

"Is yours not?"

"You make me nervous too..." she paused. "I don't know why I feel this way, but laying here in your arms feels so right to me. It's scary because it's never felt this right before."

"Maybe...it's because it is right," I told her.

She lifted her head off my chest, and I could tell she was looking at me. She climbed up to my face. I could feel her breath. Finally, no games, no nothing. It was pure openness and vulnerability; we kissed.

I pulled back. "Oh my gosh."

"What?" she asked.

"I was right a week ago in the car." She tilted her head in confusion. "You really are a bad kisser," I flirted.

"Shut up," she chuckled, leaning in to kiss some more. Just as I thought would happen when we were in the car.

We made out for hours, then we would talk, and then we would continue to make out until around 4 a.m. When I opened my heart, I just wanted her to understand. I wanted to give, and because of that, lying there with each other, making out, and talking was better than any sex I'd ever had.

We fell asleep in each other's arms.

That night, I realized that I tended to try to fulfill my need for love through the quantity of women I could get. But putting it all away for one woman brought out feelings that were indescribable.

The beauty of this is that when I finally connected with someone on this level, I realized that all of those rejections, those heartbreaks, and other relationships in the past didn't compare to the feeling I had with her in that moment. Man must taste the bitterness of defeat, heartbreak, being played, and rejection in order to taste the sweetness of true love.

To find love we have to get our hearts broken a couple of times. To get love, we have to be played by people, like Haley and Melanie, and be rejected over and over again. To find love, we must first know what it feels like to be truly broken. To give someone everything you have but find out it's not real.

To know who 'the one' is, we must first know who 'the one' isn't.

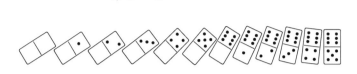

Chapter XI

Yuanfen

The Game of Fate

[Yuanfen: A Chinese phrase translated as "destiny" or "fate."]

What determines a man is not by what he wants but by what he's determined to struggle for. His level of commitment to what he believes he wants and the reward for his commitment is turning that dream into reality.

Londyn and I were together the next night and the night after that.

She made me pancakes in the morning. I scheduled a date for the hibachi grill. I picked her up, and this night would get interesting.

When I picked her up, I asked her, "How many times did you change your outfit for me?"

"Only four times," she said.

I was ready in ten minutes.

She looked incredible. She wore tight blue jeans, a grey turtleneck with a black vest over it, and to finish it off, a red scarf that made her plump lips stand out.

On our way there, she said, "I've never been on a real date before."

"What?" I was stunned, but this wasn't the first time I'd heard this.

I realized that I'd been to the hibachi a lot. When the chef is cooking it in front of you, he will flip some food, and you have to catch it with your mouth. I caught mine, and Londyn took a few tries to catch hers. I teased her every time she missed. When she finally caught it, I grabbed her knee and it tickled her. Our chef took a doll out that was like a spray gun and started to spray sake into our mouths. She chugged it for twenty seconds straight. When I said, "Wow, you're so good with your mouth," she choked on it and gave me a look.

While we were eating dinner, a girl walked past our table. "Hi Connor," she said. I turned my head to see Haley's roommate. The last time I saw her was on Valentine's Day when Haley ditched me for her ex-boyfriend. Maybe she found the stuff I left on the roof. If not, then it had been up there for a while and was probably covered in snow.

"Hey," I called back as she walked away. Then I looked at Londyn.

She stared back at me expecting an explanation.

"So, what did you think of the yum yum sauce?" I asked, attempting to ignore what just happened and the look she was giving me. I couldn't escape.

"Who is that?" she asked. "Is that one of your *other* girls?"

I tried to laugh it off. "Uh no, I used to be friends with her, why?"

"Well, she sat down with other people, and they are all eyeing us."

I didn't turn around. Instead, I just smirked. "They are probably eyeing *you* for the same reason that I eye you when you're not looking – to look at you." I looked her up and down.

She rolled her eyes and smiled. "You're such a flirt."

When we got up to leave, I helped Londyn put her jacket on. I turned around and was about to walk with her when I met eyes with someone. Haley was sitting there with four other girls including her roommate. They were all staring.

The chef had just created a huge flame on the grill, which lit up all of their faces. As soon as the flame was lit, he extinguished it. Her face went dark. I thought I felt something for Haley, but I guess I was the only one who felt it.

Londyn turned around. "Are you ready to leave?" she asked.

"I've been ready, babe."

She smiled, and I took her hand. On our way out, I let out a soft laugh.

320

"What?" she asked.

I was ready to leave the past behind me – Gary, the women, and everything, not the restaurant. I was ready to create a future with Londyn. I wanted to start fresh.

Part

The Detox of Life

I sensed that life had a natural cleansing system to rid us of those who are toxic in our lives. Just as the body detoxes us of diseases, life tends to tell us when it's time to walk away from those who are holding us back.

Haley wasn't going to make it easy for me to detox her away, however. She called me in tears the next night at around 11:30.

"Can I see you?" she sobbed.

"For what?"

"I made a mistake. I'm sorry. I've been working up the nerve to call you for a week now." She started to pour her heart out to me. "My roommate found everything." She started to cry again. "She found the card and the champagne, and everything else on the rooftop."

"Didn't you... Didn't you leave me for your ex?" I replied.

"Yes," she said. "I thought I missed him, but I was stupid. I shouldn't have ever let you go."

"You forgot about the flowers on the swing set."

"What?" she sniffled.

"I didn't just make the rooftop great," I told her. "I laid flowers on the swing your father used to push you on. I was going to take you there first, and then you also forgot about the reservations I made for you."

"You did all that?" she whispered.

"But most importantly...you forgot me."

"I'll do anything for you," she begged and began to cry. "That other girl won't treat you the way that I will!"

I felt bad for her, but that's the only thing that I felt.

"You're right," I said. "She won't treat me how you would. She won't leave me. She won't play me. She will put me first. She won't forget about me."

I could hear her crying. I let up a little bit. "I'm sorry, Haley, but it's just too late."

"But I still love you," she professed.

"Goodbye Haley," I said.

After I hung up, I realized that I might have never been with Londyn if it wasn't for Haley making that decision on Valentine's Day. Without Haley, I wouldn't have known that total vulnerability is what builds strong relationships. Perhaps I wouldn't have had what it takes to break through to Londyn's heart.

Life works the way dominoes tend to fall. When it's falling, we may feel uncertain, scared, or out of control. But after it's fallen, we realize that it creates a bridge leading you to something better.

People come into our lives for a reason. Haley reminded me of Romans 8:18 – "The pain that you've been feeling can't compare to the joy that's coming." Everything falls apart right before an invaluable gift manifests.

After I hung up on Haley, I also told the other girls who I was seeing that we had to stop. Some of them didn't handle it well, some cried, and others posted sad quotes and references to me all over social media, but Haley handled it the worst after our talk.

A couple of days later, I was at a Starbucks in Indianapolis. When I finished, I walked outside to my car, and there was a bright-orange piece of paper under the windshield wiper. I was pissed because from far away I thought it was a ticket even though that was where I always parked. When I pulled it out, I realized it was a folded notecard. I slid the note out from the wiper and opened it.

It was a drawing of me with X's for both of my eyes like you'd see in a cartoon character who died. Right below it was the handwritten message: "Asshole. You're making a huge mistake." I'm not a lawyer, but this definitely felt like a threat.

The only person who knew I was there consistently was Haley, so I knew it was her.

I looked around, scanning the area to see if she was around or watching me. Then I walked around and checked my car for dents or scratches she could've left. Everything was okay, so I left. Later when I was with Londyn, she saw the note. "Oh my God," she gasped.

"I know," I said, chuckling. "Doesn't my hair look awful in this drawing?"

"That's what you're worried about?" she asked as if I was stupid. "Your hair?"

The one person I regretted calling most was Gary, but I knew that it was time to walk away from this community. Being in the clubs and doing that work would hurt my relationship with Londyn. To me, this was more valuable than anything I was getting from Gary.

I realized what Jay realized when he left. The only way to beat this game is to walk away from it.

"I think it's time that I leave this community," I told him. He handled it surprisingly well.

"I thought this day would eventually come," he told me. "So, you've found a girl?"

"I have," I responded.

"Knowing you, she must be quite the catch. You were my favorite, but if relationships and love are your goals then I shouldn't hold you back from that."

"Thank you," I whispered. It was hard to part from him and this world.

"Relationships are one of the biggest challenges in life," he told me. "Here's my advice: *Remember that bad times never last but strong relationships always will.*"

Part

Romeo Romance

I went out to a familiar bar with Londyn and her friends to secretly celebrate my parting from Gary, the business, and my past lovers but it was full of drama.

"You are a pimp," said the guy who saw me dancing with the two soccer players a few weeks back. "You're with a new girl every time I see you!"

I looked at Londyn, who was already looking at me with her eyebrows raised. "I don't know what this guy is talking about," I mouthed, shrugging.

She glared at me, mouthing the word, "Sure," and sarcastically nodded.

He got close to me. I could smell the alcohol on his breath. "Teach me everything you know." He started getting a little too close to Londyn, so I stepped in between them.

"Wait here," I said to him. "We'll be right back."

We weren't coming back.

I walked Londyn, Megan, and Kennedy to a different spot in the club. While they went to the bar, a hand grabbed the sleeve of my leather jacket. *I hope this isn't Alysa,* I thought.

I turned around to see Haley's roommate. The one who answered the door for me when I was supposed to pick her up on Valentine's Day.

"Easy on the jacket," I scolded her, wiping off my sleeve just as Ace would do. "Are you here to thank me for making your Valentine's Day better?"

"Well, no," she answered. "But we did enjoy it, yes. I'm telling you that you're treating my best friend wrong."

I knew she was talking about Haley, but I played dumb. "Oh, that guy?" I asked, pointing to the drunk across the bar. "He was just acting weird and getting way too close. I hope you understand why we walked away."

"What?" she snapped. "I'm not talking about that guy; I don't even know that guy!"

"Oh," I awkwardly intoned. "Then who?"

"You know who," she snapped. "I'm talking about Haley."

"What does she have to with anything?"

"You don't know how much you'll regret this. She cares about you so much, and you're treating her like an asshole. She doesn't deserve that."

"I'm an asshole? For caring about her?" I asked. "I'll regret what? Someone who I can't trust, who's deceiving?" I wasn't going to let myself be labeled as that. "You saw everything I went through for her. I spent money and time on her, but she cared about me so much that she ditched me for another man. Explain that to me. Give me one good reason why I'm wrong about any of this and I'll take back everything. I'll take her back."

She said nothing.

After a few moments, Londyn – after a couple of shots – grabbed my arm and pulled me away. "You're mine," she stated, pulling me in for a kiss. I think that jealousy like this, to me, is hot. This is how Londyn showed her deep desire for me. I find it to be one of the most attractive things when a woman will fight for what she wants, unafraid to pull you away from other girls.

Londyn was all over me. She clung to me, made out with me, and everyone around high-fived us. Then Kyle walked in and saw us. He told me later that he was slightly surprised to see this based on the difficulty she was giving me a couple of weeks before.

The music switched to a slow song, and a few couples stayed on to dance. Londyn tried to walk away towards the booths because she was self-conscious about being one of the only ones on the dance floor. I pulled her back in.

"Connorrr," she whined. "Everyone is going to look at us."

"Forget everyone around us, and just look into my eyes," I whispered. "This moment feels so right, so let's make it special."

She looked me in the eye. My boots stuck and unstuck to the drink-covered wooden floor. The room was barely lit, and her face lit up on and off with the strobes. It set a dark and mysterious mood.

Her tone changed. "What are your intentions for me?" she asked.

"To make you fall in love. Then we will get married and go on our honeymoon to the Bahamas." I then told her the sad story from way back about when I was a kid when it was always my dream to go there except that our boat didn't dock and we sailed away as I watched the island shrink.

"Aw," she said. "I want to take you there."

"Please do, and when we go, we'll hit a bar on the beach as the sun sets, and everyone will love us," I playfully mused. "We'll get invited to a party that night on the beach. I'll look at you, and you'll look at me. We both know we're going. This will be the start to three years of romance before I decide to finally break your heart."

She started laughing and hit my chest. "I've never been in love before."

I looked in her eyes. "You're going to fall for me," I said. "I'll be the first..." I paused, looking away. "And I'll also be the last," I assured, looking back into her eyes.

She was speechless. For the first time, the mouthiest girl in the world had nothing to say. She just stared at me with eyes of intense desire. Almost like she was hurting for a kiss.

"Kiss me," she whispered, eyeing my lips and my eyes up and down. I grazed her cheek and we kissed, and then she buried her head in my chest. While she was there, she started to fiddle around with the collar of my sweatshirt. I thought she was fixing it, but instead, she bit my collarbone. It felt like electricity went down my arm and into my right leg. I swayed and almost fell because I never had a girl do this to me before. I grabbed a pillar next to me for balance.

I'd never even heard of this move.

"What was that?" I blurted.

"I watched a movie with Megan the other day, and I saw a guy do this to a girl, so I wanted to try it on you," she giggled.

I looked at her skeptically. "What kind of movies do you watch?"

She laughed. "It was just some romance."

"I thought you said you weren't really the romantic type."

"It was just a movie!" she snapped. "I'm not."

I just smirked and looked her in the eye as if I was denying what she was saying. She took me over to a table after the song ended, and we talked one on one. It was beginning to merge from winter to spring, and the spring showers began to pat against the window and glide down in streaks.

"Tell me something about you that I don't know," she said.

I explained to her the situation that went on with my family. My parents hated each other, and I always thought, growing up, that they didn't care about me. I later realized they just showed their love to me differently. This was a story about how I let go of my expectations and attachment for love.

Expectations & Suffering

It was my track and field senior night in high school when all of the graduates were celebrated.

After the track meet, the seniors lined up on the track with their families in front of the stands when they were individually announced. The bleachers were decently packed, and I was excited to be recognized.

I sent out invites to my closest friends and my family. I wanted them to be there for me, and I realized that this was how I wanted to feel loved by them. If they came and clapped for me, and took pictures with me – just be there for me – it would make me feel special.

After my parents divorced, a lot of love was replaced with hate and resentment.

I explained to Londyn how I struggled with my relationship with both of my parents. When I was a kid, whenever I would ask my mom for help with paying for clothes, she would always break down and cry. I eventually learned to stop asking her. We were going through bankruptcy when I was in grade school, and I was wearing clothes that I grew out of years ago and clothes with holes in them. The kids would laugh, saying, "Your pants are flooding," which meant they were short, but it was because I couldn't afford new clothes.

On the other side of the coin, when I would ask my dad, he would get angry, cuss me out, and possibly even hit me. One time, he hit me so hard, my retainer flew out of my mouth.

To get onto the track and field team and other teams in high school, I helped my mom paint and clean rich people's houses in order to come up with the $150 fee.

Don't ask me how I was eating because times were tough. I was either eating chicken-flavored ramen from the pot or I stole food from events, but my mom didn't know about that.

"So, don't tell her that," I told Londyn, winking at her after telling her all about my checkered youth. "She'd like to meet you though."

"Wait," Londyn paused. "You told her about us?"

"Yeah."

"Why?"

"Uh," I stuttered, avoiding the question, "let me finish my story first."

I remembered one day we were cleaning this gorgeous abandoned penthouse condo in Indianapolis that cost about $800,000. There were curved hallways, crystal chandeliers, obsidian countertops, and I remember that a professional painter came in to paint murals in the rooms. One of the rooms of the children who used to live there had a wall-sized mural showing a beautiful sunset behind a tree in the mountains. The tree was black with a purple glow slowly fading around it.

I was supposed to be cleaning that room, but I just sat there and stared at it. It was so beautiful, but I was so jealous at the same time because I wished I could have had that in my room. The rest of the time my mom and I were cleaning this condo, I was complaining.

Eventually, she broke down and started crying.

I always hated seeing my mom cry. I felt like shit, so I held her tight in my arms and cried with her. We were both hurting. "Don't worry mom," I said, wiping a tear away. "One day, I'll buy you anything you want."

My senior night, was a trial to see who was really down for me. To me, that night meant the world. To me, that night would show me who was all in for me and who wasn't. I thought that night I would feel wanted and valued to them. The day came, and the only friend who came was Adonis.

I was getting texts about an hour before my race from friends and family saying they were sorry but something came up. I knew nothing came up; they just didn't want to come. My heart started to sink because the way I viewed it at the time, if they didn't come then I obviously didn't mean enough or wasn't valuable enough to them.

My heart wasn't broken just yet.

Among family members, my dad, mom, stepfather, and brother all showed up. They were going to be the ones to walk with me in the ceremony.

Moments after my race, all of the seniors were getting ready to line up with their families. This was going to be my moment. Even though my dad and mom hated each other, meaning that there would be tension having them standing right next to each other, I still needed them there.

My mom, stepdad, and brother went up to me right before the walk.

"Hey, we're not feeling well," they told me. "So, we are all going to go home. Is it okay if we miss the ceremony?"

I nodded. "Yeah…that's fine," I whispered.

But it wasn't fine.

As these words were coming out of their mouths, I could feel my heart breaking more and more. Part of me wanted to stomp the ground and demand they be there to walk with me, but the other half of me wanted them to want to be there with me. I didn't want to have to beg anyone. I wanted my friends to want to be there too. I just wanted to feel wanted by somebody.

I turned around and walked away. Tears began to accumulate and tried to spill out, but I forced them back down. The only person who walked with me was my father. I wrote down something special I wanted the announcer to say about my mom, my stepfather, my brother, and my father. There was a bouquet for my mom.

Even though the relationship with my father was always rocky, we bonded deeply in that moment. The announcer called my name and began to read what I'd written about everyone who wasn't there to hear it. Lastly, he called my name, and I put my hand up to wave to the crowd, but my head faced down.

I was bawling.

Tears were rolling down my cheeks as I held the bouquet for my mom, but my hair was so long it covered my eyes, so nobody could tell.

I cried because I felt so worthless. In this moment, I felt I wasn't loved by anyone except for my father and Adonis. It didn't mean the others didn't love me, it was just how I perceived it.

My dad noticed, and he put his hand on my shoulder. "I know I might not have been the best father and that I haven't always been there for you," he said, "but I won't miss moments like these from now on even if I'm on my deathbed."

It was because of that moment that I learned to truly stop expecting anything from anyone. The only person who was with me in my hardest times – when I was crying, hurting, and felt like I couldn't take it anymore – was me. There may be people who have been with you through a lot, but nobody has been through every moment with you except yourself.

People have a perception of how a mother, a father, or a significant other should be, but instead, I learned to accept them and love them for who they are, not who I want them to be. I believe people suffer when they want reality to be something other than what it is instead of accepting reality and who they are.

I needed to realize that they are who they are, and I needed to learn how to accept that and love them through it instead of focusing on how my needs weren't being met.

In reality, you may feel frustrated when you aren't being loved by someone, but when you take a look at the full picture, you may realize that the other person may feel just as frustrated. They might be trying their hardest to give love to you in their own way, and maybe you aren't receiving or accepting it. They may not know any other way.

Love is patient and takes time to grow.

Part of love isn't only giving but learning how to accept the love others try to give.

They were loving me as best they could with what they had to give. I couldn't be upset with the effort. My mom bought me a dog when we were going through bankruptcy, and it was really one of the only things I had because right after the divorce, we had to sell all of the toys my brother and I had to stay afloat.

Both of my parents loved us in completely different ways, but that helped me learn how to not only love in my own way but embrace fully when someone else is attempting to show their love to me. It helped me learn how to let go and accept others for who they currently are as well as accept myself for who I am.

I think that night needed to happen because afterward, my father told me that he was going to seek emotional guidance from a counselor. He and I tended to be prideful, but we both realized that half of the battle is realizing that there is one to begin with.

Even if my mom and I never discussed it, I think she knew that it impacted me deeply that they left because she never missed an event of mine after that night.

All someone can really do is love without expectations because if you love somebody expecting to get something in return, it's not love.

Part

The Talk in the Mist

Inevitably, Londyn wanted more from me.

After I told her that story, she moved her chair over close to mine and examined my face.

"You have the perfect smile, the brightest eyes, perfect lips and hair…" She paused. "But now that I've gotten a good look at you, I see that you have flaws too." It was a weird way to compliment somebody.

"Um, thanks."

She reached her fingers out towards my face. "What's this?" she asked.

She was reaching for the slight indent under my left eye that I'd had since I was a child.

Right before she touched it, I grabbed her wrist. She jumped.

"Don't touch," I whispered, looking down at the table.

"What is it?" she pestered. "Is that a birthmark?"

I stood up and grabbed her hand. "Let's get out of here," I urged.

"And go where?"

"Let's go to your place," I said.

I dragged her along as she continued to ask me questions about my face. Persistence was one of her strengths. She was the first girl to ever notice that mark. Perhaps one day, I thought, I'd tell her more about who I am and about my scars…or perhaps I wouldn't.

We hadn't had sex yet, but I knew it was coming soon.

We began to run down the city sidewalks in the rain. Within a few steps, I was already soaked. At my car, I didn't unlock the doors.

As the rain was roaring down, Londyn yelled, "Unlock it!" She tugged on the handle as if it was going to magically open.

"Come kiss me instead," I yelled back.

"What? Are you crazy?!"

"We're already soaked," I said as the rain started to calm.

I walked over to the other side of the car. When I placed my hand on the side of her face and looked her in the eyes, everything went silent. The rain was pelting the hood of my car and the sidewalks, and a car alarm was going off down the street, but in our heads, it was silent. It felt like time stood still when we kissed. Her mascara smeared down her cheeks in black streaks. I melted. I was cold moments before, but now it was as if the rain was steaming off our skin.

Whenever we kissed, I couldn't get enough, and it felt so warm. It felt so right. I spun her around and aggressively put her back against my window and we started to make out. I ran my fingers like a comb through her wet hair. She grabbed the back of my head. This could be one of the top two romantic moments of my entire life, the other being the time when she drank the sake for twenty seconds.

"I've never kissed a man in the rain before," she whispered.

I opened the door for her and helped her in.

When we got back to her house, I grabbed a towel from a closet and wrapped it around her. I led her into the bathroom where I combed her hair and blow-dried it.

In history class, I learned about a famous trade route called the Silk Road. I don't remember much about it, but I knew that the shine of her hair reminded me of silk, and the way it straightened reminded me of a road.

She laid on top of me and we started making out, but she stopped and sat up.

"So why did you tell your parents about me?"

"Why is that such a big deal?"

"I just feel like you would only do that if it was serious between us."

"I thought that there was no 'us,'" I responded, air-quoting the word 'us' like she did on the washing machine a while back. "Isn't that what you said?"

She started blushing. "I feel different about us now." She'd said that word again.

"What do you mean?" I asked. She got off me, now lying side by side with me. I just watched her mouth move as she talked.

"I've never felt this before with a boy," she said. "I told you I've never fallen for a guy, but it feels like I'm right on the cliff about to jump off."

"You're falling for me?" I asked.

"It feels like it, but I don't want to unless you feel the same way."

What she didn't realize, and something I was trying to deny, was that I was already in love with her.

I was fighting myself, though. Every time I had fallen in love, I either ruined it or it ruined me.

"What are you trying to say?" I asked. "It sounds like this has been on your mind for a while." I heard Kyle say this to his girlfriend, and it seemed to work in getting her to communicate.

She bit her lip nervously. "What are we?"

"Please don't ask me that," I responded.

"Why?" she snapped.

"Because I don't know what I want."

I lied.

In my heart, I knew I wanted Londyn to be mine, but in my head, I didn't want to open myself up and let someone have the ability to break me all over again.

She moved away from me slightly when I said that. I could tell it wasn't what she wanted to hear. "I'm falling for you too, Londyn," I said. "But I'm resisting and trying not to give in."

It was interesting how at the beginning of the book, and my life, I was constantly seeking love, but now that I felt it and now that it was real, I didn't want to reach out and accept it from Londyn.

"Why won't you let me in?" she asked, putting her hand on my chest.

I took her hand and moved it away. "Let's talk about something else."

"Why?" she asked, sitting up to face me. "You said that night, the first time we kissed, that maybe we both just need to let go. Was that just a lie?"

I looked away. "No, I truly believed that."

"Believed? So, you don't anymore?" she retorted. "Why can't you be with me? You told me to let go of my past and to trust you, but you're not willing to do that for me? I've opened up to you, I've trusted you, and now that I'm giving you all of me, you want to walk away?"

She was pouring her heart out to me.

"I do want you, but I'm conflicted because part of me just feels like I need time," I said.

She laughed and rolled her eyes.

"You are just like every other guy," she sneered.

Those words hit me hard. After a few moments of silence, she began to cry.

"Come here, let me explain myself," I gently intoned.

I wrapped my arms around her fragile body. She smacked my hands away.

"Just leave," she cried. "I need to take some time to myself too."

"Listen, I wish you would…"

"Just please go," she interrupted.

I put on my clothes that were still damp from earlier, and she laid down facing away from me. On my way out of her house, I felt like it was wrong to leave, and that I should've stayed and done something. But I didn't know what else I could do.

I had one idea left that was risky. I left my $300 red USATF jacket there on purpose because I figured she would text me and tell me it was there. Or, knowing her, she'd possibly burn it. I hoped it was the former and I could convince her to see me in person so we could talk further about this whole situation.

I stepped outside. It seemed that the rain had long stopped but was replaced by a dense fog. I could barely see my car parked on the street 15 meters in front of me. It was an eerie feeling, and it was so quiet that my mind was playing tricks on me; I believed I heard whispers.

It seemed the world laid quiet, and unclear, as did I.

Confliction feels foggy. I knew that I was in love with Londyn, but part of me didn't want to be and tried to deny it. It seemed that I was a hypocrite. I told her to let go of her past and trust me, but I couldn't do that for her. I thought I learned how to love and be open, but it seemed when I truly had it, I was more guarded than ever.

After Melanie, Haley, the people who I thought were my friends, and everyone else, my heart was locked away.

When Londyn was beginning to break through the cage I locked it in, I decided to run away. They say that everything we desire is behind fear, and at first, I always desired true love, but now I feared to be vulnerable and open. Why did it work like this? At first, I chased love and never got it, but now that I didn't want it, I began to overdose on it. I turned my back on love because I realized I didn't need it, and in this exact moment, I found it.

I feared that I might have lost it now after that night's conversation.

Part

Scar

48 hours had gone by with no communication. My plan wasn't working. Kyle and I both agreed that I should probably call her and apologize. On the third day, a Thursday, I decided to pick up the phone.

"Hi," she said.

"Hey, I think I owe you dinner and a talk."

"No thanks."

"You're right," I said. "Let's just skip dinner and talk instead."

"Why do you want to talk to me?" she asked.

"We had a misunderstanding, and I want to explain everything."

"There's nothing to explain, Connor. You don't want me. You just want to charm me, lead me on, and have me fall in love with you, but after I do, you'll leave. You think dinner and a talk would just fix everything overnight?"

"I messed up, and I'm sorry. I miss you, and I want to make things right with you. I'm trying really hard for you, Londyn, and it's because I care. It's because I *luh*…"

I stopped myself.

"You *what?*" she asked.

"I need to tell you something, but I want it to be in person," I said. "If you don't want to see me, I understand, but just know that I've done everything I can to see you and make it right. But I can't do that without you there to listen."

"We can go out Saturday night," she said. "Plus, I kind of need to give you back the jacket that you forgot at my house."

When Saturday came, we met downtown, but she ignored me much of the time.

When I tried to dance with her, she would for a second and then walk off. When I tried to joke with her, she would make a "humph" noise as if she was fake-laughing. She was clearly upset with me.

When she danced solo, guys eyed her.

"I'm going to get us a drink, and then we are going to sit down and talk," I told her when a song ended. "What would you like?"

"I'll try a Long Island to see if I like it as much as you," she said.

The only connection we had all night was when she held onto my hand as I walked away toward the bar. They casually split apart when I got too far away. It was cute. A song came on, and I watched her move her body to the music, dancing alone. She was still eye candy to me. I ran into somebody as I walked away because I was checking her out. I apologized and went to the bar.

Londyn was wearing these black jeans that stretched around her curved legs and disappeared beneath her tan boot line. She wore a light-blue, stiff denim jacket. Her hair tightened into a ponytail then fell as gracefully as a waterfall as it flowed out of the band it was held in. To me, even with all of the people there, it seemed as though there was always a spotlight on her.

She was also the spotlight to another guy.

While I was walking back with two Long Islands, I noticed some guy lurking around her. He was like Alexander. Stalking her and ready to make his move at any moment. It didn't feel right. I started to hustle through the people.

Her back was faced towards him, and the people divided for me at the right time. I could see exactly what happened.

I was too late.

He came up behind her while she danced, put his hand out, and reached between her legs from behind. He grabbed her ass and wrapped his fingers underneath to grab her pussy.

He literally assaulted her right in front of me.

Londyn jumped and turned around, expecting it to be me, but when she realized it wasn't, she pushed him away and started yelling at him.

I dropped both of the glasses when I saw this.

They shattered simultaneously.

Londyn was steaming, and my blood was boiling. I moved the remaining people aside who were between me and this guy. I didn't know what I was going to do, and even though I wasn't fully together with Londyn, the image of another man feeling her up made me erupt.

I grabbed the guy by the collar of his cheap dress shirt.

Londyn grabbed my arm. "Connor! Stop!" she yelled.

I reached back, then swung, and his nose cracked between my middle knuckles. His nose and mouth gushed blood. He went down holding his face, and blood started to soak into his white shirt. I was going to spit on this guy, kick this guy, and break every bone in his body.

"Hey!" his friends yelled, moving through the crowd. Not only them, but security was swarming us fast.

I grabbed Londyn's hand and ran in the other direction from where they were coming from. I figured that because he was on the ground, I would be the one who'd get arrested.

Now that we were running away, I would definitely get the blame.

"Stop them!" they yelled, but before security knew what was happening by the door, we ran out. My car was around the corner, so we hopped in and waited until everyone passed.

We ducked our heads, and I held my finger over Londyn's lips.

She tried to talk, so I put my hand over her mouth. She slapped my hand away.

"What the fuck, Connor!" she yelled.

I started the engine, put it in sport mode, and drove away quickly.

"You almost killed that guy!" she continued yelling. "What were you thinking?!"

"I didn't kill him," I said. "But I should have."

A painful sting accumulated on my hand.

I looked at my hand gripping the wheel and realized I must have landed my punch crooked. His tooth had pierced the skin on my pinkie knuckle down to the bone, but in the moment, I didn't feel it because of the adrenaline. It was bleeding a lot. I switched hands on the wheel and put my knuckle in my mouth to suck off the blood.

"Are you crazy?" She slammed the dash in front of her. "You didn't have to do that to him!" She was right in a way. I didn't have to, but I thought about it.

What would a real man do?

"You're right," I said, taking my knuckle out of my mouth. "But I needed to." Then I put it back in because it was still bleeding.

Most men might have let it slide, but is that even a man if he lets something like that happen? If I loved her and was crazy about her, the animal would come out and I'd wreck shit for her. I just didn't understand; if she's supposed to be my queen, how I wouldn't fight for her. I've met few 'men' and a lot of boys, but what would a real man like Jay, Kyle, or Ace do?

I tried to put my hand on Londyn's to calm her down.

"Why," she snapped, pushing my hand off. "Why do you care!?"

She went on and on and on…

"I can't fucking believe you're defending a guy who literally assaulted you, and you're mad at me, who protected you!" I yelled back.

"I'm not yours anyway, according to you!" she steamed. "Why does it even matter who touches me, because you don't claim me as yours!"

I slammed on the brakes. We were on a main road, and cars honked as they went around us, and the lights streaked past.

"You're going to kill us!" she yelled. "What are you doing!?"

I pulled over to the side with my blinkers on, put the car in park, and looked at her.

"You're mine," I said. "I don't give a fuck if it's your family, some gay guy, or an asshole from the club, nobody is allowed to touch you the way I do. Nobody is allowed to hold you the way I do. Kiss you how I do and talk to you how I do."

I leaned in, grabbing the side of her head. We made out for a moment before she pulled away.

342

"Have you lost your mind?" she spat. "What are you even saying?"

"I don't care if you thought what I did was wrong or right, and maybe it wasn't…"

"It wasn't," she interjected. I ignored her because I thought I was right, but trying to win through logic wouldn't work.

"I don't know why I did it, but the image of another man touching you…my body just reacted on its own. If I didn't care about you…if I didn't desire you, and want you…I wouldn't have done anything." I paused and then continued. "I'm saying that I want you to be mine. Just you and I, and it's what I truly want now."

"Oh, now you want me," she mocked. "Where was this?"

"Love is something I've never known. I've only known what it feels to be broken by it, but with you, I can't help but feel it. I don't know what it feels like, but what I feel when I'm with you makes me believe in it." I gripped my steering wheel tight.

"I don't know how to love either, Connor," she said. "I've never felt this way before."

I looked at her, and we stared into each other's eyes.

"I miss you when you're not around," she said. "I think about you constantly. I was afraid that I scared you away the first night we spent together, but here we are again… Just tell me how to love you, but I can't if you won't let me," she whispered.

My heart thumped a little harder when she said that.

"Let's figure it out together…" I told her, leaning in, which she did as well. We began to make out.

She didn't like the warrior side in that moment at the bar, or at least, she said she didn't. But looking back, she'd love me deeper than she ever had because I fought for her.

343

Part

Panic

The first time we made love was in a car.

Instead of the word 'fucked,' it was 'made love' because that's what it felt like.

While we made out, I rubbed her and she whispered, "I'm literally so wet right now."

These were some of my favorite words. She reached over and felt on my pants. "You are literally so hard!"

"What are you going to do about it?" I smirked.

In the back seat, she blew me while I rubbed her clit. After a couple of minutes, I moved her to sit on top of me. She looked me in the eyes when I started to rub my dick against her. I put it in, and she rode me in the back seat, slowly.

My tinted windows were fogged over after fifteen minutes, but while she was having her way with me, I noticed her face light up.

She stopped while I was fully inside of her, wiping her hand on the back window.

"Oh no," she said.

No doubt about it, the lights of a Charger, which meant it was probably a cop.

I realized we were parked in the street.

"Get your clothes on fast!" I exclaimed. "It's a cop!"

I threw on my pants without the underwear and a jacket without the shirt underneath.

I couldn't believe I was always late to school when I was younger.

This time it took me eight seconds.

As the cop began to walk up to our car, Londyn was just putting her shirt on, and I rolled down my window while scrambling to put my shoes on. By accident, I put the left shoe on my right foot and my right shoe on my left foot.

"You're kind of parked in an awkward position," the officer joked.

"Trust me, sir, I know," I responded, implying the inside joke to Londyn that he had walked up while we were having sex. She slapped my arm.

"Is everything alright?" he asked.

"My car was making a funny noise, so I immediately pulled over, and I was just about to check it out."

"Let's take a look," he said. "Pop the hood."

He shined his flashlight on everything and then shined it on me. I thought he was looking down at my feet because my shoes were on the wrong feet.

I'm so busted, I thought.

"Is your hand alright?"

A sigh of relief came out. He was looking at my busted hand and not my feet.

"Yeah, I just cut it badly on something sharp when I was digging around in the engine because I barely had light," I laughed awkwardly.

Londyn asked what we were doing, and I showed her the scar on my knuckle. In front of the police officer, she took my hand, cleaned it off, and wrapped it up. In this moment, I felt so warm and loved by her.

"You should be okay to drive," the officer said. "I'm going to head out. I just got called for backup." I shook his hand with my left hand, the one without blood on it, and thanked him.

As he walked away, he turned back around. "Next time you get dressed, put your shoes on the right feet." He knew this whole time what we were actually doing. Londyn made a face and sat back in the car.

I feel bad about lying, and I don't support it, but what could I have even said? "Yes, officer, I hit someone in the face earlier and probably broke his nose. Then we ran away because I didn't want to get caught, and we were just having sex in the middle of the street when you walked up." I bet that would have gone over like a lead balloon with him. I hope he can understand now, if he reads this book, that Londyn's and my hands were tied...

Mine were tied metaphorically, but Londyn's were physically – if you get what I mean.

The Labyrinth of Love

Love is perfect because of its imperfection.

When I was in elementary school, I had an obsession with the *Percy Jackson* book series.

Specifically, I loved Poseidon and Hades. In one of the books, there was something called 'The Labyrinth,' a maze with a beast that tears teams and people apart.

I always viewed relationships as a labyrinth. Only the most committed and dedicated partners are able to figure out its challenge together. It's designed to expose the relationships where the couples aren't fully committed by splitting them apart and to award the relationships where the couple works together to figure out its maze. Every turn you make determines whether you will be rewarded with deeper, stronger, and more intimate love versus the feeling of slowly splitting apart.

As the weeks began to go by, it was rocky. Relationships are difficult, but Londyn and I wanted to find a way to make it work. I wanted our love to be deep, and I wanted to connect with her and continue to connect.

The trials and the challenging times were also what defined the moments and the feelings I'd remember forever with her.

At the start of summer, our unspoken love for each other would be tested.

I was at university getting my master's degree, but I wanted to take steps toward creating a career for myself revolving around relationships and dating.

I had an opportunity to attend some events that would transpire over the course of about a month worldwide that would feature Jason

Capital, Tony Robbins, Gary Vee, and many others.

The downside was that the events started in 48 hours, and to me, it was a once-in-a-lifetime opportunity. Some of these events were the final ones for these self-help and personal-development stars.

I'd never have another chance like this. I knew, on the other hand, that distance and extended time apart can kill a relationship.

I wondered how Londyn was going to handle this. I pictured in my head that I would try to bring it up casually, yet every scenario seemed to end in a loss.

I thought that I would take her to her favorite restaurant, Texas Roadhouse, to try to make amends in hopes it could cover for this sudden change of events. I picked her up and tried to play it cool. But as we sat at dinner, she could read me like a book.

"You're acting strange," she said. "What is it?"

I took a hot roll from the basket, ripped off a piece, and dipped it in the butter.

"There's something I'm not really sure how to tell you, Londyn," I said, playing with my roll. "I guess I just need to say it."

"I'm listening," she said, leaning in close.

Without telling her, I drained about $8,000 from my savings and signed up for multiple events. I showed her the emails.

"According to this, you would leave tomorrow?" she hesitated. "Why didn't you tell me?"

I looked down at the table.

"What are you going to do?" she asked.

"I think that I need to do this," I said. "It doesn't mean that I don't care about you, and it doesn't mean that I'm leaving you forever. I see a future with us, and I want to be with you for a long time."

She reached out her hands across the table, and I held them.

"I'll miss you, and I would do anything for you to stay," she said. "But if you think it's important, I don't want to hold you back from it." This was the woman I needed. The one who wanted me to stay but saw how important it was for me to do this.

"Could you take me to the airport tomorrow?" I asked.

"Of course."

We were up until midnight packing my bags, and then we laid down together. She held onto me tighter than she ever had, and we basically stayed up all night talking about how much we were going to miss each other.

"You can't leave," she whined.

"You'll talk to me every day, right?" I asked.

"Yes," she said, pouting. "Better not talk to other girls out there either."

The goodbye at the airport the next morning was difficult but impactful. We held each other for a few minutes.

"You're going to change the world; I believe in you," she said, holding me tight.

"How do you know?" I asked.

"Because you're unlike anyone else I've ever met."

This was the first time the mouthiest man in the world, me, was speechless.

I kissed her forehead. "I'll be back before you know it." I started walking but stopped and turned around. "And don't bite any collarbones while I'm gone."

She rolled her eyes as I walked away. I went up the escalator and could still see out the windows. She stood there watching me. Just like the time when I first met her when I walked away for Haley and we made eye contact as the elevator doors shut. This time, I would only walk away from her to build something for myself. I'd never leave her.

The labyrinth that we had to face was the distance.

Over time, I tended to see patterns in my family's and friends' relationships, and one was when the men sacrificed everything for their women – their careers, what made them happy, and their friends. Every time, it eventually led to a dead relationship.

I felt this calling in my body's inner compass to pursue a new life and a new mission, and I already knew what would have happened if I'd stayed home with Londyn instead of choosing to pursue my dreams.

In summary, it was what David Deida said about a man's purpose in *The Way of the Superior Man*:

"Every man knows that his highest purpose in life cannot be reduced to any particular relationship. If a man prioritizes his relationship over his highest purpose, he weakens himself, disserves the universe, and cheats his woman of an authentic man who can offer his full, undivided presence."

While I was away in multiple states including Wisconsin, Florida, Illinois, and more, I had dinner with Londyn over video chats almost every night.

For men struggling with long-distance relationships, a good start would be to have Facetime or video dinners with her where you tell her what to get or cook for herself and she does the same for you. I treated every dinner like an actual date, but I was dying just to touch her, kiss her, and feel her.

Even though we were hundreds of miles away from each other, our relationship deepened every day.

The week before I returned home, Londyn texted me: "I'm longing for you... The night you come home, I'll let you do anything you want to me... You can have all of me... I'm yours."

The night I returned home was the night before July 1 – my birthday.

We hadn't told each other we loved one another yet, but that night it would finally manifest...

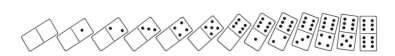

Chapter XII

Kara Sevde

Blinding Love

[Kara Sevde: A Turkish concept defined as 'black love' or to be deeply in love.]

Swans are known to be one of the only animals to mate for life, and if their mate happened to die, they can die of heartbreak.

I loved Londyn, but I didn't know how to just say it.

The night I returned, Londyn was celebrating Kennedy's acceptance into medical school, but she was getting impatient. They were out at a bar for the celebration, but she knew that I had landed already. She didn't want to be rude and leave.

"I want to see you tonight," she texted me. "As soon as I can leave, I'm coming straight to your arms." But I didn't want to wait, and when I found out where she was, I had an Uber take me because, after a day of flying, I didn't feel like driving.

As soon as I stepped one foot inside the building, she turned her head and looked at me. It's as if she could almost feel me there.

Disbelief first, then denial, and finally joy all formed on her face within a few seconds.

I couldn't help but smile.

She was the most beautiful girl in the world to me. Everything about her. Her perfect teeth behind her model-like lips. The way her eyes looked so dark, lined with mascara, but sexy. The way she put her silky brown hair in a messy bun. The way she wore her skintight black dress that showed off every curve like smooth clay pottery. She still couldn't believe that I was real.

Without a word, we hugged.

"What are you doing here?" she whispered.

"I couldn't wait another second."

For the rest of the evening, she clung to me like a koala.

As we sat next to each other, she started rubbing my inner thigh. I was talking to Megan across the table, midsentence, when Londyn grabbed my dick under the table.

"Woah!" I gasped. She snuck a touch on me.

"What?" Megan asked, looking confused.

"I'm sorry, I'm just really excited." I gave Londyn the look, and she looked back at me with a mischievous look. She wanted to play, so I was going to play.

Megan asked me a question, and I looked at Londyn. "I'm not sure. What do you think, Londyn?"

I was going to get her talking to return the favor. When she started talking, I repositioned my arms to where they were now under the table. My right hand and fingers wrapped around Londyn's inner thigh, very close. As soon as I put my hand there, Londyn, in midsentence, stuttered and cracked a smile. She knew what I was doing, but I looked at her as if I was very engaged in the conversation so nobody would pick up on our game.

I took two fingers and began to finger-walk up her inner thigh as she talked. She began to lose track of what she was saying.

"That's really interesting," I said, rubbing her over her jeans. "Please tell us more."

Londyn put her hand on me, and I was as hard as a diamond.

"Oh my gosh!" she blurted. Then we looked at Megan sitting across from us.

Megan looked at me, and then at her, and then back at me. "You guys are weird," she said as she stood up to walk away.

I leaned in close to Londyn and put my hand on her collarbone.

My lips grazed her ear.

"When we get home, I'm going to rip your clothes off as soon as we step in the front door," I whispered. She could feel the warmth of my breath on her ear. She closed her eyes and took a deep breath as if she almost couldn't handle it.

"Can you please just do it to me now?" she begged.

"Let's leave then," I said.

She slid out of her seat to use the restroom, and as she walked away, I watched until the view of her was blocked by a man who sat down right in front of me.

"Long time no see," the man said, looking me in the eye.

My eyes squinted, my eyebrows clenched, and my jaw flexed. This would be the last place I thought I'd see…

"Noah," I growled. "It has been a long time, hasn't it?"

He sat across from me wearing a grey wool coat, a beanie, and an arrogant smile. Over the years, he perfected his looks with a sharp jawline, a shadow of facial hair, tan skin, an easy smile, and hypnotic brown eyes. He was like the inverse of me. I wore darker colors, and women told me I had dreamy blue eyes and the best smile.

However, it seemed we differed in another way. After Noah had dropped out of IU's business program, he wanted to become the world's greatest pickup artist and start a business around that. But it failed because he had screwed so many people over that nobody wanted to do business with him anymore. At least that's what I had heard from Gary and connections from IU.

"What do you say?" he asked. "How about some pickup for old times' sake? Whoever gets the hotter girl has to pay $100 to the other. It'll be just like the good old days."

Londyn was walking back from the bathroom. I slid out of the booth and made out with her. "Wire-transfer the $100 to my bank," I told him with a smile. "I'm retired from that stuff."

I never got the $100.

The Heart's Truth

The word 'love' is over-vocalized but underperformed by most.

There are people – like Noah – who will use you and then toss you aside for a better opportunity. Others tell you to follow your dreams, and once you do, they try to tell you how stupid you are for doing it.

The world is heartless, and when you give the world your heart, most likely it will try its best to crush it. But sometimes, you have to get your heart crushed in order to learn and grow. After you get your heart broken, you have to pick up the pieces and rebuild it stronger.

The right people will cherish you, treat you as if you're priceless, and not use your vulnerability against you.

"Who was that guy?" Londyn asked, clicking her seatbelt into place. I explained to her everything that happened. She asked to see a picture of my ex, and when I showed her Melanie, she said, "Wow, she's really pretty."

I said nothing.

After a few seconds, Londyn asked, "Do you think she's prettier than me?"

This was a tricky question.

"Babe, to me, you are the hottest girl I've ever laid eyes on," I assured her.

She said nothing.

She still wasn't convinced, so I needed to speak the truth from my heart.

"I remember the first night I ever saw you," I told her. "I saw you walk in, and I just couldn't take my eyes off of you. I knew you were *'the one'* from the moment I saw you. Even though you denied me a thousand times," I exaggerated, "I just couldn't give up."

She broke into laughter.

Women love hearing about your perception of them the first time you ever met them. The drama, the story, hooks her. It's for the same reason that you would enjoy hearing a woman tell you that you are the hottest thing she's ever seen.

"If that guy slept with her while you were dating, why didn't you punch him in the face?" she asked.

"No reason." I tried to play it cool, casually saying this as I looked out the window.

"There's always a deeper meaning behind a person's actions and words, so tell me the truth," she said. "Why did you punch that guy who touched me when we weren't even dating, but you acted like you didn't care that your ex cheated on you with him?"

"Probably because you mean more to me than any girl ever has."

She looked at me and started to blush.

When I was the villain, I learned a lesson when I tended to sacrifice my people for my benefit in the club. When you stab someone in the back and screw them over, you in turn leave your back wide open to be stabbed by someone else. I did to others what Noah did to me, and in that process, I hurt a lot of people and pushed everyone out of my life.

As soon as Londyn and I stepped inside, we scratched up the paint on my walls. We knocked lamps over. Paintings came off of the wall. We were all over each other until we finally found my bedroom. I pressed her against the door and put her arms up. I whispered in her ear everything I planned on doing to her.

"You have the voice of an angel," she breathed, gripping the back of my head, "but the tongue of a devil." I didn't exactly know what that meant, but it sounded romantic. It reminded me of what one of my mother's old friends said about a weird talent I had.

When I was a young kid, I showed them that I could touch my tongue to my nose.

She smiled and said, "You know, one day a woman will love you for that." My mom slapped her in the arm and gave her 'the look'.

355

When I asked what that meant, she replied, "You'll find out one day."

Today was the day that I found out what she meant.

I nibbled Londyn's jaw, and she bit my collarbone.

I took off my shirt, and she felt down my body.

I unfastened her belt and slid it out loop by loop as she did with mine.

I knew that every girl has a freak in them, but not every girl has the right kind of man who can bring it out.

One small candle lit the corner of my room.

The weak flame could barely light our faces, and the shadows danced on the walls. It set the mood of uncertainty, mystery, and romance.

I kissed up her thighs, looking her in the eyes to see her reaction.

"I hate you," she said, but she loved it.

In the moment, my mouth moved on its own. "Too bad, because I love y–" My mouth slammed shut before I could finish the sentence.

"Connor..." she whispered, sitting up. "You what?"

I looked away. "I... I'm not sure."

She caressed my cheek, gazing into my eyes. "You love me?"

I paused for a moment; the only sound that filled the room was the raindrops pelting the skylight window. My voice broke the silence.

"Yeah... I love you." A flash of light illuminated the room for a split second followed by a crackle of thunder in the distance.

"I love you, Connor," she said, glancing away. "But I don't want to."

I squinted my eyes. "You don't want to?"

"Because eventually, we will have to leave each other."

In a year from now, she would be leaving to go to school.

I thought that if we do love each other then maybe we could make it work, but I heard once that you should leave tomorrow's problems for tomorrow's you. I didn't know what our fate would be – for her to leave me would break my heart – but right now, in this moment, it was worth it.

356

"Every time we kiss, one of them will be our last no matter what, Londyn," I told her. I learned this from years ago when I watched Hakan's friend pass away before my eyes.

I began to elaborate on this thought. "Whether it's marriage, and we grow old together and pass away, or whether our last kiss is tonight. Eventually, everything has to come to an end."

I used to believe, long ago before my parents' divorce, that love is supposed to last forever. Love is free-flowing, just as Joel Kramer says, so we shouldn't fear it but be glad that we got the chance to experience it together.

"Love will come and it will go," I told her. "All I know is that right now, I love you. It's here, so let's dance within it."

"I love everything about you," she responded, leaning in for a kiss.

We made love over and over again for hours. After a while, on the outside, it didn't look like love. I had scratches, bite marks, and probably bruises all over me. These were the marks of our love. Even the broken man can love if he can piece himself back together. She was like the perfect fit to my puzzle piece. There are many pieces in the box, and they say there are many fish in the sea, but it seems that there's only one at a time that fits perfectly like this.

I looked at the clock. "It's 4:30 in the morning," I blurted.

"That's fine," she said. "It's summer, we're living, and it's your birthday."

It was as if we thought the same, we saw the same, and we were one. No matter what would happen with us, this night would remain in my heart forever.

Love had branded me, and it would leave its mark forever.

The Piece That Took the Most

It was another week of déjà vu. First Noah, then another.

In the morning, while she was asleep, I pulled the blanket over her to make sure she was comfortable. I left early to do some writing in a coffee shop, and even though I'd only slept five hours, I felt fully rested.

I sat by the window and people-watched as they passed by on the sidewalks.

My heart stopped when a man walked past. It was Ace. A beautiful woman held onto his arm, laughing and smiling. I pinched a bead on the bracelet he gave me years ago. I was about to get up, but I stopped myself when I noticed a diamond ring, fitted to her ring finger, that sparkled in the morning sun.

It had been years since we talked, but I just wanted to go up and talk to him. I believed he wanted absolutely nothing to do with me, however. My heart was reaching for him, and I wanted to see if he was married now. I gritted my teeth and squeezed my hand into a fist. My eyes filled with tears. I wanted to find out everything about him that I'd missed over these past few years…that I should have been there for.

After a few minutes, I ran out of the coffee shop and looked in the direction they went. I looked store to store, but he was gone. I was too late. I walked back to my car and drove away.

I was gone for a few hours, and when I returned home, Londyn had left but she left a note that read, "I'll be back soon."

She returned with a load of wrapped presents.

"These are for you. Happy birthday!" she screamed with the biggest smile on her face.

She spoiled me with shoes, designer clothes, and a watch.

Out of everything, I probably loved the card she made me the most. She used a lot of colors including my favorite, orange, and stapled them together into a small book.

"The glue is fresh, so be careful with it," she said, sitting cross-legged next to me.

I didn't know what she meant until I opened it.

The first page read, "July 1st has become one of my newest favorite days… Words cannot describe how much you mean to me and the impact you've had on my life… I've never been so happy…to be your girlfriend, your best friend, and lover, and I want it to be forever… Here's a timeline of when we first met to the rest of our lives…"

She printed out a Google Map of Bankers Life Fieldhouse (The Pacer's Stadium) where we first met, cut out a heart shape from the map, and glued it to the card. The next page displayed the same heart shape but with the location of where we had our first kiss. Then our first date at the hibachi grill and its location. Our first dance and where we made it exclusive together. On the final page was my address with the caption, "The first place you told me that you love me."

As I was reading this, it reminded me of when I was growing up.

My parents tried to show me their love, but I didn't know how to receive it. I craved it, but when I got it, I rejected it. It made me uncomfortable, and I never knew why.

A part of love is not only giving it but learning how to receive it as well because people show love differently. How one might tend to show their love might be completely different from how you think love should be shown.

Londyn was trying to love me as hard as she could, and if I treated this like I didn't care then it might shut her down. It made me uncomfortable for some reason, and I didn't know why, but I tried my best to show how grateful I truly felt.

"This is incredible," I said. "No one has ever done anything like this for me before."

She smiled and perked up. "Really?" I sat and admired the makeshift book for a few more seconds, and then she rubbed my arm with a giggle.

"You're cute," she said.

"What do you mean?" I snapped automatically. I shook my head. "I mean…what are you talking about?" I started to smile.

She smiled, shaking her head.

I guess I still wasn't good at it, and she saw this, but she could see my heart.

I was touched.

Managing Emotions

The condom broke.

"What do we do?" Londyn asked, panicking.

"We need to go now," I fretted.

We got dressed quickly and hopped in my car.

I stopped at a local CVS, turned off the car, and looked at her. "Are you coming in with me?"

"Why are we here?"

"You have to take the morning-after pill," I said. We didn't have time to lose.

"You act like this has happened before," she snapped, crossing her arms. "I'm not going in there; they are going to judge me."

I sighed and got out of the car. I put my hood up so nobody could get a good look at my face. The pill cost something like $60 and was in a locked container with an alarm on it. I had to bring it to the checkout desk for the person to unlock it. It was 11:30 at night, and I saw something that I didn't want to see – a line to check out.

These next few minutes, I felt the most judged I've ever felt. I stood in line with people who greeted me. They looked at what I was holding, then my eyes, then away.

Finally, I reached the cashier, as a few people started to fill the line up behind me at the register. I hoped we could make this quick, but the woman at the register said, "Just one second, I need to get some paper from the back." I tried to lean awkwardly over the register so I could cover up the container, hoping nobody would see it.

My ruse was blown when the woman unlocked the container. "You need to be at least eighteen to buy this; can I see your ID?" Because the store was quiet, everyone in line heard what she said. This brought everyone's attention to me. I could feel their judgment radiating.

I paid and hustled out of the sliding doors to the car.

"What took you so long?" she asked. I stopped ripping apart the box and looked at her.

"Do you know how awkward it is to stand in line for this?" I asked, handing her the pill.

She stared at the pill. "How am I going to take this without water?"

I sighed and walked back into CVS again. I grabbed a small water bottle and stood in the line behind everyone who had just seen me walk out with that pill.

"Back already?" the same woman at the register asked.

I looked away. "Yeah."

"You know, if this happens frequently…" She paused abruptly as if she'd made a mistake. "I mean, if you come here often, you could sign up for our rewards."

"I think I'll pass for now," I rasped, clearing my throat. "But thanks."

I hopped back in the car and gave Londyn the bottle of water. Finally, she took the pill, and now we left our destiny to time.

I was sure that I was going to be a father because she didn't get her period for two weeks. I was doing my best to stay calm.

For two weeks, we were waiting and waiting for her to get her period, and it wasn't coming. For weeks, she was on edge. For those weeks, she was constantly throwing jabs at me. "Why would you do this to me… We're never having sex again… The pill says it's only 99-percent effective, which means I could still be pregnant."

If I was going to be a father, then I needed to be there for the kid. My mom bought my stepfather a plaque that read, "Anyone can be a father, but it takes someone special to be a dad." I didn't want a kid now, but if I was going to have one then I needed to give the child love with everything I had.

It was a beautiful morning. Full of sunshine, chirping birds, and Londyn's nags about whether she was pregnant. We sat down at my kitchen table just after I had made us waffles. I spread peanut butter over the top of mine, and it melted into the crevasses. I cut a piece off, dipped it in syrup, and ate it while Londyn continued to pester me.

"How am I going to explain this to my family, Connor?" she asked.

I only had one option left – a pregnancy test. I went back to the same CVS with her, and we went through the same argument about her not coming in with me. I sighed, then I got out of the car.

I wasn't sure what I was looking for, but I thought I'd found it when I read on the directions that she had to pee on the stick and that it was 99-percent accurate. I stood in the line, and this time the small box didn't stick out like the giant container the pill came in, so I felt a little less awkward. When I got to the front of the line, I realized it was the same woman from the last time. I hoped she wouldn't recognize me.

"Welcome back," she greeted, recognizing me. She scanned the pregnancy test. "Did you still want to pass on the rewards card?"

"Just give me the card," I snapped, rolling my eyes. I filled out all the information and put the card on my keychain. My first points on the card were a pregnancy test, and they would also be the last because I was never coming back. It would take just sixty seconds to get the test results. When we got back to my place, Londyn went into the bathroom to conduct the test while I got on my knees and prayed.

I heard the bathroom door open, and I jumped up as if I wasn't doing anything.

"Well?" I asked. "What does it read?"

Silence filled the room.

"Connor, I can't believe it…" she whispered, looking down at her feet.

My heart dropped. I was certain her next words would be, "I'm pregnant."

"Gotcha!" she laughed. "It says negative."

I raised my finger as if I was about to say something. Then I just got up and walked away.

I definitely joked like that with her, but when I got a taste of my own medicine, it was bitter. She skipped across the living room and hugged me from behind.

"Is this your way of telling me you're sorry for giving me hell these past two weeks?" I asked.

She giggled. "Yeah."

I dried the dishes from breakfast and put them away while she washed the waffle maker in the sink. As I was putting a plate away and behind me, I heard her drop the waffle maker in the sink. I turned around to see her holding her hands over her face. She started to cry.

In that moment when she hurt, it seemed that I hurt. But I didn't even know what I was hurting over. Thirty minutes ago, she was mad at me; five minutes ago, she was happy and giggling; and now, she was crying as if she was watching a soap opera.

Londyn's emotions were all over the place. She had a mouth when she was angry, but when she cried, it was so innocent. I've seen women who have been hurt badly by men and who have built high walls to defend against opening up to anyone ever again. But imagine how powerful their love is behind those walls.

Behind Londyn's seemingly random emotions had to be a deep love for me waiting to be awoken.

A woman is like a treasure chest, and inside is a love deeper than we can imagine. However, to open that chest, she needs the key, and the key is the right man. Women cannot be women without men, and vice-versa. A key to nothing is useless, while a chest that can never be opened is a curse. Behind these tears she cried was a woman who could love me, but I needed to figure out how to love. I needed to be that man who has the key to open it.

Love was something I never was good at...but I had to give my whole heart.

The G's of Love

Love is giving without expecting anything in return.

For a woman to cry in front of her man shows how much she trusts him, how much she's open, but also how much she needs him in that moment.

I turned off the water to the kitchen sink and brought her in close to me. As tough as she was, she felt so fragile in my arms. I didn't hold her because it was right, but it was what my body seemed to do on its own because my heart felt her needing me. I carried her to the couch in the next room. I held her until the cries turned into sobs.

"I would cry, too, if I broke your waffle maker," I gently teased, rubbing her head.

"It's not that!" she snapped, digging her face into my chest.

"What is it?"

"I don't know," she sobbed.

At least we narrowed the reason down to anything but the waffle maker.

"I just love how detailed you are," I said sarcastically like I was talking to a child.

"I don't know why I'm crying; I just feel like I've been so hard on you," she said. "You've dealt with me so well, and I just feel like I don't deserve you."

"Isn't that what a relationship is?" I asked. "Life has brought us together, and it's testing me constantly to see how committed I am to you. If I would leave when it gets hard or give up on you, what would that say about me and how committed I am to you?"

"I don't know," she sniffled, shrugging her shoulders.

She knew; she just wanted to hear more. Her crying stemmed from uncertainty. She needed to feel my strength and sense how committed to her I truly was.

I took the back of my finger and wiped a tear away.

"I told you that I love you, Londyn. I made a commitment to you to love you at all times. Not just the good times, but through all the times. The bad ones, the good ones…" I paused, looking her in the eyes. "And even the times when you challenge my patience." I softly smiled.

I was using a technique called the 'pattern interrupt' in which you say or do something to break the current state she's in.

She cracked a smile and dug her face back into my chest.

"Do you think I'm crazy?" she asked.

"Oh, babe…" I said delicately, cupping her cheek, "of course I do." I smiled.

She gasped and hit my arm. "I'm not crazy!" She turned away and acted like she was pouting.

"Pouting, huh?" I asked, attempting another pattern interrupt. "Why is it that I fell in love with the most stubborn one of all?"

She broke out laughing. She couldn't keep up the act for long.

The pattern interrupt is the gift of man. When she gets into a mood, it's hard for her to break out of it by herself. It's like she sees in colors, and when she's angry, everything is dyed in red. Help her, and give her your gift of breaking through and releasing her from her emotions and guiding her back into the woman she truly is. Be the key to her treasure chest.

I kissed her forehead. "Life is way too short to live unhappy."

"You know, these past two weeks were actually kind of fun," she said.

"Fun?" I asked as if she was losing her mind. "What about this was fun?"

"Maybe in the future, we could have children," she said. "I was kind of liking the idea of being a mom."

"Oh yes, please," I said sarcastically. "Because I would love to experience you like this for nine months straight." I said this even

366

though deep down, I would love it.

She laughed. I realized, from this moment, that in a healthy relationship, love shines its brightest when there are three things present. Three words beginning with the letter 'G' need to happen in order to experience love to its fullest depth.

The first of the three I discovered: *Giving.*

Londyn had multiple sides to her. Like a Sour Patch Kids candy, she would be sour, extremely sour – but then twenty seconds later, she would be sweet. On occasion, it could be frustrating, and part of me would begin to get annoyed. I realized that my feelings of frustration with these emotional cycles came from a place of selfishness. If love is about giving, and you're focused on how difficult it is for you, then you're not giving her what she needs.

This poisons the relationship.

Criticizing her and saying what's she's doing wrong comes only from the selfish mind, which causes her to shut down even more. There's no room to give when your mind is focusing on what you're not getting.

These emotions from Londyn were a package deal. Sometimes I thought, *I wished it could all be so simple. No outbursts, no problems, and it's peaceful all the time.* As soon as I thought this, I realized how bland the relationship would be. Londyn drove me wild sometimes, she pissed me off, and she was crazy, but this was a woman. So random, illogical, and inconsistent, but on the opposite side of her anger, hurt, or tears was a love for me so deep that I couldn't put it into words – when I broke through.

Even in relationships, women test their men. The most loving women are, ironically, the ones who will test their man the most. To many, it may seem like constant jabs and pestering, but this is a gift she gives her man. She knows his weaknesses, and she is obnoxiously intolerant of a man who gives in to settling on average. She wants the best version of him to come out at all times.

A man needs to give that version of himself constantly – loving through the nuisances, the random emotions, and especially during the times when he doesn't feel like it. It takes true commitment from the man, but without true commitment in anything, you will never achieve depth.

I learned quickly that a woman will throw her worst moods at a man to see whether he can handle it or if it's a weakness of his. If he cannot handle it, it will keep reoccurring more and more until he can.

This is, in fact, part of the labyrinth that splits relationships apart because a lot of men give up when they haven't given their full gift to her. Feminine nature will always be complex from a man's point of view.

In this moment, when I wiped her eyes, the man in me wanted to try to fix something. I thought that because she was crying, there was a problem. For a man, the logical thing is to find the source of a problem so he can then fix it. But a woman isn't a furnace that's stopped working or a cracked window. You fix those problems, but when you try to fix her, she only becomes angrier or hurt. The problem gets bigger.

When a woman feels like you are trying to fix her then, from her perspective, she thinks you're viewing her as broken. Like she's a cracked window, and she sees you just replacing her with someone else. She believes she isn't worthy of your love because, to you, she's a broken problem. Londyn just wanted to observe my ability to open her and feel certain that I wasn't going to leave her.

A man shouldn't try to change her or fix her. That's a battle that will never end. Instead, choose to commit to her and fall in love with her – flaws and all. That's also what giving is. It's extended without an expectation that she will change.

She showed loved differently than me, but most people give love in the way they would like it in return. I had to observe her, and part of commitment is learning how she gives love because that's most likely how she wants you to show your love to her.

I realized that for someone you love, *don't give anything less than everything.*

Righting My Wrongs

"You should just call him," Londyn argued.

Ever since I saw Ace, the feelings were eating at me to talk to him.

I stood up and looked out the window at the beautiful city skyline. "I'm not going to do that," I said, looking at her through the reflection of the window.

She gave me a look. "You said that you've fallen in love with the most stubborn woman, but it seems that I've also fallen in love with the most stubborn man."

I smirked and rolled my eyes as I stared at my reflection in the window. My phone began to vibrate, and Londyn looked at it; her eyes got really big.

"Who is it?" I asked, turning around. I was hoping that it wasn't an ex-girlfriend of mine.

If it was then I would have some explaining to do for something I hadn't been doing.

"It's Ace."

"Ha-ha, you're hilarious, Londyn," I said, faking a laugh.

She nodded her head, passing me the phone. "Seriously."

I held the phone in my hand and stared at the name because I thought it wasn't real.

"Answer it!" Londyn snapped.

His voice was clearer and more powerful than ever. "I know we haven't talked in a while, and I'm a few weeks late, but I wanted to tell you, 'happy birthday!'"

"I've been thinking about you," I spilled. "Is there any way we can meet up?"

"I saw you get into your car at the mall on your birthday, and my fiancée kept telling me to go up and talk to you…but I just couldn't do it," he responded. "I thought you wouldn't want to talk to me."

"Wait," I interrupted. "Fiancée?"

"I got engaged," he said after a short pause.

I didn't say anything.

"I'm leaving for California tonight, and I'd love to see you before I leave."

"You're leaving?"

"If you're not doing anything, you can come over tonight," he offered. I looked at Londyn, and she stared back at me.

"I think you need to go make things right with him," she whispered.

"I'll be over shortly," I said, hanging up.

Light & Dark

He was still at the same place after all those years.

He stood at the front door waiting for me. The last time I walked out that door was when I found out Melanie was cheating on me and, overnight, my life fell apart.

I was nervous, but I had to face this mess that I made and make it right. As I walked up the steps, it felt like I was walking over those pieces that I left here. I could pick them up and try to rebuild everything I destroyed with Ace, but I thought I'd leave them on the ground.

I was a new man, and this time I thought I'd rather just start fresh. It was time to restart, not rebuild.

What do I say? I wondered.

The other half of my mind answered in Londyn's voice: "Whatever is in your heart."

Ace and I shook, and then I gave him a hug. I tried to figure out the words to say – how to say I was sorry. It felt I was trying to force a watermelon through a small hole.

"Where's your fiancée?" I asked.

"In California," he replied, shutting the door.

"I wish that I could've met her before you both left."

"Maybe if you come to California."

We went down into the basement and sat in his home theater. I sat in the same recliner I did years ago. Ace sat in the chair where Alexander sat when he showed me the messages that were proof of Melanie cheating on me.

We talked for hours about his life, mine, Londyn, and how he found his passion for cars.

"How did you propose?" I asked. I usually ask everyone about their love stories and how everything unfolded. I couldn't help myself but ask; it was my passion.

"Why?" he smirked. "Are you going to propose to Londyn?"

"I don't think that I'm the marrying kind," I responded, playing with a thread on my shirt.

He was one of the few who knew about my past. My parents' divorce and how it tore me apart. In my heart, part of me wanted to experience everything with Londyn. I loved her, and eventually, this would mean marriage, but to me that was a big step. I inherited a curse from my family that destroyed love, but maybe it was my purpose to learn how to be the man who could put an end to that curse.

I thought that if I slightly let go of my love with Londyn, I would re-create what I saw my parents do to each other when I was a young boy. However, if I held on too tightly, I would squeeze it to death as I did earlier in my adult life.

"I see you with a family," Ace said. I'd never given the idea a thought until he mentioned it. I was perfectly fine being in this love story with Londyn, but I believed that with every love story, there's either an end or it lasts 'happily ever after.'

"Is anyone else coming?" I asked Ace, changing the subject.

"I texted Adonis, and he opened it but didn't respond," he sighed.

He claimed that it was okay, but I knew him too well, just as he did me. I could tell he was hurt by this. This was one of the major turning points in his life. Marriage and moving across the country with a woman. However, none of our old friends came. Tonight, to him, was what my senior night on the track was to me. Tonight, it was the same story for Ace, but this time I was the only one of our old friends who showed up for him.

I knew this moment was the best time to tell him the truth.

"I know I haven't been there for you as much I should've been, and I'm sorry," I told Ace. "But from now on, I will be." That's what my dad said to me years ago on my senior night, at least. It felt like a weight had lifted from me after making this promise.

"I appreciate that," he said. "I'm sorry too." He paused for a moment. "People haven't supported my decision to go through with this and move out there, but I feel like it's the right thing." Ace was seeing something that nobody else could see. He had a vision in his heart and felt a calling to start a new life out there with this woman.

Who was I to judge this? I didn't want to sway his opinion. As a friend, all I could do was support it fully and believe in his vision because nobody else seemed to.

Finally, at 11 o'clock, it was time to take the first steps into his vision. It was time for him to hit the road. My heart sunk. He left everything behind except for a few bags with clothes, his dog, and his car. He rolled down his window after the engine purred to a start.

"My fiancée told me that maybe I should've tried harder to stick with you when I told her about what happened between us," he said.

My heart thumped.

"Londyn said the same to me about you," I smirked.

"This feels right," he assured me, nodding his head slightly. "I know now that this isn't a 'goodbye,' it's just a 'see ya later.'"

I smiled. "Just save the 'best man' spot for me at your future wedding."

He smiled and rolled up his window. He took two fingers and snapped them together like scissors. He mouthed the word 'cut' behind the glass. I did the same thing back. It felt like I had finally taken a step back in the right direction with Ace and with my own life.

I'd truly miss him and his one-of-a-kind personality.

He drove around the corner, and as he did, the moonlight lit up the sidewalk and the streets. As he drove out of sight, a cloud began to cover the moon. It looked as if the moonlight was chasing him when a wall of darkness from the cloud swallowed everything in its path.

The cloud moved past quickly, and a line of light chased the darkness away. I should've been sad, but I smiled. Even though I hated myself for what I did to him, life told me in this moment that it was necessary for us.

The Sun's Presence | The Moon's Beauty

When you look up at the moon, every night it seems to have a different shape and is in a different location. Women are like the moon. They change their mood constantly.

Men have to be the sun. It's always there, radiating each day. Even with clouds in the sky, it never fails to shine through and light the world. A man should never stop radiating his full presence of love to his woman. His love should be abundant just as the sun's light is everlasting.

I tended to live in my head growing up. I was constantly thinking about either the past or the future. From waking to falling asleep, my mind could never turn off. Presence is the opposite of being so caught up in your head. It's living in the moment, but it was my weakness.

I never felt my mind turn off until Kyle taught me, indirectly, what it felt like.

"Watch this," he said. We were driving on the highway in his BMW.

"Watch what?"

"I got my ECU tuned today."

"ECU?"

"Basically, the computer that runs the car," he said. "I used a program to modify the way it distributes fuel and air to the engine so I can make some real power."

I had no idea what the fuck he was talking about.

"I had to throw some upgraded parts on and make sure things are running smooth," he continued, "then I got some extra horsepower."

"So how fast can we go?"

"Let's find out."

He stepped on the accelerator, and my head flew back into the headrest. We went from 70 miles per hour to about 120 in four seconds. It was like a rocket. The speedometer still climbed with ease as we began to roll faster and faster.

We hit 130, and then 140, weaving through the traffic on the highway. They honked, and it looked like they flipped us off. I couldn't tell because we passed them too quickly. I swallowed to wet my dry throat as sweat accumulated on my forehead.

We hit a top speed of 156 miles per hour.

This was one of the scariest moments of my life. One pebble, one wrong twitch of the wheel, and we would be dead. This was what total focus and presence was. In this moment, we weren't thinking about anything. Our entire focus was on what was happening right before our eyes.

I'll freely admit that this wasn't the stupidest thing I have ever done, but it definitely wasn't the wisest. We weaved between two trucks, coming within a couple of feet of hitting them.

"Holy shit!" Kyle screamed, beginning to laugh. He slowed the car back down to about 100 miles per hour.

When we slowed down, I realized I had been holding my breath the entire time.

"Oh my God," I exhaled.

After I let my heart calm down and my breathing slowed, I came to a realization. I'm not in any way telling you to hop in your car and go as fast as you can to come to the same realization as I did. But in that moment, I felt what true focus and presence was. While we were going that fast, I had no thoughts going through my head. I was fully there and involved in that moment with Kyle.

This reminded me of Londyn and any relationship for that matter.

Sometimes, a woman will become angry, bitchy, and moody, and it's only because she is starting to feel your lack of clarity, presence, and focus.

Women will say things like "It doesn't matter," "Leave me alone," or "It's fine." But as men, we can feel in our guts that it's not.

However, most of the time men walk away and fool themselves into believing everything is actually fine. When she says this, she's challenging you to pursue her with all of your love in that moment.

It's *not* fine, and she wants to know you care enough to open her back up. When she pulls back, she's calling to you.

Most men are very masculine when challenged by another man.

For example, while I was in the car with Kyle, we searched what our Chinese Zodiac animal happened to be. His is a Tiger and mine is an Ox. He automatically said, "The tiger would beat the ox in a fight." Out of anything he could've said, he said that. I naturally responded, "Maybe, but if the ox gets one clean hit with its strength, with those horns, that tiger is catfood." We went on for five more minutes about a topic that didn't matter at all. He challenged me; I fought back – that's being a man.

When a woman says "I'm fine," men read it literally and believe it's all okay. In reality, it's another test. She is seeing if you care enough to find out what's really bothering her.

Over time, if her man neglects her, she will close off and become bitchy, moody, and down. Without deep and loving intimacy from you, she hurts. A woman's life is largely based on connecting with you. Feeling the depth of your love is her oxygen.

For a man (but also for many women), it's his climb to becoming the best at what he does. A man can get resentful and frustrated toward his woman not because of her but because he feels like he's failing. This is a direct reflection of his inability to penetrate her moods and tests – and to convert her mood into love once again. He feels that the only option is to leave, but this would only mean he's given up.

One of my favorite quotes is from Stephen Covey: "Most people do not listen with the intent to understand; they listen with the intent to reply."

Most people hear, but they don't listen. Men hear what she's saying and take it directly to heart. That's not listening. To me, hearing is shallow, but listening to someone is feeling what they are feeling, understanding what's burdening them.

376

Her life is the present, which means men need to learn how to embrace it with her fully. Looking in someone's eyes when they are explaining something to you or asking high-quality questions goes a long way in making somebody feel like you truly care about them. Especially when she's been closed off and hurt over time, she will need that.

A relationship is like a plant that needs consistent watering and nutrients. It needs the presence of the sun – where you are able to give her full certainty that she is the most special person in your life and consistently show her this is true through your actions – the watering that helps it grow.

Growth

Fire has two metaphors. First, fire is used to destroy, murder, and burn things away. However, you can also use fire to warm yourself and burn a new path. Fire can inspire a deeper love.

There will come a time in a relationship that you tend to fall into a routine. A man will get stuck in his work and grow complacent with his woman. The signs of this are when she starts to become snappy, bitchy, and moody. It is a warning sign to you that you are becoming complacent and she's feeling your lack of love and certainty for her.

Sometimes, she will say things that hit below the belt, but it's not because she doesn't love you. It's because she's hurting. She feels like your effort to connect with her and consistently open her has disintegrated.

This is especially true if, like my family, you failed to give her that connection over time, she will become extremely closed off. She'll probably say some very nasty things.

A man needs to be constantly nurturing the relationship with romance, dating, and avoid falling into a routine. *Routine is the absolute death of a relationship.*

There was a time when dating Londyn that I grew complacent, and I failed to consistently date her, and over time she developed a mood. Luckily, I caught it early on, so it didn't grow out of control. She had built up resentment, however, and she was like a cannonball at first.

"You don't follow through with what you say you're going to do."

"You treat me like I'm not special."

She once gave a whole speech about how I was a really bad boyfriend. She acted like I'd been a bad boyfriend to her the entire time we were together. A man can't call her names, ignore her, or shut down in the face of her anger. In her storm is where the fire is that will bring you two together, stronger than you'd ever imagine.

This is the labyrinth. It all depends on what the man chooses to do. Use her fire and turn it into passionate loving again.

"How did that make you feel?" I asked. "What else is on your mind?" I listened. "I love you… I don't want to fight," I said. "I want to make things right with you. I'll do whatever it takes."

Give her your full presence and your entire heart when she's hurting. *Words always have a deeper meaning and stem from somewhere within.* Stand like a diamond wall, and feel everything she's saying. Talking and venting are the medicines needed to mend a woman's broken heart.

If you've hurt her over time, then apologize from the heart. I once heard that when you argue with your significant other, it's not actually her who you are arguing with. You are arguing with the part of her past that hurt her before. Don't fight her past because you're not her past. You're her present. She feels deeply. She feels insecure and uncertain in this moment. A woman will snap at her man not because she doesn't love him but because she loves him deeply and is hurting.

I would say something like this:

"I'm sorry. I probably treated you like other people who have hurt you. I know that you're hurting, and I've let you down, and as your man, you expect more from me. Thank you for opening up to me. I can't promise that I'll be the best boyfriend. I'll piss you off, make you mad, and hurt you. But I can promise, and I do promise, that I will do the very best that I can, from this day forward, to make every moment special with you."

Look into her eyes and feel both you and her. Don't say it but feel it, and speak it from your whole heart. Breathe into your entire body.

What you say is worthless if you don't mean it. Make her feel desired by you because you know with absolute certainty that you will be there for her, that you will love her and take care of her through everything. Then make love to her as if it's your first time but also your last time – every single time.

It will take time to understand what she needs in certain moments. Part of the battle is learning through these times how to love her. Also, if she is able to show you this fiery and wild side to her, it shows how open she is to you and how much she trusts you. She doesn't show that side to everyone, so use it to enhance the relationship.

Women are unique in that aspect. She wants your total, complete attention on her, especially in the times when you don't want to give it. She picks fights to feel your intensity and focus so you can break through to her. She creates a problem that she doesn't know how to solve to see if you can – to see if you love her enough to find a way to solve the problem, not surrender to it.

A woman chases connecting with the man while the man chases to put his flag at the peak of the mountain.

An example would be when Londyn and I had a conversation about the night I ran down the sidewalk to see her. While I was running, I ripped my boots. All I saw was damaged footwear, and to me it meant nothing. But to Londyn, it meant not only something but everything. She held her heart. "Aw, you messed up your boots to see me – you really did care." I smiled and shook my head. She was such a girl.

If the roles are reversed, neither will feel truly fulfilled. Constantly throughout the relationship, she challenges her man to continue to grow, and opening her up should be his mission in the relationship.

When you seek to open her constantly, she feels that connection she needs from you. Sometimes a man will win a woman and think, "Oh, I've got her, so I don't need to do anything anymore." Problems don't go away, they only rearrange, and you have to figure out the solution once again with new pieces. When she is closed off, he needs to be aware and look into her eyes, tickle her, or snap her out of that mood with some sort of pattern interrupt.

Treat every day as if you are trying to win her love all over again.

As the months went on with Londyn, I began to realize that these cycles would continue. But these cycles are necessary for a relationship to grow deeper.

That is the essence of the second 'G' – Growth. Just like a plant, the more you water the roots, the bigger it grows. Focus on the roots of a relationship, not the fruits. Consistently break through her moods to make her feel cherished, special, and loved by keeping her in a love story – as Hakan would say.

The quality of the relationship can always be better.

Love isn't a destination as most think it is; it's a journey.

Part

Soulmates

In the beginning of time, according to Greek mythology, humans were created with four arms, four legs, and a head with two faces. Fearing their power, Zeus split them into two separate parts. He called the two halves 'soulmates' and condemned them to spend their lives in search of their other halves.

I believed that Londyn was my other half. Our love began to grow deeper as the months passed. In the heat and inspiration of love, I made a choice.

She invited me to one of the biggest fairs in the state. It was held in her hometown, so I met her entire family. During sunset, we rode the Ferris wheel, and the golden light reflected off her amber eyes. It lit up her smile, and my heart was fully open.

She laughed, and I just stared at her.

I was madly in love.

Ace's words echoed in my head as I got lost in her eyes. He asked me, "Are you going to propose to Londyn?"

Back then, it wasn't the time. But in this moment, it felt right.

I kissed her.

"It's like your lips were made for mine," she said, blushing. "They are perfect for mine."

"You're perfect for me," I replied.

That night, while she was asleep, I designed a ring.

I collected stones when I was younger. I had diamonds, emeralds, rubies, and sapphires in a case back home. Londyn's birthday was in May and mine in July. I sketched up a drawing of a white gold ring with a trinity-cut diamond in the center. On the outside of the diamond laid one ruby on the left side. On the other side was an emerald. (May's birthstone is an emerald, representing Londyn on the ring, while the ruby is the birthstone for July, my month.) If we decided to eventually have kids, I left space to add their birthstones outside of ours.

It was one of my most beautiful creations.

I didn't know how I would propose to her, but it didn't take long for me to make a plan.

On the last night, Londyn's family invited me to go on a New Year's cruise with them. On the lake, right outside the city of Chicago, we would watch the fireworks. I could see the vision in my head. I would get down on one knee while the fireworks exploded over the city's skyline. I would pull out this ring and then ask her to marry me as the clock struck 12.

After everyone was asleep, I sat down with Londyn in the basement. I told her how excited I was for this cruise.

"No man can ever replace my dad," she said. "He will always be the number-one man in my life."

This felt like a test to me. She seemed to imply that her father would always be more of a man than I am.

I smirked. "It seems you're failing to see something."

"What?" she asked.

I grabbed her wrist, pulling her into me. I sat her on my lap, so she was straddling me, and looked into her eyes.

"You have a father, but I'm your man. Let me show you the difference." I began to make out with her.

After I returned home, I had the ring made. It took several weeks, and I didn't tell a soul about it. This was what I felt was right. Just as Ace saw something that nobody else could see with his fiancée, I saw something that only I could see with Londyn. I didn't tell Ace, Kyle, Jay, or my family. I didn't even tell my cat.

I knew what I wanted, and my heart was telling me to do this.

The week the jeweler was going to have the ring finished, Londyn's brother happened to be getting married. She asked me to be her date for the wedding, and of course, I obliged. I had never been to a wedding before. In the church, while Londyn was getting ready to be one of the bridesmaids for the wedding party, I had time to talk to her mom and dad. Even though it was raining outside, love filled the air.

I asked her mom about how they first met.

"Well, we were high school sweethearts, and her father actually dumped me on Valentine's Day for another woman," she told me.

"How could anyone dump a woman like you?" I asked, flashing a charming smile.

"I like you," she chuckled. "You're such a sweet talker."

"Please continue," I said.

"In college, her father and I eventually got back together," she said. "He asked for me back, and even though he broke my heart, I still loved him. I gave him another chance. We've been married ever since."

I could hear the hurt in her voice when she talked about it.

Londyn explained later about how her mother had hearing problems growing up. In school, she was getting bad grades, and her family made her think she was stupid. In reality, she just couldn't hear very well.

Her mother, just like me, felt like she was never enough.

She didn't get that love and reassurance that children need. When her high school sweetheart left her for another woman (before having a change of heart), she probably saw herself as worthless. I felt for her.

Londyn's father truly did care for her, though. He took care of her and made sure she didn't have to get a job. He was also a genius, a multimillionaire who started with nothing but dirt.

He reminded me of Kyle when he asked to take me to lunch in his Audi R8, and then hit about 90 miles per hour on a side road. I'm not sure why, when I'm in a car, people want to turn it into a drag race every time. Maybe it's because I ask the same question every time.

"How fast can this thing go?"

When I was out to lunch with him one on one, I wanted to know everything inside his brain. He was like an older version of Gary. We sat in a booth while a rainstorm blew the trees side to side.

"When I talked to your wife, she told me about how you used to get made fun of for having clothes that were too small when you were in grade school," I mentioned, attempting to start conversation. "You used to fight people because of it, and you were poor. You remind me of myself, and I wanted to ask how you did it. How did you come so far from nothing?"

"Well, I could give you the generic version," he said. "For example, be the best at what you do, never settle for mediocrity, and follow your heart." He paused for a moment.

"Honestly, my wife is my angel," he said. "She saved me."

"Saved you?" I asked. "From what?"

"From myself," he replied. "She gave everything for me. I realized that if you give your full effort in everything you choose to do, logically you'll never fail... Well, I guess that's not accurate. You'll fail, but statistically, over time, you'll be successful. There's no way you couldn't be."

He was a finance guy. One of the best investors in the world.

I had a stereotype that finance people tended to just do a lot of cocaine and cared about nothing except their money. Her father shattered my perception because looking at him was like seeing a reflection of myself. He had nothing but came so far. Life and passion flowed through him. I wondered if it was partially because of Londyn's mother, who believed in him every step of the way.

"You see a lot of people who give the bare minimum in life with everything they do," he said, driving to the wedding. "As a result, they achieve the bare-minimum results."

Seconds 'til Zero

Prior to the wedding, I saw Londyn getting ready.

I walked into the room, and she started to cry. She slammed her makeup down on the counter and stared at her reflection.

"I look terrible," she cried. "I can't get my hair right, and now my makeup is smearing."

I sat for a moment and listened to her complain. "It's not your makeup, Lo," I gently told her. "It's your smile; it's that playful personality. It's the sparkle in your eyes and the little girl who comes out. It's when you're breathing freely and laughing openly. That's when I can't help but love you." I held her, and she pouted in my chest. This was something I heard Anthony Robbins say in his *Ultimate Relationship Program.*

"I guess I'm just emotional because my brother is getting married," she said.

I sat in the middle of the church as the ceremony took place. Londyn wore a red dress, and I winked at her as she came down the aisle. She rolled her eyes.

I watched Londyn's parents in the front row while her brother kissed the bride. I wondered what it was like to see their child get married. I wondered if I would ever feel what it would be like to watch my child eventually get married... if I ever had one. Londyn, her sister, and her mom cried at the reception during the first dance. They looked at Londyn's father when a song came on and wanted to see if he would cry. He didn't. He just sat and smiled softly. I admired that for some reason.

Londyn, after a few shots of alcohol, said to me, "I have wedding fever."

"What?"

"This makes me want to get married too," she reiterated.

"Oh, babe," I smirked. "I already have the ring ready for you."

"Yeah, right!" she exclaimed, slapping my arm.

She thought that I was kidding from my smile and how I usually act. Little did she know it was actually true. But I was scared. A night after the wedding, and the night before Londyn and I would come home, something unexpected happened. That night, I walked out of my room to get water around 11 o'clock. I noticed downstairs that the light was on in Londyn's room. Her door was cracked open, and I heard faint voices in the room. I crept downstairs and leaned in close to see through the crack. I barely saw Londyn on the bed with her mom and sister.

"That means I will have to break up with Connor." Londyn was sobbing.

I shook my head because I couldn't have heard that right. I put my ear close.

My heart began to thump faster and faster.

"If that's what you're going to have to do, then that's what it has to be. You have to do what's right for you. We love Connor, but I know that the distance might not be able to work," her sister said.

"Why does this have to happen now?" Londyn cried. "It doesn't matter because, no matter what, I'll have to leave Connor."

"Are you thinking of breaking up with him soon?" her sister asked.

My breathing stopped. What would she say?

"I... I don't know," she stuttered.

I couldn't believe what I was hearing.

I finally understood. Londyn was thinking about leaving me because after winter ended, she would be leaving to go to school far away. We both felt like long distance wouldn't work, but I didn't know it was eating at her like this.

Eventually, in a few months, she would have to make a choice.

Maybe she felt that if she broke up with me now, she could break our hearts early so they could heal instead of dragging this on until spring. But I didn't know if I could ever heal from that. Her love had rooted past the point of return into my heart and soul. If we ended things, it would be like ripping a bush out of the ground, destroying the entire surface. The process of ripping it all away would leave me with nothing… It would kill me.

"We invited him on the New Year's cruise," her mother said. "I think we should wait to decide after that. It doesn't start until next spring; he at least deserves that."

I accidentally leaned too close and touched the door. It creaked open an inch, and all three of the girls turned their heads in my direction.

"Is anyone out there?" one of them asked.

I stood with my back against the wall and out of sight. One of them began to walk towards the door to check and see. I had to get out of there. I tiptoed down their spiral staircase into the basement. There was no trace that I was ever there. I went to the basement so I could go outside into the garden.

When I was young and watching my parents' divorce unfold, I tended to go deep into the woods behind my mother's house where there were beautiful creeks, birds, and wildlife. It was isolation, and even though I always hated isolation, it ironically was where I was also the most comfortable.

There was a special spot behind my mom's house where, deep in the woods and every spring, a small patch of red tulips grew. Only about ten tulips grew there and, after a few years of living there, I found out why they grew there of all places. The owner of that land died in the early 1700s and was buried in the exact spot those tulips grew from. He died of a virus, and his wife planted the tulips where he was buried to always remember him. Those tulips grew strong every year, and every year around that same time in the spring, I would pick one and bring it back to my mother.

That's how I showed her I loved her. That red tulip I brought back was a symbol of my love. Even though red is typically a color that is used to reference pain, suffering, and brokenness of a divorce, to me, the red represented that I'd love her through those times.

As I sat in Londyn's backyard, I looked in the sky, and the moon glowed red. This time, the tulips were replaced by a blood moon. It was an omen. That our relationship was stabbed and bleeding out.

Londyn meant everything to me… She meant the world to me.

Thousands of crickets chirped as a faint breeze rustled the trees.

I wanted to spend the rest of my life with her.

I wanted to grow old with her and watch as our hair began to fade into grey together. I wanted to wake up every morning, watch the sunrise together, and enjoy the little things in life, just as my grandparents did. To have children with her and hear their little feet run through our house that we built together. I wanted to give Londyn and our family everything that I wished I had when I was a child. To go to the pumpkin patch and carve a pumpkin because we were too poor to be able to do those kinds of things.

I wanted to see the world with her and watch sunsets with her on different islands. In my head, I saw us together…forever. I wanted our final moments alive to be together. We argued once, oddly, about who should pass away first – me or her. I wanted her to die in my arms, before me, as a grandmother. I didn't want to die first and leave her with that pain. I wanted her to be the love of my life until the very end…

As I stared up at the blood moon, I felt cold. I didn't know what was going to happen with us after I heard her words, but I knew that life had a plan for us. It was already written in my destiny what was to come, but we both didn't know what it would be. I had a choice to make though, just like Londyn. Part of me wished that I didn't hear the conversation, but later I realized how important it was for me to hear it.

Part of me wanted to back away because the end was in sight.

Maybe I could just run away before it came to that decision in order to cushion the blow for her. She was thinking of how to make it easier on me, and I was simultaneously thinking of how I could make this decision easier for her. She just didn't know that I knew. I knew that running away would be certain death. I didn't want to rush to the end of our relationship even though the signs told me it could be coming and that it was very near.

I only had one option at this point. I didn't know what was going to happen in the end, but I still owed a promise to Londyn. I told her that I couldn't promise her I'd be the best boyfriend, and I couldn't promise that I'd always be perfect, but I promised her I'd give her everything I have.

I could give her every last drop of love that I possibly could and hopefully...just maybe...it would prevail.

Quite possibly, the ring being designed could change everything, or maybe it wouldn't, and we would still go our separate ways. As I said, I wasn't sure of what was going to happen, but going forward, I had to squeeze out every last drop of my love. If this ended, and I didn't give it everything I had, then I would hate myself.

When I gave my mother those flowers, it was because I loved her. This blood moon was also a symbol.

At the end of the night, this moon would be gone. Perhaps it was telling me to give her all of my love while I can because soon she would be gone. Red is a symbol of death but also passion. The future was scary, but it was on its way. Either I could run away or embrace whatever destiny life had written for me and love it until our last breath.

It was late, and we were going to leave early, so I stood up to head back inside. I looked at the sky one more time, and I saw a shooting star incinerate into the atmosphere.

Those are rare to see, and maybe it was a sign that love is rare.

When you have it, truly own it.

Part

Across the Stars

John Williams' *Across the Stars* was my favorite orchestral piece because it was the theme that played when Anakin and Padme fell in love, but it also symbolized the end. We knew that it was going to; we just didn't know when.

We left together the next morning. I gave the family hugs and said, "Until next time," with a wink. We drove home and sang all the way. We shuffled music, and an old song came on that I hadn't heard in years. "This is my favorite song ever!" I gasped.

It was the same song from long ago: "Hemorrhage," by Fuel. He sang, "Don't fall away, and leave me to myself..." I looked at her when he sang this line, and she looked at me. I put my hand on her hand. She gripped it tight. Whenever I saw her face, I saw a clock that was ticking. Every second that passed, it ticked closer to the end. After the song ended, she turned down the volume to zero.

"What would happen if we had to break up?" she asked.

"Why would you say that?"

"No reason. I just like hearing your answers to stuff. What would you do? Like would you be okay?" she asked.

"Oh babe," I said, smirking. "You know that I can't live without you."

"I'm serious, Connor," she laughed, changing her tone back. "Be serious."

"I-I'd hurt...a lot," I whispered, staring blankly out of the window.

When she dropped me off at my house, she asked to come in, but she couldn't because I needed to pick up the ring.

"I need to pick something up, but we can go out later," I told her.

"I can't come with?" she asked, giving me a funny look.

"I told you I have to go get the ring for you." I winked.

"Shut up," she said, rolling her eyes and smiling. "You wouldn't do that."

"You're right," I whispered, looking away. "Maybe that would be crazy."

She left, and that's when I saw the ring for the first time. The jeweler wore a glove, so he didn't leave a fingerprint on it. It was one of the most beautiful pieces of jewelry I'd ever seen. It sparkled. It shined. It was better than the vision of it that I saw inside my head.

I paid for it and left. It was secured in a white leather ring box. I couldn't help but open it over and over again to look at it. I set it in the cup holder and let out a deep breath. "Am I even going to be able to give this to her?" I asked myself.

When I got home, I put the box on my dresser and laid on my bed. I stared at the ceiling. I wondered if Londyn was laying in her bed thinking about me at the same time.

I drifted off to sleep, and I woke up to my phone going off. Londyn was calling me.

It was around midnight. "Is everything alright?" I asked, answering the phone.

"No, we need to talk," she sobbed. It sounded like she had been crying.

"What is it?"

"I'd rather just do this in person," she said.

My heart dropped. The time was now… I thought I had more time.

"You're leaving me…aren't you?" I whispered. I heard nothing in the silence on the other line, but it told me everything I needed to know.

"Londyn?" I asked.

"I'd just rather talk about us in person."

She used the word 'us,' and the last time she used that word was when we were first falling in love. Now, it felt like she was only using that word to describe what we used to be, or I should say, what we still were. But time was running out.

In life, we are guaranteed two things: the beginning, which is life's first promise, but there also has to be an ending – the second promise from life to balance things out. It is the same with love. If you fall in love, then eventually it will end. Some people's love lasts until the day they die, and that's when it ends. Some last one night. Everyone's timeframe for love is different, and I didn't want to accept that it seemed our love clock was on its final hour. It was ticking, with every second, closer to zero.

IV Descent once sang, "I'm holding... I'm holding on... I'm scared about the moment to arrive." I finally felt what he was feeling. This moment he sang about would change my life.

This feeling was so similar to a time long ago when I learned a lesson – when I saw Blake die in that car accident. If it was my last day with someone, how would I treat them? I asked myself this question as I looked back on our relationship. Did I treat every day as if it was my last with her, or did I become too comfortable? My heart sank because why did it feel like I could've loved her harder.

It seemed like I was realizing this too late...

I grabbed my keys, my wallet, and right before I walked out, I saw the white leather box. I opened it to see the beautiful diamond, emerald, and ruby ring that seemed to sparkle even without light. I pulled the ring out and put it gently in my coat pocket.

Anxiety wrapped around my heart. I didn't know what I was going to say, but I knew that I was going to say whatever it takes because I loved her... I had one hand on the wheel while the other spun the ring around in my pocket.

I realized what I was missing as I drove in silence. I never told you what the third and final 'G' of everlasting love is. Possibly because it took everything I had to understand.

The third and final 'G' stands for '*Gratefulness.*'

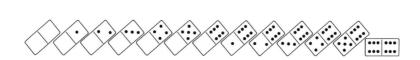

Conclusion

The End

A True Beginning

Two weeks later, I held the card that Londyn made me months ago for my birthday.

I sat on the wooden railing of a bridge that my mom built behind her new home. It was elevated over a pond she made, and I watched the goldfish below me kissing their lips together at the surface, hoping I would throw food to them. In the distance was a small lake. The color of the fish matched the burning gold-orange sky as the sun began to set on the horizon. It reflected off the fish's golden scales, which glistened like jewels.

They sparkled like Londyn's ring.

A stronger breeze ran through the leaves of the trees. They swayed. A few of the leaves snapped off the branches. They flew in the air in a spiral pattern, and then when the wind let up for a second, fell to gently float on the surface of the water.

The clouds, colored like pink lemonade, moved fast in the sky as if they were racing.

I missed her, and when I read the card, it took me down memory lane. I felt I was the only person ever who, after a breakup, would go back through old pictures and notes to relive those moments. I thought I could escape reality, and I did – for a few moments – before fantasy was ripped apart by truth. I'm sure everyone gets these feelings even if they won't admit it.

I spent my nights reminiscing and mourning until around 2 or 3 in the morning.

I thought I was alone to watch this sunset. As I watched, I could read this card and remember us. When we were together, I held back my feelings, but now I felt every word.

I flipped it open to the first page.

"Even though it took the amount of time it did for us to find each other, I built a timeline starting from the day we first met," she wrote.

On the next page was where she printed a Google map, cut into a heart, and glued it to the paper. The paper was flexible, but the heart in the center was stiff.

I remembered seeing Londyn for the first time. How beautiful I thought she was. I felt something I had never felt before. I could tell she was different. I remember leaving her for Haley and then remembered how fate brought us together.

I remembered how difficult it was to get just one kiss, and when I thought she was going to kiss me for the first time, it was just her kissing my forehead.

I smiled a little bit as I remembered how fun it was, and how funny we both were together. Finally, after weeks of hot pursuit, I got a kiss from her, and it was worth the wait. I chuckled a little bit because I remembered a time when we were in bed together and she thought my shorts were her bedsheets. She started yanking on them. I said to her, "If you want my pants off that badly, you could just start kissing me – not rip them off, you know." She laughed.

The next page on the card read, "Our very first date." It showed the location of the hibachi grill where I took her. Around the time of that date, we also had our first dance. This was what the next page read. When we danced for the first time, I told her, "I'll be your first but also your last."

She was speechless. It was one of the best days of my life.

"I put some of my favorite memories with you in here from when we first met... I love you so much," she wrote on the final page of the card.

But it wasn't forever…

Londyn called me over to her house, and I knew in my heart that our time was up. I didn't want it to be.

As I drove to Londyn's house, I didn't know what was going to happen, but I couldn't let it end like this.

When I arrived, we sat next to each other.

"What do you want to talk about?" I asked.

She began to cry in my arms. She told me that she was sorry. That it wasn't me, but it was this decision. She said that seeing me with another woman would hurt her so bad, but I wasn't thinking about any other girl.

I held her so close, but our hearts seemed miles apart. She dug her face deep into my chest and held me.

"I'm breaking up with you, but I can't let go," she cried in my shirt. Her tears soaked in.

"I thought it was going to be us forever… What about building a house together?" I asked. "What about us, kids, and a dog? When you see this in your head, am I not next to you anymore?" I was falling apart. I was spilling everything for her.

She was bawling her eyes out. "I do see you; I only see you."

"But we're in love…right?" I asked, looking her in the eyes.

"I'll always love you…" she cried.

"Then what are we doing?" I fumed, pushing her off me. "Why are we just giving up after all of this – because of distance?" I continued to rant. "What do I have to do? I'd do anything for you, Londyn, so tell me what I have to do to…"

She wiped her tears away. "You need to let me go." Mascara smeared her face.

I sat down on the floor with my back against the wall. She was ripping out my heart, but I didn't want to let go. The ring felt like it was burning a hole in my pocket. I reached in to grab it. This was the only thing I had left. Would this be reckless? Why did I feel stupid?

I closed my eyes. *Pull it out and propose,* I said to myself in my head. I paused.

Sometimes what we're holding onto so tight is what we have to let go of most. The best expression of love you can give someone is for them to feel free. Forcing this would be selfish. I couldn't, even though my entire body was screaming for me to try anything.

She cried for what seemed like hours in my arms. I had to stay strong for us until the very end. I could've given her this ring or said everything I could to make her stay, but it would only be to protect myself. I comforted her, petting her hair back.

"Everything is going to be okay," I said.

"Is this the end?" she asked.

I nodded.

"Will you be okay?"

"Yeah..." I whispered.

I told her I'd be okay, but it felt like I was collapsing inside. I walked away, got in my car, and put it in drive. I looked at her one last time. I gripped my steering wheel until my hand turned white. I drove away, and in my rearview mirror, I saw her still standing on her doorstep. I wondered if she thought it was a mistake. I wondered if she'd ever think about me.

I shook my head, knowing it didn't matter anymore anyway.

I opened my eyes. I kept replaying the breakup in my head over and over again like I was replaying a scene in a film. I wondered if I could've said something different. The sun had almost set, and the stars began to emerge one by one as I sat on the railing. A drop fell off my jaw and landed on the card Londyn made for me. It seeped in and spread on the paper. I petted the spot with my thumb as the drop made the paper wrinkle. I was crying. I gritted my teeth and shut the card with a snap. I was hurting so bad. It had been weeks since we broke up, but I couldn't stop reliving it in my head.

I still couldn't let go...

I took the ring out of my pocket. I flipped it like a coin with my thumb, caught it, and threw it into the lake. It sunk to the bottom where it would rest for eternity.

I heard the back door open and shut. I looked and saw my mom coming out. I wiped my eyes and tried to calm myself, but it was too late. She had already seen me crying.

I guess I wasn't alone. She came and leaned on the railing next to me as I sat.

"Did Londyn make that for you?" she asked, pointing at the card.

"Yeah…" I whispered, staring at it.

"I always thought you were a player," she joked. "I guess you aren't after all."

I smiled, letting out a soft laugh, and shook my head. I looked away.

"I wonder if she ever thinks about me," I said. It seemed that wherever I went, Londyn was always with me because I couldn't get her out of my mind. We hadn't talked since the breakup.

"I've never seen you like this before," she replied. "You really cared about her."

"She means nothing to me," I snapped, looking away. She meant everything to me…

"A part of love is also learning when and how to let go." My mother paused and then continued. "You know, when you were younger, you were always so happy."

I continued to stare at the card, but I listened.

"When you were just born, I left you with your grandparents for a week while I was in Colorado. When I returned, I walked up to your crib. You were fast asleep, but when I whispered your name, you opened your eyes. When you recognized it was me, even though you couldn't talk, it seemed that the whole room lit up. It was like you hadn't seen me in years."

I rubbed my nose and eyes.

She continued. "You didn't need to tell me how much you loved me because in that moment, I felt it. The way you smiled at me and the way you wanted me to just hold you was all I needed for me to know. I'll never forget that day because your smile was the only smile I've known that could light up a room like that."

I fought back tears listening to this.

"Even when we were at our worst, living next to the train tracks and poor," she went on, "you still smiled for no reason at all. Every day I woke you up, you were always smiling from morning until sundown. I asked you one morning, 'How are you always so calm and happy?' and you told me, 'What's not to be happy about?'" She put her hand on my shoulder.

Even though we were struggling, I was losing friends, and I was hurting so bad, I still found a reason to smile. I smiled over nothing at all.

"When did you…" she paused, *"forget how to smile like that?"*

A strong gust of wind whipped through our hair when she said this. She brushed her blonde mane aside. I looked at her, and we both had the same blue eyes. The blue eyes I had that women said were charming, dreamy, mysterious, but intense – the eyes I got from my mom. I felt all of these emotions as I stared into hers. I guess our eyes were both beautiful from the pain of the past. The images burnt into our eyes were what made them beautiful. She was strong just as another woman who I'd soon meet...

Just like that, so soon after she joined me, she walked back into the house. The sky was slowly losing its light, and all the yard lanterns began to illuminate the garden.

I was alone with my thoughts in the dusk. *When did I change,* I asked myself. *When did I forget how to smile?* I wondered why I smiled before, and what I saw in life that prompted me to smile. Is that what caused me to be so strong in those times?

In my life, at first, I regretted everything and wished life could have been different. In those moments when I was being rejected, when I hurt, and when it felt like my life was falling apart, I wished it could've been different. I felt regretful, but I realized without those times, I would've never become the man that I am today.

There was a time when I bought soccer balls and wrote on them for girls to get them to date me, and it never worked. There was a time when I had no hope. During my childhood, I was so emotionally torn down from my parents' divorces, the financial constriction of bankruptcy, and having all of my friends cut their ties with me. It even left physical scars on my body. I named that part of my life *'Toska,'* a Russian word that translates to 'a pain so deep that it can't be put into words; a spiritual anguish and suffering.' These were the times that turned me cold.

I believe that's what I felt growing up, and it left me scarred for much of my life. My heart was crippled, but I still picked up the pieces and found my way out of that suffering.

I believed I was worthless, and this belief was shown through the way I walked, talked, and acted. 'Odraz' is a Czech word that translates to 'reflection.' Jay showed me that most people believe they aren't good enough, whether that's for a girl or to pursue their dreams. These beliefs that we place on ourselves shine through and come out in the way we talk, think, and act around others. When we fix those inner conflicts, it fixes the results on the outside.

I desired deep obsession from a woman. I never knew what it felt like to truly be wanted, so I set off on a journey with Jay to figure out what it would take. I found myself in a skating rink, feeling it for the first time. 'The Mind's Eye' was when I was able to attract Caitlyn, the kind of woman who I didn't have a chance with before. Flirting, attraction, and even happiness or sadness is based on an interpretation. It is how we choose to view our situation, and then our response is based on how strong or weak that interpretation is.

Caitlyn was special to me, and when we opened up to each other, I couldn't deny that I felt strongly for her. That's why it impacted me more than I thought when I realized at IU that she was lying to me the entire time. That's why I named her part, 'La Douleur Exquise', a French phrase meaning, 'The pain of feeling like you found your soulmate, but realizing you aren't theirs' – in other words, to want someone who does not want you. It triggered transformations in both me and Noah when the girl he loved chose me over him.

This turning point led me into Gary's hands. 'Hotwired' is an English term meaning 'to bypass the ignition system in order to steal it.' I felt that when I talked to a girl, every second passing was another second that she was falling for me. Like I was stealing her heart from the way I could use my words. After Caitlyn, I viewed this as a game. I didn't want to lose anymore, so I put my heart, emotions, and pride aside to learn all of the secrets behind seduction.

I was a villain. 'Kilig' is a word from the Philippines describing 'excitement and the feeling of achievement within romantic settings.' I loved the clubs, but I realized how much greed was taking over my mind. It felt so wrong, but it felt so good. I could make the most beautiful woman fall for me. Hakan, Letter-Z, and everyone else only fueled me. We were all falling into a world of cold darkness. I loved the pool parties; I loved the power and I became addicted to it all. Inside, I was slowly rotting and felt like I was numb. Every heart I broke, or led on, or sacrificed sent me down a dark and lonely path. I started to lose myself.

I even almost sacrificed Melanie, right when I told her I loved her, for another woman. 'Cavoli Riscaldati' is an Italian term translating to 'reheated cabbage.' It is used to describe an attempt to save or restart a relationship that can't be revived. It took Hakan's best friend, Blake, for me to recognize how greedy I was, and for the first time in a long time, I committed fully to Melanie. When I saw him pass away in that car accident, it traumatized both of us.

After I fully committed to Melanie, it was taken away from me when I discovered Melanie in bed with my best friend. *'Onsra'* is from a language in India meaning 'that heart-wrenching moment you realize that a love won't last.' Not only that but all of my friendships as well. It split Hakan and me apart, and then I saw Alex and Noah teamed up against me. *I realized that you may want someone to be in your entire story, but perhaps they are only meant to be a chapter.*

Going through heartbreak, all I could focus on was revenge, but when I achieved it, I didn't take into consideration the price. The cost of greed was one of the people who meant the most to me – Ace.

'Jinxed' is an English term meaning 'misfortune.' After I pushed everybody away through carelessness and greed, I felt more alone than I had ever felt in my life. I didn't want to end up like Letter-X, and that's fortunately when Letter-V saved me. Through him and Ace, I realized that true relationships and friendships should be cherished and protected because they are irreplaceable.

Alysa showed me that one choice impacts everyone around you like a ripple effect. To be open to love, we must risk being hurt. We must first walk through rejection, and be played... We have to give our all for somebody and find out that they weren't all in for you...

Love tends to appear when we aren't looking for it.

Which is why I named chapters 10 and 11 'Koi No Yokan,' Japanese for 'the feeling upon first meeting someone that you will inevitably fall in love, and 'Yuanfen,' Chinese for 'destiny or fate.' I met Londyn and felt like she was that person.

If it's meant to happen, then fate will magically remove things perfectly in order for it to happen. It removed Haley, teaching me a lesson first so that I could apply it to Londyn. Without Haley, and learning that I needed to open up in order to love, I might have never connected with Londyn.

Jay taught me to stand for what I believe in, and that through persistence as well as hard work, you will achieve your grandest dreams.

Kyle showed me how to keep pushing through difficult times and to have faith in yourself. Also, he helped me realize that usually the world's biggest smiles are created from the world's deepest pains.

And finally, Londyn...

Londyn taught me many things, but above all, that love is worth fighting for. When I thought of that, I looked down at my knuckle. The scar from when I hit that guy in the face was permanent.

She showed me that I could focus on getting bigger and better things out of life if I could let go of the community that was beginning to be toxic in my life.

Real success is to be able to give all of your love without holding it back.

I named the final chapter 'Kara Sevde,' which translates to 'black love.' It describes a feeling when you're in love so deep, it's almost blinding. As I grew, I learned new things, but it seemed that I also lost an important lesson. Now that I think about it, I said that the third 'G' for everlasting love is 'Gratefulness,' but I never described how it helps love get to that level.

This breakup took place just before I met Dana – the woman in my introduction. I was seeking an answer. I wanted to figure out what I was missing from my life and why I still wasn't happy. That's why I found myself miles away from home listening to the best speakers in the world.

That's when I saw Dana sitting at the table. She told me the story of her late husband and son. I noticed as I talked to her that she still smiled. She was so happy even after she saw her husband get shot and killed, and the only thing she had left to remember him by was their son, who died hours later.

Some of her last words before we parted ways were, "He taught me to live life day by day... I feel like someone hurt you long ago... You're searching for something."

What was I searching for?

Jay once said, "Why is it that when I wake up, it still feels like something is missing?" What I was missing was what I described after I saw Blake pass away in the car accident years ago. Somewhere, I let this lesson go, and only when our relationship began to come to an end did it all came back to me.

"Live as if you were to die tomorrow. Learn as if you were to live forever." – Gandhi

Gratefulness is celebrating every day we can breathe. If you love someone, never hold it back. Cherish every moment that you can look into her eyes, that you can hold her and feel her. Make love to her, every time, like it's your first time...but also your last...because one of these times it will be your last time.

Breathe her entire body and soul. Focus on giving every drop of love you have to her and there's no way you won't prevail.

Life is too short to take anything for granted. Not only for your lover but for your own life. Life is too short to live bored, unhappy, and angry. When you reach your time to die, don't look back and think, *I wish I could've done...* Instead, you should be able to say, "I gave life everything I had."

Instead of worrying about how long you live, worry about how you live. With Londyn, I was hurt, but I realized I gave it everything I had. I couldn't help but be grateful for her and for life granting me true love. She made me realize what I was missing. I was searching for happiness but failed to recognize it when it stood right before my eyes the entire time...

I forgot how to enjoy life and focused entirely on shallow things.

I learned that a smile is free... Peace is free; we just have to seize it. Happiness lies within.

Just like the dominoes, these individuals were all a part of my path. They would always be a part of me no matter how I looked at it because they all steered me in different directions.

Without them, I'm not sure who I would be. They were all a part of the man who could write this book. I could regret that they were a part of me, but if I regretted that, then I would hate myself because they were me in a way. Our past, added up, is who we currently are. Peace comes from accepting and loving who you've been and realizing who you are now.

After that day, I began to see the world differently. I began to love others differently.

When you love someone without dependency, or expectations it seems to be endless. I wanted to make every moment special with whoever was supposed to cross my path next.

I began a new journey to figure out how to smile but to smile for no reason at all.

Smiling not because I had something but smiling over nothing at all, because that's what it's all about...

I named this book *Waking The Core Of Man* to help people learn about attraction and dating, and how to love not only others but themselves – but most importantly, to show that selfish desire can tear your life apart.

I had an artist chalk and paint the covers of this book. Some people believe that the front cover is a sunset, and others think it's a sunrise. I never decided which one it is. The sunset people see the ending to a love story with Londyn. Because the back cover is night, they believe it's me going into a dark time after the heartbreak. They say the colors detail the pain.

However, others believe it could be a sunrise from the back cover. The back cover's nighttime theme represents how I went through those dark and challenging times in order to find peace within myself. They believe that the sunrise represents the start of a new journey and the beginning of a new life.

Perhaps the covers are based on what Lao Tzu once wrote:

"New beginnings are disguised as painful endings."

What do you think?

But I won't leave you on that note…

Two years later, I was with Kyle at a football game tailgate. He was with a girl who he eventually began to date seriously, and I was walking with them through the crowd of people.

Out of nowhere, we heard a woman yell, "Kyle!" When I realized who it was, my body turned into jelly, and my chest filled with butterflies.

It was Londyn.

She looked at me, and my mouth turned dry. I walked away without saying a word as she and Kyle began to catch up.

I needed air. I went to the bathroom and leaned on the sink. I raised the sunglasses to my forehead and splashed water in my face, then looked myself in the eyes.

Why am I seeing her again? Why did fate decide it was going to be today? I asked myself.

Why, after two long years, did I feel like this? I thought I was over it and that I moved on, but when I saw her, my insides melted. It felt like we had just broken up yesterday. A flood of emotion and memories consumed my body. I knew I had to go talk to her; almost like I was being called to do at least that. My hands felt cold. My body felt numb. I stepped out of the bathroom.

I tried to play it cool. I walked up to her to give her a hug.

"Long time no see," I said, smirking. She looked me up and down. She was still as beautiful as the first day I saw her.

"I'm going to, uh…" Kyle said, "leave you two alone." He scurried off.

I looked Londyn in her amber eyes. I was nervous. We talked as if we had just seen each other yesterday.

"I'm finally a Physician Assistant!" she cheered.

"Congrats!" I said, raising my hand to high-five her.

She high-fived me, and our fingers curled together like we were holding hands. She pulled her hand away as soon as they did.

"Sorry," she blushed. "That was just a natural reaction."

"You're as pretty as before," I flirted, pulling her hand back in. I kissed it, smirking.

"You haven't changed," she said, shaking her head and smiling. "You're still the same."

I raised my sunglasses casually to my head so she could look into my eyes.

"Good, so you still think I'm hot." I winked. It was an inside joke dating back to when she called me hot on the washing machine years ago. She picked up on it.

She rolled her eyes like she always did. "You've always been such a sweet talker."

"O-only for you," I stuttered and blushed.

"Right," she mocked, rolling her eyes again. "You're telling me you haven't dated any other girls since me?"

"Maybe I have, but you know they aren't you…" I smirked. "You've dated?"

"I did, but it didn't work out," she replied.

"Oh man," I said sincerely. "I'm so sorry to hear that." A smile grew on my face.

"No, you're not," she snickered. I laughed and looked away.

"Listen," I said, pulling her in for a hug. "I've got to go but if you…"

"I've missed you…" she whispered, interrupting me. "A lot."

She rested her head on my chest. "I mean, I've thought about you a couple times," she snapped, trying to hide it like in the old days.

This felt like the day when I hadn't seen her in months. We held each other like we did when we were in love. I pet her hair as she wrapped her arms around my back.

I hadn't dated or even talked to a girl for a year and a half.

I took time to heal, and just when I was going to jump back in, fate had a different idea. Maybe years ago, destiny was preparing us for this. Maybe I had to right my wrongs first so I could fall in love second.

I've always been a slave for love… I once heard that everyone is a slave to something, and love happened to be the thing I kneeled for.

She never knew that I was going to propose to her…

She never knew I had a ring…

She never knew my plans for her…

"Londyn…" I whispered.

She rested her chin on my chest and looked up into my eyes.

It felt like the day we danced when she was hurting for a kiss from me.

I leaned in… I looked at her lips…

She leaned in… She shut her eyes…

I missed this too. Perhaps this time I could make those plans become a reality. Perhaps this time we could finish our love story.

Maybe this time it would be different…

In case you ever want to get in touch
or if you ever need me, on social media I am at
@selnakim
If this book opened your eyes,
especially if it helped turn your life or relationship around,
I would appreciate it if you would take the time to give it a positive
review on Amazon.
Also, share it with those who may benefit from my work.
I read every single review.
It also spreads the message to others who might be in need.

If you're serious, need help fast, and want more,
email me at
questions@awakeningalpha.com
or go to my website at
AwakeningAlpha.com.
That is where I schedule all of my speaking events,
one-on-one personal mentoring,
and private coaching via phone or face-to-face.

Remember that a candle cannot light the wick of another candle until
it is first lit itself.

Thank you.